Empowering Students
with Hidden Disabilities

Empowering Students with Hidden Disabilities
A Path to Pride and Success

by

Margo Vreeburg Izzo, Ph.D.
Program Director, Special Education and Transition Services
The Ohio State University Nisonger Center
Columbus

and

LeDerick Horne
Poet, Speaker, Advocate, Entrepreneur

·P A U L·H·
BROOKES
PUBLISHING CO ®

Baltimore • London • Sydney

Paul H. Brookes Publishing Co.
Post Office Box 10624
Baltimore, Maryland 21285-0624
USA

www.brookespublishing.com

Typeset by BMWW, Baltimore, Maryland.
Manufactured in the United States of America by
Sheridan Books, Chelsea, Michigan.

Cover image ©istockphoto/Christopher Futcher.

Library of Congress Cataloging-in-Publication Data

The Library of Congress has cataloged the print edition as follows:

Names: Izzo, Margo Vreeburg, author. | Horne, LeDerick, author.
Title: Empowering students with hidden disabilities : a path to pride and
    success / by Margo Vreeburg Izzo, Ph.D., Program Director, Special Education and
    Transition Services, Ohio State University, Columbus, Ohio; and LeDerick
    Horne, Poet, Disability Advocate, Entrepreneur.
Description: Baltimore, Maryland : Paul H. Brookes Publishing Co., 2016. |
    Includes bibliographical references and index.
Identifiers: LCCN 2015045157 (print) | LCCN 2016005114 (ebook) | ISBN
    9781598577358 (paperback) | ISBN 9781681251110 (pdf) | ISBN 9781681251141
    (epub)
Subjects: LCSH: People with disabilities—Education (Higher) | Students with
    disabilities—Psychology. | College students with disabilities. |
    School-to-work transition. | BISAC: EDUCATION / Special Education /
    Learning Disabilities. | FAMILY & RELATIONSHIPS / Learning Disabilities.
Classification: LCC LC4818.38 .I99 2016 (print) | LCC LC4818.38 (ebook) | DDC
    378.0087—dc23
LC record available at http://lccn.loc.gov/2015045157

British Library Cataloguing in Publication data are available from the British Library.

2020   2019   2018   2017   2016

10   9   8   7   6   5   4   3   2   1

Contents

About the Blank Forms   vii

About the Authors   ix

About the Contributor.   xi

Foreword   *Dan Habib*   xiii

Preface   xvii

Acknowledgments   xxiii

1   Why Do So Many People with Hidden Disabilities Struggle?   1

2   The Path to Disability Pride: Assisting Students as They Dare to
     Dream   31

3   Mentoring: Guiding Students Toward Disability Pride.   63

4   Transition: Planning for College and Careers   89

5   College Life: Valuable Life Lessons in the Classroom and on
     Campus   115

6   Daring for the Dream Career: Living a Life of Value   133

7   The Last Transition: Disability Pride and Quality Relationships
     with Bill Bauer   151

References   163

Index   173

About the Blank Forms

Purchasers of this book may download, print, and/or photocopy Figure 2.1 and Figure 6.1 for educational use. These materials are included with the print book and are also available at **brookespublishing.com/izzo/materials** for both print and e-book buyers.

About the Authors

Margo Vreeburg Izzo, Ph.D., is Program Director for Transition Services at The Ohio State University Nisonger Center. She has extensive experience designing and directing projects that improve the transition from high school to college and careers with funding from the U.S. Department of Education, National Science Foundation, and numerous state and local agencies. Dr. Vreeburg Izzo has developed educational curricula for students with disabilities; conducted numerous trainings, focus groups, and interviews with teachers and students; managed the development of web sites, videos, and other dissemination products; and published more than 35 peer-reviewed articles, books, or book chapters on disability and transition issues. She received the Mary E. Switzer Fellow from the National Institute of Disability Rehabilitation Research in 1996. As Past President of the Division of Career Development and Transition, she provided leadership to national, state, and regional committees to improve the quality of education and transition services. She also is a mother, wife, grant writer, and a person with attention-deficit/hyperactivity disorder (ADHD). She believes that people with hidden disabilities are more likely to succeed when they can exercise self-determination in choosing their path to college and careers. In the pages to come, learn more about Margo's life with ADHD and her personal and professional mission to help all people with hidden disabilities lead meaningful lives. For more information on how to contact Margo, visit www.MargoIzzoPhD.com.

LeDerick Horne, labeled as neurologically impaired in third grade, defies any and all labels. He is a dynamic spoken-word poet, a tireless advocate for all people with disabilities, an inspiring motivational speaker, a bridge builder between learners and leaders across the United States and around the world, and an African American husband and father who serves as a role model for all races, genders, and generations. LeDerick is the grandson of one of New Jersey's most prominent civil rights leaders and uses his gift for spoken-word poetry as the gateway to larger discussions on equal opportunity, pride, self-determination, and hope for people with disabilities. His workshops, keynote speeches, and performances reach thousands of students, teachers, legislators, policy makers, business leaders, and service providers each year. He regularly addresses an array of academic, government, social, and business groups and has had appearances at the White House, the United Nations, Harvard University, the National Association of State Directors of Special Education, and the Pennsylvania, Wisconsin, Nevada, and Alabama State Departments of Education. His work addresses the challenges of all disabilities, uniting the efforts of diverse groups in order to achieve substantive, systemic change. Go to www.lederick.com to learn more about LeDerick and his work.

About the Contributor

Bill Bauer, Ph.D., is Professor of Education at Marietta College, a small rural liberal arts school located in the rolling hills of southern Appalachian, Ohio. Bill has a sensorineural bilateral hearing loss, yet a severe hearing impairment has not held him back. He was a former elementary school teacher, school principal, and superintendent. His doctoral degree is in rehabilitation counseling, and he has a private practice at a local hospital and serves as a consultant to many disability-related organizations regarding transition and life span development. He completed postdoctoral work at the Ohio State University Nisonger Center and received the Lifetime Achievement Award from the People First Association. Bill contributed greatly to this book's final chapter, which incorporates his many years of experience in working with youth, adults, and families with hidden disabilities as well as physical disabilities, sensory impairments, and mental health conditions.

Foreword

"EMPOWERING STUDENTS WITH HIDDEN DISABILITIES: A PATH TO PRIDE AND SUCCESS"

In 2003, I sat at my son Samuel's hospital bedside in the intensive care unit as he lay in a medically induced coma. He was three years old and had developed pneumonia from complications following surgery. During this time, one of my son's doctors encouraged me to be a photojournalist in the midst of my fear. "You should document this," he said.

Soon after I began working on my first film, *Including Samuel*, and Samuel's life is the central thread through the film. Making this film helped me face my fears and biases head-on, both as a director and as a father. I wanted to show the general public why I felt so strongly that inclusive education is the most important factor in giving Samuel and other children with disabilities the opportunity for a happy and fulfilling life. As a journalist, I didn't want to sugarcoat the issue. I wanted the film to be as complex as the reality of successful inclusion.

As I took the *Including Samuel* documentary nationwide, I started to understand how our experience parenting a child with a very visible disability—cerebral palsy—differed from parenting a child with a hidden disability. At almost every screening, someone would pose this question in some form: "What about kids with hidden disabilities? Can they be fully included like Samuel?" These hidden disabilities can include depression, learning disabilities, anxiety, attention-deficit/hyperactivity disorder (ADHD), bipolar disorder, autism spectrum disorder, eating disorders, PTSD, and a host of other mental health challenges.

At a screening in Buffalo, a mom spoke up and told the story of her son, who had autism, one of the hidden disabilities that LeDerick Horne and Margo Izzo discuss so powerfully in this book. She explained that his routine had to be carefully managed every morning—just the right food, just the right clothes, just the right type of communication. If anything was off, he'd have a "meltdown" once he got to school. And then, she said through tears, she'd be judged as a "bad mom" because of her son's challenging behavior.

That experience was one of many that led me to create the film *Who Cares About Kelsey?*, which focuses on Somersworth High School student Kelsey Carroll. When Kelsey entered high school, she was a more likely candidate for the juvenile justice system than graduation. She had a diagnosis of ADHD and carried the emotional scars of homelessness and substance abuse, along with actual scars of self-harm. As a freshman, she didn't earn a single academic credit and was suspended for dealing drugs. Many wrote her off as a "problem kid"—destined for drug addiction and jail.

The resulting film, *Who Cares About Kelsey?*, shows what successful school transformation looks like on the ground, in a real school, through the eyes of a student. The film follows Kelsey's transformation into a motivated and self-confident young woman. Along the way, critical figures in her personal and educational life shape her coming of age and play important roles in an education revolution that's about empowering—not overpowering—youth with hidden disabilities.

LeDerick and Margo write about the "Kelseys" of the world through their powerful lens of decades of personal and professional experience. I got to know LeDerick first as a passionate poet and masterful facilitator. In 2010 at a youth inclusion summit inspired by *Including Samuel*, he led a group of 20 students with and without disabilities through the process of designing a national campaign called "I am Norm," which to this day continues to "Redefine Normal and Promote Inclusion," as the campaign tag line states.

I met Margo at an AUCD conference when I presented the *Who Cares About Kelsey?* film along with Kelsey. Her support for the film meant the world to me, since Margo has worked at Ohio State University for 32 years and has been directing projects related to the transition from school to college and careers since 1985. That alone would be enough to spark this book. But perhaps her greatest motivation for this book is her daughter Anna. Anna's story is an integral part of this book and is a testament to how a student living with a hidden disability can be empowered to succeed.

LeDerick and Margo understand intimately that youth with hidden disabilities are often misperceived as being troublemakers instead of as complex children who need supports from the adults in their homes, schools and communities. They understand that effective support and interventions can ease the pain of these students, raise graduation rates and help students connect with their community through mentors and peer groups. They also know that students with emotional and behavioral disabilities are more likely to be victims of violent crime than perpetrators, and that without appropriate interventions, they are at increased risk for dropping out of school, for incarceration, homelessness, and for long-term reliance on government assistance.

Here are a few things to consider while reading this book.

1. **Hidden disabilities are extremely prevalent**. Over three million students in the United States have diagnosed hidden disabilities such as learning disabilities, ADHD or emotional/behavioral disability (EBD). One in every 10 youth in the United States experiences a mental health disorder severe enough to limit daily functioning in the family, school, and community setting.

2. **Hidden disabilities can wreak havoc on learning.** Students with hidden disabilities receive below average scores on reading and math assessments, compared to students in the general population. For example, one-third of students with LD have been held back (retained) in a grade at least once.

3. **Punitive approaches are disastrous.** Punitive discipline policies, like "zero-tolerance," which emphasize the use of suspension and expulsion in addressing problem behavior, don't get at the root causes of behavior. Studies also show that these policies do little to improve school safety and disproportionately impact students with disabilities and students of color. What they can result in is traumatic experiences for students and adults, as you can see in another one of my film, Restraint and Seclusion: Hear Our Stories (www.stophurtingkids.com).

4. **Post-school outcomes for students with EBD are dismal.** National studies show that students who are suspended or expelled often drop out of school, which frequently leads to juvenile delinquency, arrests, and prison. Students with EBD are twice as likely as other students with disabilities to live in a correctional facility, halfway house, drug treatment center, or on the street after leaving school.

Now that I've provided four major downers on this topic, let me offer four hopeful points:

5. **Here's a too-well-kept secret: behavior is a form of communication.** When a child is "acting out," it is generally *not* because he or she just want to be "bad," but because the child are trying to tell us something and does not have the language or communication tools to express him or herself effectively.

6. **Sometimes simpler is better.** Parents and educators can take crucial, relatively simple actions to help children with hidden disabilities. Parents: Spend 15 minute a day listening unconditionally to your child; do person-centered planning; have a discussion with your child about his or her needs and their strengths; refuse to allow others to underestimate your child. Educators: meet with a child one to one to brainstorm positive solutions to behavior challenges; calling a family member at home to tell that person that things are going well; share one new resource related to mental health each month with colleagues; create space at a staff meeting to share success stories.

7. **No need to reinvent the wheel.** There are *many* longstanding, evidence-based educational approaches that your school should implement to dramatically improve the outcomes for students with hidden disabilities. Parents should ask their schools about approaches like differentiated instruction, extended learning opportunities, universal design for learning, functional behavioral assessments and transition planning. Like most successful educational practices, these approaches were incubated in the field of special education, but can be crucial for the success of every child—label or not.

8. **Having students with disabilities in general education enriches the school.** Thirty years of research is clear that inclusive education will

result in better academic, social, behavioral and postsecondary outcomes for students with disabilities. But just as important, I've never
seen a study that shows that inclusive education diminishes the experience of students without disabilities in any way. In fact, studies show
that "typical" students often improve their academic achievement in
inclusive settings when they learn alongside students with disabilities.
And as I discuss in my TEDx talk, "Disabling Segregation," the social
and emotional benefits of learning in a school that represents the true
diversity and different-abilities of the world are profound, even if they
can't be easily measured on a standardized test.

By working together on this book, LeDerick and Margo stay true to the
inclusive values they hold dear and exemplify the "Nothing about us, without
us" theme from the disability rights movement. The book is full of examples
from people who have lived the experience of having a disability. They write
about the importance of helping students to feel disability pride and accept
who they are as people and students. They understand that without that acceptance, these students will find it hard to disclose, use supports, and develop
the skills needed to become affective self-advocates.

I agree with LeDerick and Margo that educators, families, and community
members need to help students with hidden disabilities feel proud of how their
minds and bodies work, teach them to embrace their challenges, give them the
supports and accommodations needed for them to reach their full potential,
and provide ways for these students to connect with the disability community.
My family has been fortunate in that Samuel, now 16 and a sophomore in high
school, has experienced inclusive education with educators who had high expectations for him, and created classrooms rich with innovative, universally designed instruction. It's no coincidence that he is consistently on the honor roll,
involved in a host of extracurricular activities and now has his eyes on college.

Transitioning to college and career is a particularly difficult time for all
students and it can be particularly challenging for students with disabilities,
so it's wise that LeDerick and Margo spend part of this book discussing how
educators can focus on their student's strengths during transition.

Above all else, LeDerick and Margo's work centers on helping students
connect with their strengths and interest in order to achieve their goals for the
future.

This book is based on a clear, essential premise: despite many societal
forces working against them, people with hidden disabilities contribute a great
deal to the world. Educators and others have the unique opportunity to help
the next generation of people with hidden disabilities realize their potential.

Dan Habib
Filmmaker and Project Director
University of New Hampshire Institute on Disability

Preface

SOME WORDS FROM LEDERICK

Since graduating from New Jersey City University in 2003, I have been fortunate to work with a number of organizations and agencies dedicated to improving the lives of people with disabilities on the national, state, and local level. The New Jersey State Department of Education's Office of Special Education was the first agency to offer me the opportunity to share my story, poetry, and advice to help improve the transition outcomes and self-advocacy skills of high school students with an individualized education program (IEPs). Through my work with the New Jersey Department of Education, I was introduced to the IDEA Partnership that is housed within the National Association of State Directors of Special Education. The youth leadership and development work I did with the IDEA Partnership centered on promoting and supporting groups throughout the nation that believed youth and young adults with disabilities need to have a meaningful role in governing the organizations that provided support for people with disabilities. Then, in 2005, I was asked to chair the governing board of a new nonprofit, which is now known as Eye to Eye. The head of this organization had the novel idea of using the power of art, mentoring, and storytelling to empower young people with learning disabilities/ADHD. Over the years, I have been invited into some of our nation's best schools and learned from advocates with and without disabilities, and I have been able to take part in cutting edge initiatives in the field of education. Beyond my poetry, this book is my first attempt at writing down what I have learned about disability culture, education reform, self-advocacy, and what is needed to help young people with disabilities develop their fullest potential.

A college professor with attention-deficit/hyperactivity disorder (ADHD) and a poet with a learning disability decide to write a book. This may sound like the beginning of a really bad joke, but if there is any power within the pages that follow, that power comes directly from the unlikely partnership described in this playful line. Margo and I met in Washington, D.C. at the 2010 Office of Special Education Programs project director's conference. I was invited to deliver an opening keynote for this annual gathering of approximately 1,000 researchers who were working on innovative ways to improve the quality of education and transition outcomes for students with disabilities. I spent an hour sharing my personal story as an individual with a learning disability who had survived a myriad of challenges faced by many young people as they utilize special education services and make the transition to adult life. I also provided suggestions on reforms that I felt were needed to ensure that all students receive a quality education. Margo was one of the first people to walk up to me after my presentation. Our first conversation together would be one of many, and it began a deep alliance and shared commitment to improving the lives of people with disabilities.

Margo and I began to work together regularly over the next several years. She invited me to The Ohio State University, where she was directing a number of projects to increase academic and transition outcomes for students and young adults with disabilities. I became more and more impressed with her work each time I returned. She was a project director who was able to create and manage teams of diverse professionals who were doing groundbreaking work in the field of transition at both the high school and college level. For example, one of Margo's projects developed transition curricula to assist high school students in researching and developing their own transition plans for college and careers. Another one of her projects facilitated student learning communities to assist students with disabilities who were majoring in science, technology, engineering, and mathematics (STEM) fields to develop self-determination skills so they could advocate for needed accommodations and supports. In addition, Margo directed a project that created Ohio's Statewide Consortia of five college programs that provided comprehensive transition services to enhance employment outcomes for students with intellectual disabilities. These college students with intellectual disabilities benefit from the educational and social aspects of college life while preparing for employment. Another project used online mentoring to help high school students with IEPs develop their transition plans.

Outside of working together, Margo and I also began to build a friendship that was based, in part, on our shared experiences as people with hidden disabilities. Her diagnosis of ADHD and my diagnosis of a learning disability made for interesting conversations as we frequently talked about the benefits and challenges that came with the ways our minds worked. It was during one of these conversations when Margo first suggested that we collaborate on a book that would capture our ideas, stories, and advice. We both realized that in the field of disability studies, and specifically within education, there was not enough advice for educators that comes directly from the people who have lived with a disability. We both believed that the combination of our professional experiences with our respective passion for research and writing would give us the ability to create a book that would have the potential to make a lasting effect on how students with hidden disabilities perceive themselves as they prepare for the adult world.

MARGO'S MOTIVATION

I went to school before the Education for All Handicapped Children Act of 1975 (PL 94-142) was passed and before students with ADHD were diagnosed and provided with IEPs to ensure that they received a free appropriate public education. My mom and my teachers had high expectations, and I went on to college, majoring in psychology and special education. I started my career teaching high school students with emotional and behavior disorders. My passion for transition was fueled when I was teaching these high school students. I felt a tremendous responsibility to teach them the skills they needed to work and live in their communities. So, I pursued a master's degree and a doctoral degree to discover how to deliver quality education and transition services.

I realized that the school climate for my daughters was much different than when I had gone to school. Schools had shifted to a high-stakes testing environment in which students had to pass state graduation tests to receive their diploma. I recognized that my daughter, Anna, had many of the same characteristics that I had as an elementary student, but her grades were good, so I did not worry. I also knew that postschool outcomes for students with disabilities were significantly poorer than for students who were not identified, so I did not want Anna to be served by special education. I spoke with her middle school teacher, who pointed out that my daughter may need some additional supports, such as medication and extended time, as the curriculum got tougher and the stakes got higher. We visited our pediatrician and completed the diagnostic surveys to qualify Anna as a child with ADHD who could receive medication—but from the school's perspective, Anna did not need specialized services and did not qualify for special education.

I noticed that Anna's self-esteem was dropping during this time. As she approached the rigors of high school, she resisted taking her medication, and her grades dropped further. The school counselor recommended special education services to gain the additional supports Anna needed to become proficient in more challenging subjects. Anna's self-esteem lowered even more. Once she qualified for special education, the system recommended the easiest subjects, and her teachers' expectations dropped. I felt that we were in an unending downward spiral that was drowning out Anna's potential. Although Anna and I had very similar learning styles, our high school experiences were totally different, in part because the levels of expectations were not the same. The system stopped believing that Anna could learn.

I kept thinking that Anna and I had such similar academic struggles. Memories of my challenges with organization, impulsivity, and focusing on one task made me begin to wonder: Was it possible that I also had ADHD? I started to become more and more convinced. It was at this point that I decided to undergo the psychiatric testing, and, to no surprise, I exhibited many ADHD characteristics and received a prescription for medication. With the receipt of this news, I became determined to be a positive role model for Anna. I was not going to let Anna stop believing in her abilities. She is now completing her master's degree at The Ohio State University while she works full time and is planning her wedding.

As I interact with high school students with disabilities, I see so many who have similar experiences to Anna's high school journey. Students give up their dreams, in large part, because teachers have given up or maybe are just afraid to expect too much. How are students going to believe they can learn if teachers do not believe in them? It may be tougher for students with disabilities to learn, but those students and their teachers cannot give up just because it is hard. This is where LeDerick's story and my story intersect. We both believe that students with disabilities, and especially those with hidden disabilities, deserve to dream about a future in which they make the transition to colleges and careers that capitalize on their strengths, preferences, and talents. This book is dedicated to those students and adults with hidden disabilities and hidden potential who have disability pride and who dare to dream.

OVERVIEW OF CHAPTERS

The goal of this book is to broaden educators' understanding of disability from an asset-based approach in order to assist students with hidden disabilities in accepting their disability, reaching their goals, and gaining disability pride. Each chapter provides guidance to help students strive to stay in the game—the game of learning, working, and living to their potential. We provide many stories from our own lives as well as others who have walked the journey from struggling student to self-determined self-advocate. Some highlights from the upcoming chapters follow.

Chapter 1 provides the current state of students with hidden disabilities. A number of disability categories are described, and Tips for Teaching are suggested to address some of the challenges that students experience.

Chapter 2 introduces the Path to Disability Pride and demonstrates, through a series of case studies, how people with hidden disabilities come to incorporate disability into their self-concept. Find out how LeDerick, after many years of feeling shame, eventually learned to embrace his disability and why Margo's daughter, Anna, became a strong advocate once she got to college.

Chapter 3 defines and describes various models of mentoring, including Eye to Eye, a national organization that matches college and high school students with dyslexia, ADHD, and other learning disabilities with younger students who have similar learning differences. The chapter also covers other organizations run by people with disabilities who strive to increase disability awareness and pride. The authors share both research results and personal testimonials that demonstrate the impact of mentoring. These testimonials show how self-determination and a positive self-concept are fostered and reinforced by mentors. Mentoring helps students who often feel alone in connecting to a larger community of people who lend support to students through critical junctures and transitions.

Chapter 4 provides an overview of self-directed transition planning so educators and parents can empower students to take charge of their own transition to college and careers by engaging in activities that promote disability pride and positive transition outcomes. Read success stories of how these state and local events changed the course of kids' lives. Finally, gain many free resources and curricula to teach students to plan their own transition to college and careers.

Chapter 5 explores the rights and responsibilities of college students with hidden disabilities. Strategies for preparing for tests, writing research papers, and advocating on campus are provided. Learn how students with hidden disabilities majoring in STEM learned about the effects of their disability and developed disability pride.

Chapter 6 discusses strategies to help students explore their own interests, passions, and abilities and learn how to explore career opportunities that turn a job into a career. Studies have shown that more than 35% of America's entrepreneurs are people with hidden disabilities. Read about how Adam, a graphic designer with learning disabilities, uses his writing/spelling software to label his designs after advocating for technology on the job, and discover how LeDerick started his own consulting business, delegating the tasks that he finds challenging.

The final chapter explores the skills needed to negotiate personal relationships, such as knowing and valuing yourself and communicating needs and wants with spouses and children. Tips on how to navigate relationships are shared through case studies and discussion. Readers also learn how to use the Path to Disability Pride framework to help students build a better understanding of their disability's role in their self-concept.

Acknowledgments

Many of the case studies and content incorporated into this book were inspired by projects directed by Margo Izzo at The Ohio State University. We would like to thank the sponsors for the opportunity to conduct research and demonstration projects that improve transition outcomes for students with disabilities.

The EnvisionIT, E-Mentoring, and Stepping-Up EnvisionIT Projects were funded by grants awarded to The Ohio State University Nisonger Center from the Office of Special Education Programs, U.S. Department of Education (EnvisionIT Phase I and II award numbers H327A020037 and H327A050103, respectively; E-Mentoring Phase I and II award numbers H327A060066 and H327A090058, respectively; and Stepping-Up EnvisionIT award number H327S120022). The Ohio STEM Ability Alliance was supported by the National Science Foundation under NSF Award Number HRD-0833561. Any opinions, findings, and conclusions or recommendations expressed in this material are those of the author(s) and do not necessarily reflect those of the U.S. Department of Education or National Science Foundation.

To my amazing daughters: Angela and Anna. You grew up with a mom who worked long hours and took every opportunity to travel, to learn, to grow, and to share the results of her latest projects with whomever would listen. Seeing you succeed as teachers, professionals, and great friends provides me with more joy and comfort than a mother deserves. Thank you for sharing your lives with me.

To my mother, Anna Vreeburg, who immigrated to the United States in 1950, had seven children with my dad, was widowed at age 39, and raised us all with a strong work ethic. Thank you for modeling self-determination from the time we were small children and for giving us the most precious gift of all: the determination to work hard, gain a quality education, and to be proud to be an American.

And to my friends and colleagues across the country whose work has inspired me to continue to discover and implement the evidence-based practices and predictors that increase the quality of life we all hope to achieve. Our dream is that all the students and adults with disabilities who inspired our work not just "dare to dream" but achieve those dreams, as well.

Finally, to my siblings and my husband: Having a family member with ADHD has its challenges and its joys. I'm thankful that the joys far outweigh the challenges.

—MVI

To my grandfather, Semmion Horne, who passed away in 2013 after 90 years of living life completely on his own terms. Thank you for showing me how much can be accomplished through faith, hard work, and the disciplined pursuit of one's goals. I have worked hard to live my life in the tradition of service and enterprise that you embodied. To my father, Raymond N. Horne, who was an awesome physical education teacher and coach and showed me that effective storytelling has the power to transform ordinary people into champions. To my mother, Brenda Lewis, who was my first advocate and who continues to inspire me with her strength and wisdom. To my wife, partner, and best friend, Metra Lundy: Thank you for being our family's rock and for encouraging me to take on the creation of this book. And to my newly born niece, Penelope, and my daughters Aniyah and Kamiylah: Meeting a teacher that makes you feel smart and important is a gift that every child deserves. It is my hope that in the years to come you are blessed with teachers that will help you to love your minds and to reach your fullest potential.

—LH

To the memory of my son, Grant, who continues to spread his love and happiness from above. To my first mentor, my mother: I still hear her echoes of encouragement, "You can do it." To my siblings, Sherry, Bonnie, Randy, and Steve, who treated me with the best sibling love I could have ever wanted. To my teachers in grade school and secondary school and my college professors who believed in me and my abilities. To my competitive swimmers, who touched my life in more ways than one for over 32 years. To my students, past and present, who inspire me on a daily basis to share the knowledge I've gained and the lessons I've learned in my journey of life. To my friends who accepted me for who I am from grade school to this day, who didn't discriminate because I had a disability. And last, to Mary Ella and Maddie, who are the "heartbeat" of my persona.

—BB

Why Do So Many People with Hidden Disabilities Struggle?

1

"Everybody is a genius. But if you judge a
fish by its ability to climb a tree, it will live its
whole life believing that it is stupid."
—Albert Einstein

People with hidden disabilities live in the community and go to school and work in every venue imaginable. Some are identified as having a disability when they are young children by parents and pediatricians. Others are identified by teachers and psychologists in schools. Others discover in adulthood that there is a label that describes many of the characteristics they feel. Some adults are never identified and land on their feet with a satisfying career and family life that provides the right balance of challenge and support.

Many students and adults with disabilities, however, do not get the right supports in school or find the right job, the right partner, or the right friends who accept them in total, especially during the awkward moments when their hidden disabilities are exposed. They may turn to drugs or alcohol during these awkward times to numb the inner voice that keeps shouting, "You are stupid!" or "You do not fit in!" They do not have a sense of belonging, but they still need to connect to a group who accepts them for who they are. It can be difficult for others to accept them when they have not accepted themselves.

The goal of this book is to help teachers, parents, counselors, therapists, administrators, and self-advocates realize that there is hidden potential behind every struggling student with a hidden disability. Parents and professionals are crucial supporters who help students with hidden disabilities gain an accurate and strength-based acceptance of who they are and how their disability affects their learning and their relationships. Helping all students—those who are struggling as well as those who are proficient—realize their potential and dare to dream is the most important mission of schools.

This book also is written for students and adults with hidden disabilities who have made (or want to make) peace with their disabilities. Every day they can pass as people without disabilities because no one can see their disabilities. Some people will use the term *hidden disabilities,* whereas others will say *invisible disabilities* or use terms such as *learning disabilities, attention-deficit/hyperactivity disorder (ADHD), intellectual disabilities,* or *autism.* Whichever term is used, the most important mission of this book is to help people with hidden disabilities accept themselves—their strengths, passions, disabilities, and challenges—and pass along the wisdom they have gained to others who get caught in the struggle to realize their potential. The goal of this book is to broaden people's understanding of disability by using an asset-based approach to assist people with hidden disabilities to identify their strengths, accept their challenges, and gain an identity full of disability pride.

HOW MANY STUDENTS HAVE DISABILITIES?

Students with hidden disabilities cut across a number of disability categories. Although the majority of students with hidden disabilities are labeled with some form of a learning disability, speech-language disorder, or ADHD, students with hidden disabilities can also include those with mild visual impairments, behavior disorders, or autism spectrum disorders (ASDs). All people with hidden disabilities share the perception of being normal by the outside world. They lack the visual indicators that shout "disability"—the signs that easily conform to society's perception of disability, such as using a wheelchair, walking with an impaired gait, or speaking with an obvious impediment. Having a hidden disability gives students the option to either hide or disclose. They have the choice to deny this aspect of who they are or incorporate disability into their identity.

The true number of people with hidden disabilities will never be known. It is impossible to count because there is not an agency or a census that can systematically assess each citizen to determine the true number of children and adults with hidden disabilities. Many people go through life struggling with certain tasks or daily activities but never receive a formal diagnosis. Schools have a mandate to identify, serve, and report the number of children with disabilities who receive special education services, so data collected by the U.S. Department of Education is a good place to estimate the number of students with hidden disabilities.

More than 5.8 million students with disabilities ages 6–21 received special education services in 2014, representing about 8.4% of the general population (U.S. Department of Education, 2014). The Individuals with Disabilities Education Improvement Act (IDEA) of 2004 (PL 108-446) regulations define each category of disability. The definitions of categories of students with disabilities, as well as the approximate percent and number of students ages 6–21 served under IDEA by disability category in 2014, are provided in Table 1.1.

Table 1.1. Federal definitions, percent, and number of students ages 6–21 served under the Individuals with Disabilities Education Improvement Act (IDEA) of 2004 (PL 108-446) by disability category

Federal definition	Percent	Approximate number
Autism means a developmental disability significantly affecting verbal and nonverbal communication and social interaction, generally evident before age 3, which adversely affects a child's educational performance. Other characteristics often associated with autism are engagement in repetitive activities and stereotyped movements, resistance to environmental change or change in daily routines, and unusual responses to sensory experiences.	7.6	442,611
Deafblindness means concomitant hearing and visual impairments, the combination of which causes such severe communication and other developmental and educational needs that they cannot be accommodated in special education programs solely for children with deafness or children with blindness.	*	*
Deafness means a hearing impairment that is so severe that the child is impaired in processing linguistic information through hearing, with or without amplification, which adversely affects the child's educational performance.	*	*
Emotional disturbance means a condition exhibiting one or more of the following characteristics over a long period of time and to a marked degree that adversely affects a child's educational performance:	6.2	361,077
1. An inability to learn that cannot be explained by intellectual, sensory, or health factors		
2. An inability to build or maintain satisfactory interpersonal relationships with peers and teachers		
3. Inappropriate types of behavior or feelings under normal circumstances		
4. A general pervasive mood of unhappiness or depression		
5. A tendency to develop physical symptoms or fears associated with personal or school problems		
Intellectual disability (previously defined as *mental retardation*) means significantly subaverage general intellectual functioning existing concurrently with deficits in adaptive behavior and manifested during the developmental period, which adversely affects a child's educational performance.	7.3	425,139
Hearing impairment means an impairment in hearing, whether permanent or fluctuating, that adversely affects a child's educational performance but is not included under the definition of deafness in this section.	1.2	69,885
Multiple disabilities means concomitant impairments (e.g., intellectual disability/blindness, intellectual disability/orthopedic impairment), the combination of which causes such severe educational needs that they cannot be accommodated in special education programs solely for one of the impairments. Multiple disabilities does not include deafblindness.	2.2	128,125
Specific learning disability means a disorder in one or more of the basic psychological processes involved in understanding or using language, spoken or written, that may manifest itself in the imperfect ability to listen, think, speak, read, write, spell, or do mathematical calculations, including conditions such as perceptual disabilities, brain injury, minimal brain dysfunction, dyslexia, and developmental aphasia.	40.1	2,335,360

(continued)

Table 1.1.   *(continued)*

Federal definition	Percent	Approximate number
Speech-language impairment means a communication disorder, such as stuttering, impaired articulation, a language impairment, or a voice impairment, that adversely affects a child's educational performance.	18.2	1,161,641
Orthopedically impaired means a severe orthopedic impairment that adversely affects a child's educational performance (e.g., cerebral palsy, amputations).	0.1	58,237
Other health impairments mean having limited strength, vitality, or alertness, including a heightened alertness to environmental stimuli, that results in limited alertness with respect to the educational environment. It is due to chronic or acute health problems, such as asthma, attention-deficit disorder, attention-deficit/hyperactivity disorder, diabetes, epilepsy, a heart condition, hemophilia, lead poisoning, leukemia, nephritis, rheumatic fever, sickle cell anemia, and Tourette syndrome, and adversely affects a child's educational performance.	13.2	768,746
Traumatic brain injury means an acquired injury to the brain caused by an external physical force, resulting in total or partial functional disability or psychosocial impairment, or both, that adversely affects a child's educational performance.	0.4	23,296
Visual impairment including blindness means an impairment in vision that, even with correction, adversely affects a child's educational performance. The term includes both partial sight and blindness.	0.4	23,296
Total		5,823,844

*Incidence and percent for deafblindness and deafness are not shown because they each account for less than 0.5% of children served under IDEA. Detail does not sum to total due to categories not shown.

From the U.S. Department of Education, Office of Special Education and Rehabilitative Services, Office of Special Education Programs, *36th Annual Report to Congress on the Implementation of the Individuals with Disabilities Education Act, 2014*, Washington, D.C. 2014.

Specific learning disabilities is the largest disability category and represents about 40.1% of the more than 5.8 million students identified as having a disability, followed by speech-language impairments (18.2%), other health impairments (13%), autism (7.6%), intellectual disabilities (7.3%), and emotional disturbance (6.2%). Students who receive special education services and have ADHD as their primary disability are included in the other health impairments category (U.S. Department of Education, 2014).

More than 75% of the disability categories defined in Table 1.1 state that the impairment must adversely affect a child's educational performance to qualify for special education services (U.S. Department of Education, 2014). Students may have any of the disabilities listed in Table 1.1, but if the disability characteristics do not adversely affect the students' educational performance, then they do not receive special education services and are not counted as students with disabilities. Therefore, the number of students who may have hidden disabilities is most likely larger than what is reported.

HOW MANY STUDENTS HAVE HIDDEN DISABILITIES?

It is difficult to determine how many students with disabilities served by special education have hidden disabilities. Students with learning disabilities, speech-language impairments, and ADHD are the obvious categories. Many students with autism or vision or hearing impairments can perform in a class without being identified as having a disability. Students' disabilities may be unknown to those around them unless they choose to disclose. If students with specific learning disabilities, speech-language impairments, emotional disturbance, other health impairments, and autism are included, then approximately 55%–85% of the 5.8 million students in special education have hidden disabilities, ranging from 3.2 to 4.9 million students (see Table 1.1).

The incidence of other health impairments and autism has increased by 0.4% and 0.5%, respectively, from 2003 to 2012. Although still considered a small percent of the population, students with other health impairments, including students with ADHD, are increasing, whereas rates of specific learning disabilities, emotional disturbance, intellectual disability, and speech-language impairments are a decreasing percent of the disability population (U.S. Department of Education, 2014).

WHERE ARE STUDENTS WITH HIDDEN DISABILITIES EDUCATED?

The majority of students with hidden disabilities ages 6–21 are educated in general education classrooms due to a trend toward more inclusive classrooms and access to the general curriculum (Sailor, 2014). Fewer than 20% of students with disabilities are educated in a separate classroom with a special education teacher for the majority of their school day (U.S. Department of Education, 2014). Students with learning disabilities, ADHD, autism, and hearing and visual impairments are increasingly educated in the general education classroom versus special education classrooms (Crawford, 2012; U.S. Department of Education, 2014). Cosier, Causton-Theoharis, and Theoharis (2013) reported that reading and math achievement for students with disabilities is strongly and positively correlated to time spent engaged in the general education curriculum. Kalambouka, Farrell, and Dyson (2007) reported that including students with disabilities resulted in either positive or neutral effects for classmates without disabilities.

> **Text Box 1.1—For More Information on Inclusion**
>
> Dan Habib advocates for inclusion in the TEDx talk: Disabling Segregation. Habib makes a powerful case for ending the systematic segregation of students with disabilities. See the video at http://www.youtube.com/watch?v=izkN5vLbnw8.

WHY ARE SOME STUDENTS WITH HIDDEN DISABILITIES NOT IDENTIFIED?

There are many reasons why students with hidden disabilities are not identified or fall through the cracks—the effects of their disability on their educational performance are not adverse enough; the costs in time and resources of referral, evaluation, and individualized planning are too much for many teachers and schools; the stigma of having a disability is so great that families do not think the benefits of receiving accommodations and supports outweigh the negative effects of being identified; and families are resistant for a variety of reasons, ranging from fear to denial.

Adverse Effect on Educational Performance

Ten of the 13 disability categories defined by IDEA 2004 state that the condition or impairment must adversely affect a child's educational performance in order to be considered a disability. Margo's daughter, Anna, a very active child who displayed some ADHD characteristics at a young age but did not qualify for special education services in elementary or middle school, will be featured throughout this book. Anna's ADHD did not adversely affect her educational performance until she reached high school, where she had six different teachers assigning homework, giving tests, and making demands on her time. With so many tasks to organize, her ADHD symptoms interfered with her ability to successfully complete all of the required tasks.

Costs in Time and Resources of the Referral Process

A legal process begins when teachers or parents complete a referral for an evaluation to determine if a disability exists. The school must first gain parental consent for the evaluation. The school district then has 60 days to conduct the evaluation after receiving consent from the parent or guardian. Finally, the school has 30 calendar days after completing the evaluation to hold a meeting to review the results of the evaluation, determine eligibility, and develop an individualized education program (IEP) if the child is found eligible for services. The time and energy that the individualized assessment process often requires are too time consuming and labor intensive for many teachers, school administrators, or parents to initiate.

Stigma of Being Labeled with a Disability

Anna was identified with ADHD in high school and was eligible for special education services. She had to deal with the stigma of being labeled as a student with a disability during adolescence—the time when teenagers want to fit in and be accepted by peers. Some schools have developed a culture in which disability is both accepted and supported, which will limit the stigma and shame that many students feel about disclosing their disability. The stigma of disclosing is often too powerful, and students would rather give up any accommodations and supports than admit having a disability. Labeling a child or a teenager should never be taken lightly. The stigma of having a disability is so strong that approximately 60% of students who had IEPs during high school indicated that they did not have a disability the year after they exited high school (Newman, Wagner, Cameto, & Knokey, 2009).

Family Resistance to Labeling

Many parents resist having their children diagnosed with a disability (Schwarz, 2013). They do not want their children to live with the shame and stigma associated with a disability. They want to resist the process of labeling their children with a disability, especially when they know that children with disabilities do not achieve the same academic and employment outcomes that students and adults without disabilities obtain. The line between who has and does not have a disability can be difficult to determine.

To Diagnose or Not: The Fine Line
Between Students with and without Disabilities

I made every effort to utilize supports when Anna had difficulty with reading in elementary school, including the reading recovery interventions provided by the school and extra help provided by myself or tutors who I hired privately. Anna received a multifactored evaluation in fourth grade to determine if she qualified for special education supports. The testing revealed that there was not a significant discrepancy between her potential and achievement. Therefore, having ADHD did not adversely affect her educational performance.

　　As her mom, I was relieved. I was aware of the poor adult life outcomes for high school graduates who were identified with ADHD because of my role in the field of special education. Also, I was aware of the low expectations of some educators regarding students with disabilities. The effect that the ADHD label would have on Anna's self-esteem was another concern of mine. I did not want her to give up her dream of a college education and a fulfilling career. In fact, these concerns are my primary motivation to write this book—too many students and adults with hidden disabilities believe that their futures are significantly compromised if they admit to having a hidden disability. The converse is often true—their futures are compromised if a disability is not diagnosed, and students do not have access to quality special education services that assist them in developing the self-determination skills they need to navigate life.

High parental expectations of children with learning disabilities are significantly and positively associated with improved academic and postschool outcomes, including academic achievement, college attendance, occupational attainment, and adjustments to working life (Doren, 2014). How can students with hidden disabilities believe in themselves when their family members do not believe in positive adult outcomes?

UNDERSTANDING AND SUPPORTING STUDENTS WITH HIDDEN DISABILITIES

How do schools and families help students with hidden disabilities so they reach their potential? What can be done to reduce the stigma of hidden disabilities? Helping all students find their individual strengths and passions matters as much, or even more, than understanding the diagnosis and the types of accommodations and supports a student will need. Extremely creative individuals can occupy two positions that appear to be polar opposites. Many people who have disabilities may be extremely creative and have abilities that are not fully developed. For example, Albert Einstein, who is often cited as having a learning disability, struggled with many basic skills, such as selecting the correct change to board a bus. Yet, he became one of the most brilliant physicists to have ever lived. No one should be defined by what he or she cannot do.

The following section is designed to help teachers, administrators, and family members understand the different categories of hidden disabilities. Also, teaching tips and information that support students with hidden disabilities are provided. Major disability categories of hidden disabilities are described, and insights into the experiences of people with hidden disabilities, including the experiences of the authors, are provided. As previously stated, a lot of overlap exists among the disability categories. For example, people who have learning disabilities and ADHD and others who have autism and ADHD are discussed. Tips for Teaching are provided throughout the book for teachers, parents, and others who work with students with and without disabilities.

Supporting Students with Learning Disabilities

"Every child gets left behind when all we focus on are tests."
—"Dare to Dream" by LeDerick Horne

Approximately half of students with hidden disabilities have specific learning disabilities, which is often shortened to learning disabilities, a neurological condition that may alter a person's ability to listen, speak, read, write, or calculate. There is no one type of learning disability, nor is there a specific profile to describe a student with a learning disability. A learning disability may be discovered at any time during a person's life based on a number of factors, such as severity of the disability, social demands, academic or employment settings, and an educator's knowledge of learning disabilities.

LeDerick Reads Aloud

I can remember the moment that began my life as a person with the label of having a disability. I had been struggling through school for several years and had to repeat the first grade due to the challenges I had learning to read and spell. I made it to the third grade before my learning disability was identified. It was a few weeks into the school year, and my teacher decided to have the class read a story out loud. Each student took turns reading a paragraph, and with the persistence of a hungry predator, I could feel the story bearing down, moving closer and closer to me, as I twisted and squirmed in my desk. My heart raced, my palms began to sweat, and my mind was flooded with the sound of my classmates' impending laughter. By the time the story reached me, and my teacher instructed me to read my paragraph, I was so afraid of what was going to happen next that I would have mispronounced my own name if it had found its way into the text. I tried to read the words, but there was no way I could decode the symbols on the page with the same grace and effortlessness of the students who had gone before me. After a few lines, and a few giggles from my classmates, my teacher told me to stop. I received my first evaluation shortly after that day. I was formally diagnosed as being neurologically impaired, and I was sent to a self-contained special education classroom for the next 3½ years.

Although being separated from my typically developing peers left me with many social-emotional scars, I know I was relatively fortunate. My first special education teacher was a dedicated and experienced instructor who genuinely cared about me. I improved my ability to read, spell, and do math with her help.

Students with learning disabilities have the full range of intelligence, and many students with learning disabilities are as smart, or smarter, than their peers. Although a person with learning disabilities can learn effective strategies to accommodate and manage the effects of having learning disabilities, these disabilities do not go away. If students with learning disabilities do not accept their diagnosis and learn strategies to accommodate it, then they may be at higher risk for school failure, depression, behavior problems, failed relationships, unemployment, substance abuse, and dependency on welfare programs. The following case study reveals how the lack of understanding and support for LeDerick's learning disability affected his self-esteem and performance in school.

Hiding Behind the Normal Mask

Although my learning disability was recognized when I was 9 years old, and I had an IEP since the third grade, I still spent most of my childhood trying to hide that I had a learning disability. My parents, teachers, and school counselors did not explain to me what it meant to have a learning disability. Our identities are like open fields. If effort is not taken to plant and nourish positive ideas about who we are, then weeds will eventually take root in our minds. Weeds of doubt, fear, and low expectations will slowly begin to cover our true selves, choking out any potential for happiness.

By the time I reached high school, I was expending an enormous amount of emotional energy each day to maintain the persona that I was normal. I looked like a happy kid for the most part, but I was suffering with depression and anxiety. I eventually was not able to maintain this farce—I had trouble sleeping, I started faking illnesses so I could stay home from school, and I stopped caring about all the things that had previously made me happy. Things got so bad that I had an emotional breakdown in the winter of my junior year of high school. I was resilient enough to know that I had to find a way to keep moving forward, even in my depressed state. I removed myself from every relationship and extracurricular activity for several months, and I spent all my free time asking myself questions such as, "Who am I?" "What do I want to do with my life?" and "What does it mean to have a learning disability?" I did not find the answers to all these questions, and I did not cure myself of depression or anxiety, but I definitely emerged from that breakdown a much stronger person. I was only able to pull myself back to a place where I could function in school and at home by developing the strong conviction that there was nothing wrong with me or with the way my mind worked, despite my diagnosis.

Suggestions for teaching reading are provided because many students with specific learning disabilities, ADHD, and other hidden disabilities have difficulty with reading. These strategies are not intended to be used only for students with learning disabilities; they are effective for teaching reading to students with and without disabilities.

Reading is an essential life skill, yet many young adults do not acquire the reading skills necessary to maximize transition outcomes. Data from the 2011–2012 school year indicated that 74% of students with disabilities participated in

---

Tips for Teaching

Effective Reading Instruction for Students in Grades 4–12

- Provide explicit vocabulary instruction by
  1. Teaching the meaning of new vocabulary words directly at the beginning of the unit
  2. Using computer software vocabulary matching games, flash cards, or small group practice sessions so students learn definitions
  3. Demonstrating the relationship among words and concepts by using graphic organizers, syntax, and context clues
- Teach explicit comprehension strategies by
  1. Showing students how to apply the strategies to different texts
  2. Providing guided practice and extended discussion of text meaning and interpretation to small groups or individual students who need additional support.
- Increase student motivation by
  1. Selecting relevant passages related to students' interests and important current events
  2. Promoting a positive learning environment that promotes students' automomy and responsibility in learning.

Note: See Improving Adolescent Literacy: Effective Classroom and Intervention Practices at http://ies.ed.gov/ncee/wwc/pdf/practice_guides/adlit_pg_082608 .pdf for more information.

From Kamil, M. L., Borman, G. D., Dole, J., Kral, C. C., Salinger, T., and Torgesen, J. (2008). Improving adolescent literacy: Effective classroom and intervention practices: A Practice Guide (NCEE #2008-4027). Washington, DC: National Center for Education Evaluation and Regional Assistance, Institute of Education Sciences, U.S. Department of Education. Retrieved from http://ies.ed.gov/ncee/wwc.

the eighth-grade reading assessment, but only 30% were proficient (U.S. Department of Education, 2014). The percentage of students who were reading proficiently on their grade-level assessment dropped each year from third to eighth grade, with a high of 39.6% at third grade, to a low of 30% at eighth grade reading proficiently on state reading assessments (U.S. Department of Education, 2014). Given that the majority of students with disabilities are not proficient in reading, they struggle to comprehend the meaning of their grade-level textbooks (Kamil et al., 2008; Lee, Griggs, & Donahue, 2007). These students are at an increased risk for being unemployed, having low-paying jobs, and engaging in behavior that leads to incarceration (Wehby, Falk, Barton-Arwood, Lane, & Colley, 2003). Seventy-five percent of school dropouts have reading problems, and at least half of adolescents and young adults with criminal records have reading difficulties (Williams, 2013).

There is clearly a need to implement evidence-based interventions that teach students the important reading skills they need in order to be successful in college and careers. Teachers must implement reading interventions that increase students' self-efficacy and maintain their attention (Cho, Roberts, Capin, Roberts, Miciak, & Vaughn, 2015). Findings from studies serve as a reminder to schools that basic academic skills are valued by employers. Schools must emphasize training in basic literacy and communication skills and provide instruction in these areas (Ju, Zhang, & Pacha, 2012). Tips for Teaching provides a summary of evidence-based strategies to teach reading, and Table 1.2 provides links to online resources for identifying evidence-based practices (Test, Kemp-Inman, Diegelmann, Hitt, & Bethune, 2015).

Table 1.2. Web sites and resources for further information

Web site description	For more information
Best Evidence Encyclopedia provides reliable reviews of research-proven educational programs in mathematics, reading, science, school reform, and early childhood education.	http://www.bestevidence.org/index.cfm
CAST is a nonprofit organization that provides many tools, reports, and ideas for improving universal design for learning (UDL) for all learners. UDL is a set of principles that provides a framework for designing instructional goals, methods, materials, and assessments that work for everyone—not a single, one-size-fits-all solution but rather flexible approaches that can be customized and adjusted for individual needs.	http://www.cast.org
Center on Response to Intervention provides information, products and support for states, districts, and schools implementing response to intervention.	http://www.rti4success.org
The DO-IT Center supports students, with disabilities interested in science, technology, engineering, and mathematics through the use of a variety of technological and universal design for instructional supports for faculty and instructors.	http://www.uw.edu/doit
National Center for Learning Disabilities improves the lives of all people with learning difficulties and disabilities by empowering parents, enabling young adults, transforming schools, and creating policy and advocacy impact.	http://www.LD.org

(continued)

Table 1.2.   *(continued)*

Web site description	For more information
The National Center on UDL includes UDL guidelines and ideas for implementation.	http://www.udlcenter.org
National Dropout Prevention Center for Students with Disabilities provides evidence-based technical assistance to help states build and implement sustainable programs and best practices that encourage school completion for students with disabilities who are at risk.	http://www.ndpc-sd.org
National Technical Assistance Center on Transition (NTACT) assists school and vocational rehabilitation agencies to implement evidence-based practices to improve transition services and outcomes.	http://www.transitionta.org
Positive behavior interventions and supports (PBIS) is a set of research-based strategies used to increase quality of life and decrease problem behaviors by teaching new skills and making changes in a person's environment. Three web sites provide information about PBIS: 1. http://www.pbis.org is the federally funded Technical Assistance Center on Positive Behavioral Interventions and Supports. 2. http://www.apbs.org is the Association for Positive Behavioral Supports, which hosts an annual conference and maintains positive behavior support standards of practice. 3. http://www.pbisworld.com is a commercial site that provides descriptions of many behaviors with suggested interventions that teachers or parents may consider.	http://www.pbis.org http://www.apbs.org http://www.pbisworld.com
Promising Practices Network provides quality evidence-based information about what works to improve the lives of children, families, and communities.	http://www.promising practices.net
TEDx provides videos on YouTube that are testimonials of individuals who are living with many of the hidden disabilities discussed in this chapter.	http://www.youtube.com /watch?v=uU6o2_UFSEY)
Think College provides resources for students with intellectual disabilities and professionals and parents on inclusive college programs. The National Center on UDL includes UDL guidelines and ideas for implementation.	http://www.thinkcollege.net
What Works Clearinghouse established rigorous standards to assess the quality of evidence supporting educational programs and practices. Numerous reports are provided on a variety of topics; Improving Adolescent Literacy: Effective Classroom and Intervention Practices is a report cited in this chapter.	http://ies.ed.gov/ncee/wwc http://ies.ed.gov/ncee/wwc /pdf/practice_guides/adlit _pg_082608.pdf
The "Who Cares About Kelsey?" web site provides information about dropout prevention, information about the documentary film, an overview of the issues, and resources to address school climate.	http://www.whocaresabout kelsey.com

Source: Test, Kemp-Inman, Diegelmann, Hitt, & Bethune (2015).

Supporting Students with ADHD

> "My name is Margo Vreeburg Izzo and I'm a program director,
> principal investigator, faculty member, and mom. And I have ADHD."
> —Margo Vreeburg Izzo

ADHD is a neurological condition marked by persistent inattention, hyperactivity, and/or impulsivity that begins in childhood and often lasts into adulthood. Common symptoms can be categorized in three areas:

1. Trouble paying attention and being easily distracted and disorganized

2. Restless hyperactivity

3. Impulsive behaviors such as acting and talking before thinking (Arnold, 2004)

Students with ADHD have normal intelligence and are just as smart as their peers. They may struggle with poor school performance and low self-esteem because they have trouble paying attention or staying organized. Students and adults with ADHD often bring positive energy and a willingness to work hard when the learning environment is organized, structured, and relevant. Many children with ADHD continue to have symptoms as adults (Schwarz, 2013). Some adults with ADHD find a great job match in which they need to multitask or have an assistant that keeps their schedule and office area organized. Other adults with ADHD work in settings where the ADHD mind can quickly scan through multiple solutions to a problem, and their out-of-the-box thinking is an asset. The following describes how Margo became identified as having ADHD.

Margo Joins the Attention-Deficit/Hyperactivity Disorder Club

I was working as a researcher and program director at a large university when I first became identified as a person with ADHD. I also was a mom of two great kids. My colleagues told me that my youngest had ADHD when she was 2 years old, but she did not receive special education services until high school. I saw this darling little girl who was very curious—so curious that she could not sit in her seat at the dinner table or follow directions very well. She was on target developmentally and even advanced in her language and motor skills. I saw a mini-me—an inquisitive little girl with a passion for living life to the fullest. When Anna was identified as having ADHD, I decided to talk to her psychologist to see if I had ADHD. I was diagnosed with ADHD and started taking Adderall in 2001, 3 years after I earned my doctoral degree. It helped immensely, but medication does not solve all the issues associated with ADHD. I am still unorganized, impulsive, and have poor time management skills. Yet, I am very creative and able to develop innovative interventions to address the challenges facing students with disabilities in schools. I have learned to manage my ADHD symptoms by becoming the director of my own program, which is supported by grants that I write and direct. Once a grant is written and awarded, I carve out the portions that are a good match for my interest and abilities and delegate the tasks that require high levels of organization and record keeping to other employees. I do my best to manage my ADHD symptoms by using executive function skills, specifically setting goals, allocating adequate time to accomplish each goal, and providing incentives for completing goals, such as breaks and activities I enjoy.

The number of children and adults who report having ADHD has ballooned since the late 1990s. Before 1990, fewer than 5% of school-age students were thought to have ADHD. In 2013, the Centers for Disease Control and Prevention (CDC) reported that 11% of children ages 4–17 had received the ADHD diagnosis (Koerth-Baker, 2013). Experts debate the many suspected reasons for the increase in the number of children and adults who are identified with ADHD.

- Federal education policies incorporated the definition of ADHD into the Individuals with Disabilities Education Act (IDEA) of 1991 (PL 102-119), providing access to special education services, including tutors and extra time on tests, especially for high-stakes tests that must be passed to earn a high school diploma or gain access to college.

- The U.S. Food and Drug Administration allowed drug companies to more easily market medication to treat ADHD directly to the public in 1997 (Koerth-Baker, 2013).

Many students with ADHD can learn strategies to be successful. Although treatment cannot cure ADHD, taking medication and learning organizational and cognitive-behavioral skills and strategies can improve outcomes for students and adults (Solanto, 2011). ADHD tends to run in families (National Institute of Mental Health, 2013). The heritability of ADHD is high across the lifespan (Larsson, Chang, D'Onofrio & Lichtenstein, 2014).

ADHD is not a learning disability, but about 40% of people with ADHD also experience a learning disability. Students with either ADHD or learning disabilities often have difficulty with learning basic skills such as reading, writing, or mathematics. They may also have difficulty with tasks that require executive function, such as planning projects, time management, impulse control, emotional control, and organizational tasks. All students, but especially students with learning challenges related to executive functions, benefit from good teaching and direct instruction to strengthen their executive functioning skills. In his book *Executive Function in the Classroom: Practical Strategies for Improving Performance and Enhancing Skills for all Students,* Christopher Kaufman provides seven core strategies for helping students with executive function challenges. See Tips for Teaching: Executive Function Skills for a summary of these seven core strategies and tips for how to implement them in the classroom.

Tips for Teaching

Tips for Teaching Executive Function Skills

1. **Provide Students with the Support They Need to Succeed**
   - When a student is completing a writing assignment, help him or her with brainstorming, organization of thoughts, and sequencing.
   - During group activities, monitor the student's attention, providing prompts in the form of an agreed-upon verbal or nonverbal signal whenever the student goes off task.
   - Provide social mentoring in the cafeteria and during recess to help with impulsive or aggressive behavior that may cause the student social difficulties.

(continued)

Tips for Teaching *(continued)*

- Post visual reminders in the student's immediate learning environment that prompt the use of reading comprehension, editing, or other academic strategies.

2. **Teach New Skills and Content Using Systematic, Explicit Instruction**
   - Present novel content in highly explicit, step-by-step ways that clearly link the unfamiliar to the familiar (e.g., you already know about nouns and pronouns, and now this is exactly how adjectives fit in).
   - Repeatedly model new skills and give students the opportunity to practice the skills with frequent and direct feedback.
   - Provide kinesthetic learning opportunities such as role play.

3. **Teach students problem-solving and learning strategies and demonstrate how these strategies should be applied in real-life learning contexts.**
   - Explicitly teach and model the use of note-taking strategies within the context of a science unit
   - Explicitly teach or model pre-reading strategies to build reading comprehension skills
   - Explicitly teach a structured pre-writing strategy

4. **Minimize Demands on Working Memory**
   - Accompany oral directions for assignments with written instructions
   - During classroom discussions, pause regularly so students have time to take notes, lessening the demands of having to write and listen simultaneously.
   - Minimize the amounts of factual information that students must hold in working memory through the use of word walls, math fact walls, bulletin boards, and graphic organizers.
   - Clearly separate the stages of the writing process, with students only being required to complete one portion of the process each day.

5. **Provide Opportunities for Guided, Extended Practice**
   - Use guided oral reading practice to increase reading fluency, stamina, and enjoyment
   - Model the use of specific writing templates and have students repeatedly use these templates in a range of writing assignments throughout the school year
   - Explicitly teach classroom rules/expectations at the start of the school year, then practice and reinforce a rule each week through role-playing and demonstration

6. **Make the learning environment as predictable and consistent as possible.**
   - Develop predictable classroom routines for assignments, tests, collecting work, and so forth.
   - Make sure to consistently adhere to classroom rules and expectations.

(continued)

7.   Teach and Model Strategies for Approaching Frustrating or Challenging Tasks
  • Help keep anxiety, stress levels, and frustration down by showing students parts of a task that might be frustrating and then modeling ways to handle the difficulty
  • Normalize feelings of frustration students might be feeling while also providing explicit directions on what to do if they get stuck.

From Kaufman, C. (2010). *Executive Function in the Classroom: Practical Strategies for Improving Performance and Enhancing Skills for all Students* (pp 79–94). Baltimore, MD: Paul H. Brookes Publishing Co; Adapted by permission.

Supporting Students with Autism Spectrum Disorder

"I think in pictures. Words are like a second language to me. I translate both spoken and written words into full-color movies. Language-based thinkers often find this phenomenon difficult to understand, but in my job as an equipment designer for the livestock industry, visual thinking is a tremendous advantage."
—Temple Grandin (2006)

Temple Grandin is a professor at Colorado State University, a consultant to the livestock industry on animal behavior, and a person with autism. She believes that the world needs all kinds of minds, and people with autism contribute to resolving major issues that people with neurotypical brains are unable to solve. Grandin tells educators to help students with autism discover their passions and then use those passions to teach the content and the social skills needed to become contributing members of their classes and eventually of society. She attributes learning employability and work skills through the jobs and internships she had throughout high school and college. Grandin was portrayed in a 2010 award-winning movie titled *Temple Grandin.* The movie shared how she learned to speak and control her anxiety and how her teachers provided a supportive environment that promoted the development of her extraordinary talents.

The incidence of ASD has tripled since the mid-2000s, with the latest estimates from the CDC indicating that 1 in 68 children have autism in the United States (Baio, 2014). Approximately 38–41% of children with ASD are identified with an intellectual disability (Van Naarden Braun, 2015), and the comorbidity of ASD and ADHD is so prevalent that the Diagnostic and Statistical Manual of Mental Disorders (5th ed) makes it possible to assign a codiagnosis of ASD and ADHD for individuals who exhibit characteristics of both disorders (Miranda, Tarraga, Fernandez, Colomer, & Pastor, 2015). Therefore, two students with ASD may respond to very different types of interventions because the autism spectrum is so broad. Also, where the student falls on the spectrum will determine to what extent his or her characteristics of autism are hidden or obvious. Regardless, students with ASD benefit from teachers who meet them where they are socially and academically and provide individualized, small-group, and large-group instruction to teach the skills they need to navigate the school environment and eventually the community. Suggestions for teaching students with ASD, building positive character traits, and addressing common behavior problems are found in the Tips for Teaching. Many of these strategies are effective with all students, whether they have ASD, another hidden disability, or they exhibit at-risk behaviors.

Many students, including those with high-functioning ASD and other hidden disabilities, have difficulty learning verbal and nonverbal communication skills. Students with poor social skills will have difficulty working with others and can be bullied, further impairing their educational performance. Specifically, students with ASD may engage in repetitive activities, resist environmental changes or changes in daily routines, and may have unusual responses to sensory experiences.

Students with ASD exhibit some common behavior problems such as interrupting a class discussion with a totally unrelated comment, having meltdowns or temper tantrums, refusing to complete work or follow directions, arguing over rules and schedules, and difficulty getting along with peers and authority figures (Grindstaff, 2012). Margo worked with a student named Tara who had ASD. The following is what Tara said:

> "I believe that individuals can overcome any obstacles when they are challenged and supported. For me, my life changed for the better when I learned to embrace my disability. I will be there to encourage others to work hard to achieve their goals."

Many teachers do not know what to do with students with ASD and other students who learn differently. Dr. Grandin shares strategies that have worked for her on her web site (http://www.templegrandin.com) and in her TEDx Talk (http://tedxtalks.ted.com). As the prevalence of ASD continues to increase, teachers need quality information for parents and professionals to teach and support students with ASD. Books such as *You're Going to Love This Kid!* (Kluth, 2010) and web sites such as the Autism Internet Modules (AIM) published by the Ohio Center for Autism and Low Incidence (OCALI, 2015) provide strategies to assist students with autism to become welcome members of their classes and communities. The Tips for Teaching section provides suggestions to support all students, but especially those students with ASD. The strategies have been embellished to connect them to current educational reform initiatives such as the Common Core State Standards (CCSS) and assessment initiatives.

Tips for Teaching

Supporting Students with ASD and Other Disabilities

- Allow students to select projects that interest them to demonstrate the Common Core State Standards.
- Use web sites with videos and pictures from the Internet to help students discover their passions and interests.
- Use hands-on projects, especially for visual and pattern thinkers, to balance the visual and auditory methods used to engage students.

(continued)

Tips for Teaching *(continued)*

- Teach social skills directly. Explain social nuances and nonverbal communication patterns for students who are concrete learners and may not understand specific social cues.

- Reinforce career exploration through academic content by giving students examples of how scientists and entry-level workers need and use basic academic skills.

- Use class, school jobs, and internships to reinforce employability skills such as responsibility and self-regulation.

- Recruit employers, scientists, college faculty, instructors, or students in the community to mentor a student who shares their passion.

- Autistic minds tend to be fixated. If a student likes cars, trains, exotic animals, or super heroes, then use these high-interest subjects as motivation to do math.

- Share positive role models of other adults with autism (or other disabilities) to promote disability pride. Autism can be a gift if people with autism gain the confidence and skills to make the transition to college and careers with a clear understanding of how they learn, where and when to use which social skills, what supports they need to learn and follow directions, and how to translate their passions into employment goals.

- Teach resilience to students with ASD and any other disabilities. Persistence is a critical skill for everyone who plays the game of life.

Supporting Students with Emotional and Behavioral Disturbance

Kelsey was disruptive and unpredictable in the classroom. As a freshman at Somersworth High School in New Hampshire, she was unable to earn any academic credits, and she was suspended for dealing drugs. It seemed like Kelsey was a more likely candidate for the juvenile justice system than graduation (Habib, 2016).

Approximately half a million students are identified as having emotional and behavioral disturbance, about 6.2% of all students with disabilities (U.S. Department of Education, 2014). These students exhibit a number of characteristics that adversely affect their educational performance: an inability to learn, build, or maintain relationships with peers or teachers; inappropriate behaviors; and a tendency to develop physical symptoms or fears associated with personal or school problems. Most students with emotional and behavioral disturbance generally can be described as unhappy or depressed. According to the U.S. Department of Education (2014), youth with emotional and behavioral disturbance

- Have the worst graduation rates; nearly two thirds of students with emotional and behavioral disturbance drop out

- Are three times as likely to be arrested prior to leaving school

- Have the highest rates of removal to an interim alternative educational setting for drug or weapon offenses

- Were suspended or expelled for more than 10 days during the 2005–2006 school year

In addition to these challenges, estimates of youth in juvenile detention facilities indicate that 85% of these youth are eligible for special education, although only 37% were receiving special education services in their school prior to placement in juvenile detention. Without quality intervention and transition services, youth with emotional and behavioral disturbance may make the transition to juvenile detention facilities, often referred to as the school-to-prison pipeline. These youth are significantly more likely to be involved with the criminal justice system (e.g., stopped by police, arrested, spend a night in jail, be on probation or parole) than youth from other disability categories (Newman et al., 2011). Unfortunately, as youth aged, their rates of involvement with the criminal justice system did not decrease, and youth who dropped out of high school were significantly more likely to become and stay involved with the criminal justice system than those with higher levels of educational attainment (Newman et al, 2011).

Let's examine what happened to Kelsey, a high school student on the path of dropping out whose story is shared through a documentary film produced by Dan Habib. Thousands of educators, parents, and students have watched Habib's film *Who Cares About Kelsey?* as they continue to search for effective dropout prevention strategies.

What About Kelsey?

Kelsey entered high school with ADHD, a history of homelessness and substance abuse, and physical scars from cutting and self-harm. She was but one of many struggling students at Somersworth High School in New Hampshire, where dropout rates were high and morale was low among both teachers and students. Punitive discipline policies like suspension and expulsion excluded students like Kelsey from their education and made them at risk for dropping out or getting entangled with law enforcement. Then, a new leadership team implemented schoolwide reforms to improve the school climate and reduce the dropout rate, including PBIS, and things began to turn around for Kelsey. After receiving intensive self-directed planning and wraparound supports at her school, Kelsey began the transformation from struggling student to motivated, empowered young woman who could articulate her goals and dreams for the future.

WHY DO STUDENTS WITH HIDDEN DISABILITIES HAVE PROBLEMS WITH CONDUCT?

Many students with hidden disabilities exhibit behavior problems. For example, Margo's poorest grade in grade school was for conduct. Acting impulsively (e.g., speaking out, interrupting others) is one of the primary symptoms of

Tips for Teaching

Strategies to Address Emotional and Behavioral Disturbance and Other Behavior Problems

The following strategies are suggested to address behavior issues that students with a variety of hidden disabilities face and are not limited to only students with autism spectrum disorder or emotional and behavioral disturbance.

Interrupting with unrelated topics

- Teach self-regulation skills by identifying clear guidelines for appropriate times to discuss unrelated topics.
- Provide an appropriate time (e.g., lunch, regularly scheduled meetings, drive time) for individuals to share their passionate topics.
- Pair individuals with others who have similar interests.
- Allow children to use their passion for specific projects whenever possible.

Meltdowns

- Teach coping techniques to use when anxiety increases.
- Have children carry a laminated card with outlined steps that they can pull out to review when anxiety increases.
- Spend a few minutes each day reviewing the schedule and preparing the students in advance of unusual transitions or class activities.
- Identify a safe place the students can go to and give them permission and praise for using their safe place to avoid a public meltdown.
- As teenagers prepare to make the transition to college and careers, align breaks and coping strategies to what is appropriate within job settings and/or college classrooms.

Refusing to complete work/assignments

- Reduce the amount of problems that need to be completed if high accuracy occurs (e.g., if a student gets all the even problems correct, then he or she can skip the odd problems).
- Use speech-to-text technology to reduce writing tasks that students might find challenging.
- Put students in pairs or small groups to work on a project together so each individual can contribute to the completion of the project using his or her strengths.

Inappropriate social skills, including poor problem solving behaviors

- Model appropriate social skills and identify good examples of social skills when modeled by others.
- Meet with children individually to discuss poor examples of social skills.
- Role play both appropriate and inappropriate social skills and discuss how poor social skills detract from a productive class climate.
- Post rules and other positive behavior support strategies in the class, and provide visual and verbal prompts when students deviate from what is acceptable.

ADHD, and medication does not always reduce this behavior. Other reasons for acting out include

- Avoidance: Students cannot do the work, so they act out to get removed from class.

- Boredom: Talking with friends is more interesting than class content.

- Need for immediate gratification: Talking with friends gives students immediate pleasure, as opposed to paying attention and learning, which may result in good grades in the future.

- Lack of confidence and giving up: Students think they cannot learn the content, so they do not try to do their work.

- Impulsivity: The student's internal engine is in fast gear, and he or she cannot control his or her body or mind long enough to focus on the content.

The consequences of poor conduct often result in lack of achievement. Students' acting out not only interferes with their learning, but their behavior also affects the entire class.

LeDerick versus the Music Teacher

I had been in a self-contained special education classroom for more than a year, and the only time my classmates and I got to leave our room was for classes such as art and music. At some point, my school hired a new music teacher. She was young and very nice, but after sitting in her class for a day or so, I decided that she was teaching down to me and my friends. Every song felt like it was something you would give to a little kid. Now, in all fairness, I was a little kid, but these songs had simple melodies, the lyrics did not tell an interesting story, and I felt insulted to be treated like I was stupid. Eventually, I could not take it anymore. I raised my little hand during one of these awful songs, and in front of the entire class, I said in a very calm voice, something to the effect of, "Your songs are horrible. We already know how to do everything you are trying to teach us." Well, after hearing my criticism, the music teacher asked me a series of questions about song structure, and I correctly answered each question with an all-knowing grin on my small round face.

Throughout my education, I occasionally challenged teachers to intellectual duels. If an adult used my reading, writing, and math impairments as an excuse to ignore my strengths and talents, then I could become very combative. After the initial exchange with the music teacher, the quality of her music lessons did not change, so I decided to confront her in another way. Because I had been in a self-contained class with the same students, day in and day out, I had unwittingly developed a catalog of the triggers that would make my classmates talk endlessly or turn their focus away from schoolwork. For the remainder of the school year, I would begin each music class by having short conversations with a few of my classmates. I said just the right words, at just the right time, to force my music teacher to stop her lesson and attend to the cacophony that I had unleashed with my classmates.

Tips for Teaching

Supporting Students with Issues Related to Conduct

The following suggestions are recommended to first address conduct and behavior issues. If these suggestions are not effective, then meeting with parents and behavior specialists may provide additional strategies and interventions to improve classroom behaviors.

- Develop self-management plans with incentives and consequences that students select from an approved list that is provided. Students earn incentives they value as they accomplish daily and weekly goals. For example, going out to eat with a teacher or gaining a homework pass that they can use to opt out of completing a homework assignment may provide an incentive to maintain appropriate behaviors during class.

- Take a class period to meet with students individually to build a more positive working relationship and provide feedback on their behavior. Demonstrate that you sincerely care about their learning. Discuss how you can work together to help the student learn the essential content of the course, and commit your agreement to writing.

- Explain the relevance of the course content, even if it is brain exercise or the course grade is used as a measure by college admissions to determine students' academic abilities.

- Develop daily and weekly goals that are outlined on behavioral contracts.

- Engage students in transition planning activities in which they become aware of their interests, abilities, and needs. Assist these students by translating course content into requirements for careers they are interested in pursuing. Know what your students' employment goals are so you can connect academics to skills in their career area.

- Encourage students in career/college research so they see how students with higher GPAs get into more colleges and earn more scholarships, whereas students with lower GPAs may only have open admission community colleges as options.

- Use social stories to describe the link between behaviors and consequences and discuss how students are in control of the choices they make.

- Teach coping strategies for specific situations. See Text Box 1.2 for examples of coping strategies involving self-talk.

Source: OSEP Technical Assistance Center on Positive Behavioral Interventions and Supports (2015).

Many students with hidden disabilities have behavior or conduct issues that impede their ability to manage their classroom behaviors. Whether their behaviors are a result of learning disabilities, ADHD, ASD, or emotional and behavioral disturbance, the first intervention to increase appropriate classroom behaviors must begin with teaching students directly and designing classroom procedures in which clear consequences are in place to encourage appropriate social skills and compliant behaviors.

Text Box 1.2—Examples of How to Improve Coping Strategies

Example 1: When other kids say things that upset me, I can tell myself:
- Just because someone says something does not make it true.
- I am staying in control of myself. I will not let others' words control me.
- I do not want to react while I am upset.
- I can speak up for myself in a positive way.
- My mad and sad feelings will change soon.
- I can go talk to _____ (fill in a safe person such as guidance counselor or librarian).

Example 2: When I have to do things I do not like to do at school, here are some things for me to remember:
- When I am at school, I may be asked to do things I do not like to do.
- I may want to quit. When that happens, I will take a break and ask for help.
- It is important that I show myself and others that I can do things I do not like to do.
- Even teachers and the other students have to do things they do not like to do.
- When I have to do things I do not like, I will remind myself that this task will not go on forever.
- Being mature means doing things without complaining.

Example 3: When I am upset, I will take a break. Here are some things for me to remember:
- Sometimes I will need to take a break from class.
- It is okay to take a break when I am upset.
- It is important to take a break so that I have time and space to calm down.
- I must request a break before leaving the room.
- I must go to the _____ (fill in a safe space in the school).
- I must stay in my break area when I take a break.
- I will do a self-check to make sure I am ready to leave the break area.
  - Am I still feeling tense?
  - Has my breathing slowed down?
  - Do I feel calm?
  - Have I quieted down?

WHY DO STUDENTS WITH HIDDEN DISABILITIES DROP OUT OF HIGH SCHOOL?

According to a 2014 U.S. Department of Education report, 80% of students in the general population graduated, whereas only 61% of students with disabilities graduated (Stetser & Stillwell, 2014). Why do nearly 40% of students with disabilities, the majority of whom have hidden disabilities such as learning disabilities, ADHD, and emotional and behavioral disturbance, drop out of school? High school dropouts reported that they dropped out of school because of school, job, and family-related factors (see Text box 1.3; Bridgeland, Dilulio, & Morrison, 2006). Approximately 30% of adults who attended adult basic and secondary education programs reported having learning disabilities, and many other learners in this population are functionally similar to individuals with reading disabilities (Patterson, 2008, as reported in Mellard, Fall, and Woods, 2013).

Text Box 1.3—School, Job, and Family Factors Related to Dropping Out of School

School-related factors	Job-related factors	Family-related factors
Did not like school	Couldn't work and go to school at same time	Had to support their family
Could not get along with teachers	Had to get a job	Wanted to have a family
Could not get along with peer students	Found a job	Was pregnant
Was suspended or expelled		
Did not feel safe at school		
Was failing at least one course		

Source: State Board of Education's Task Force on Quality High Schools for a Lifetime of Opportunities (2004).

More than 1.5 million students with disabilities drop out of high school each year. Most of these students have failed at least one class, are credit deficient, exhibit behavior problems, do not get along with their teachers or their peers, and are struggling to figure out how to survive high school. In interviews with high school students and dropouts, teenagers said

- "If the school really cares about us and wants more kids graduating, they are going to have to give us something to look forward to." High school dropout. (High Quality High Schools, 2004, p. 13)

- "If there were somebody to just say, 'Hey, what's wrong?' or 'You don't seem like you've been yourself.' That's all kids are looking for; they crave attention. I think just a little bit of that could go a long way for kids." High school graduate who is now in a 4-year college. (High Quality High Schools, 2004, p. 25)

The dropping out process takes years. Students begin to feel alienated, like they do not fit into the school's culture. They may be bullied or ostracized. They may struggle with or fail a course. They begin to self-medicate with alcohol and/or drugs. All students, especially those who question their self-worth, need positive attention and someone who cares about them. Imagine going to school day after day and being bullied or doing poorly on tests and being reminded that you do not belong. The costs of ignoring students at risk of dropping out are high. Dropouts from the class of 2008 will cost the nation more than $310 billion in lost wages over the course of their lifetime (Ohio Department of Education, 2004).

Federal legislation continues to emphasize the need to increase academic achievement and transition outcomes for all students. The purpose of education is to assist all students in becoming contributing members of the community. A number of interventions are implemented in schools to make progress toward this goal and improve the conditions for learning so all students experience a motivating and supportive environment (e.g., positive behavior interventions and supports [PBIS], response to intervention [RTI], universal design for learning [UDL]). Learners can experience an increase in their academic and transition outcomes when they are provided with conditions that are right for learning.

Many schools have improved overall school climate by implementing a set of research-based strategies called PBIS. PBIS is a decision-making framework that guides selection, integration, and implementation of evidence-based academic and behavioral practices for improving the academic and behavior outcomes for all students (OSEP, 2015). PBIS strategies are taught to administrators, teachers, and students to improve the learning environment, increase academic achievement, and decrease problem behaviors. Schools who have implemented schoolwide PBIS with fidelity have teaching and learning environments that increase achievement and are less aversive, dangerous, and exclusionary (McIntosh, Horner, Chard, Boland, & Good, 2006; Nelson, Benner, Neill, & Stage, 2006). Another web site that provides numerous suggestions is http://www.pbisworld.com. This user-friendly web site allows educators, parents, and behavior specialists to select specific target behaviors and then identify possible characteristics of that behavior. Table 1.2 provides resources that promote positive school climate and increase achievement.

 ## Kelsey and PBIS

Kelsey benefited from a schoolwide policy called PBIS, which is a system of school reforms that helps schools more effectively address issues related to discipline. Visit http://www.whocaresaboutkelsey.com for more information about Kelsey and PBIS.

A DISABILITY PRIDE FRAMEWORK

Disability is commonly thought of as a limiting condition or impairment that affects a person's physical or mental abilities. The emphasis is on the *dis* and not the *ability* within most people's cultural understanding of disability. The focus tends to fall on impairments and deficits instead of looking at the talents, gifts, and strengths of each person. The quote from Albert Einstein at the beginning of this chapter is especially relevant to broadening one's understanding of disability. Einstein, who is often cited as having a learning disability, was 4 years old before he could speak. He failed high school math but went on to be a brilliant physicist. Many famous people had trouble fitting into the box of what many professionals (e.g., teachers, doctors, psychologists) would label as normal. (See Text Box 1.4.)

Many people who do not fit into the box of normality go on to do amazing things with their extraordinary abilities. Many people today are not only admitting to having a hidden disability, but they also are openly proud of their disability and the insights and innovations their challenges have inspired. Andy Imparato, Executive Director of the Association of University Centers on Disability, who is open about having bipolar disorder, describes disability as the interaction between the person and the environment. Excerpts from an interview with Andy follow.

Question: How do you define *disability?*

Andy: The way that I define *disability* generally is that it is a political thing, more than a medical thing or a legal thing. It's a word that connects me with a movement of people who are trying to promote more universal concepts of how you design anything and who are trying to embrace diversity in a really radical way than sometimes occurs in our culture. Disabilities occur when human beings interact with society and when the society hasn't thought about it and planned for it and embraced all forms of human diversity. I find it very empowering.

Question: What are your thoughts about disability pride?

Andy: I think it is helpful for kids and young adults to have disability pride. So, I do not have any problem with people getting a label, if along with that label they get pride, and a cultural identity, and a connection to a community, and a connection to a history of this community of accomplishing amazing things, including world leaders. I do have a problem with people getting labels that are negative labels. Labels that have low expectations associated with them and that force accommodations and alterations that some people may not even want.

Question: How can teachers empower students with disabilities to embrace their disability?

Andy: I think it depends on the age of the student, but I think if teachers can help students believe in themselves, help expose them to knowing about people with their disability who achieved incredible things. If teachers are comfortable sharing their own ADHD or their own dyslexia or their own anxiety or their own depression with the class, as a way of helping the class understand that there are adults who function well as professionals, who still have these long-term symptoms and issues that they deal with; I think that is good. I think teachers need to pay a lot of attention to language. If they use the word *suffers* every time they talk about a disability, that is not really empowering language. They need to think about their frame for disability—is it cultural, is it political, is it medical, is it civil rights, is it diagnosis and treatment or a pathology. They [teachers] can really think about their language and try to consistently present disability as a natural part of the human experience and a natural part of human diversity. Tell the kids that Martin Luther King, [Jr.] said, "Only God is able." That is a good way of thinking about humanity and the limitations associated with humanity.

Text Box 1.4—Famous People with Learning Differences

Many people have had to deal with a learning difference. The following individuals are a few leaders, entrepreneurs, and scientists who provide inspiration for those with hidden disabilities.

Michael Burry is an American hedge fund manager and was profiled in the 2010 book and the 2015 film entitled *The Big Short: Inside the Doomsday Machine*. After his son was diagnosed with Asperger syndrome, Burry believes he, himself, had Asperger syndrome after reading about the disorder.

Winston Churchill: Churchill failed sixth grade and later became a great statesman and Prime Minister of Great Britain.

Tom Cruise: Cruise is an actor who starred in *Top Gun, Mission Impossible, Rainman,* and many other movies, and he has a learning disability.

Thomas Edison: One of Edison's teachers told him that he was too stupid to learn anything. He went on to be a famous inventor responsible for the phonograph and electric lighting. Edison was not identified with a disability but may have had a learning disability.

Albert Einstein: Einstein was 4 years old before he could speak. He failed high school math but went on to be a brilliant physicist who developed the theory of relativity.

Temple Grandin: Dr. Grandin was diagnosed with autism as a child and designed a cattle processing system used by more than half of the beef processing facilities in the United States. She makes the case that the world needs people with autism—visual and pattern thinkers.

Whoopi Goldberg: Goldberg is an American comedian, actress, singer-songwriter, political activist, author, and talk-show host who has dyslexia.

Andrew Imparato: Imparato is Executive Director of the Association of University Centers on Disability (AUCD) and is open about having bipolar disorder.

Steve Jobs: Jobs was an entrepreneur, marketer, and inventor who was the cofounder, chairman, and chief executive officer of Apple and had ADHD.

Daymond John: John is an entrepreneur and business executive on the show *Shark Tank*. He launched his clothing company "For Us By Us" (FUBU) that grossed over $350 million in annual sales. John has not let his dyslexia define him. For more information, see http://dyslexia.yale.edu/daymondJohn.html

Ari Ne'eman: Ne'eman is the President and co-founder of the Autistic Self Advocacy Network (ASAN), an advocacy organization run by and for Autistic adults seeking to increase our representation of Autistic people across society. Learn more at ASAN's web site: http://autisticadvocacy.org/home/about-asan/leadership/

J.C. Penney: Penney was in a psychiatric hospital when he was 56. He owed more than 6 million dollars. He was a multimillionaire, however, when he died at the age of 92.

Tim Tebow: Tebow is an American football quarterback who was the winner of the Heisman trophy and two NCAA national football championships. He has learning disabilities.

Stephen Tonti: Tonti is an actor and producer who believes that ADHD is a difference in cognition, not a disorder. He was featured in a Ted Talk where he discusses ADHD.

One of the goals of this book is to help educators expand the scope of what students with hidden disabilities need to make the transition to college and careers as healthy, confident human beings. Students need to make peace with their disability and develop pride in who they are, their abilities, and their disabilities in order to reach this goal. When disability is reframed, it becomes easier to see that society draws the line of normalcy in a fairly arbitrary way. As a result, students with hidden disabilities, unlike other forms of disability, may find it difficult to determine on which side of the normalcy line they belong. From a legal point of view, it is not difficult to understand the benefits of using disability accommodations to ensure people receive access to the curriculum and supports needed to learn essential skills. Imparato, however, challenges educators and people with disabilities to embrace disability as a positive identifier. If students with disabilities are supported and nurtured by their family, doctors, educators, and service providers, then they can develop disability pride and connect to a long history and a diverse community of people who share their challenges and triumphs. Educators and parents should empower their students to feel proud of how their minds and bodies work, instead of feeling shame and exerting energy to hide their disability and pass as normal.

EMBRACING DIFFERENCES AND DISABILITIES

"Having a disability is not a bad thing. It can even be something to be proud of. We are all different and all have different abilities. Every child can be an ambassador of ability to our families, schools, and communities. We each have ideas, experiences, and skills that can serve everybody else."
—Victor Santiago Pineda

Victor Santiago Pineda is an educator and filmmaker who works with young people who have disabilities to inform them of their rights. He developed the A World Enabled initiative with his foundation to educate the public about the abilities and potential of young people with disabilities (Pineda, 2014).

Stephen Tonti, a student from Carnegie Mellon, won a student speaker competition with his speech, "ADHD as a Difference in Cognition." Stephen is proud of having ADHD. He believes that ADHD is not a disorder. Instead, he defines ADHD as attention-deficit/hyperactively different. He learns differently, and he accomplishes much more than his typically developing peers as long as he has some choices. He states that he will read a 500-page book of his choosing faster than a one-page article that someone else is forcing him to read on a topic in which he has no interest. See Stephen's award-winning speech at http://www.youtube.com/watch?v=uU6o2_UFSEY for more information about his accomplishments.

Once children and adults with hidden disabilities stop hiding their disability and become proud of who they are, they can then use all that energy to focus on developing their abilities and their potential. This does not mean the disability should be ignored, but it should not be the only way we define people. Students need to accept and embrace the challenges presented by their disability. They need to learn to manage their disorganization and impulsivity, master the assistive technology (AT) that helps them comprehend reading materials, or consistently use the medication that increases their ability to focus so they can confidently face each day.

People with disabilities must accept themselves. That often starts with parents, teachers, and friends accepting them for who they are. How can students reach their full potential if they are spending so much time and energy hiding their disability? How can these students shift the focus from what they cannot do well to what they can do well?

> **Text Box 1.5—Stephen Tonti's award-winning speech can be found at**
>
> http://www.youtube.com/watch?v=uU6o2_UFSEY. One can also explore other TEDx videos on depression, suicide, Asperger syndrome, and loneliness. In addition, have students select a video, read the blog, and add their original thoughts on who has a disability to the blog. Expand an understanding of disability by reframing how disabilities are minimized or maximized in different environments by using some of the examples that Tonti's video and other videos share.

FROM DISABILITY TO DIFFERENT ABILITY

Margo explained to Anna that her brain is wired differently. "It's not that you can't learn. You just learn differently. You are smart and have great potential—we need to work together with your teachers and support staff to figure out what your passions, interests, talents, and dreams are, and then help you learn best so that you can pursue your dreams." The people with disabilities listed in Text Box 1.4 are recognized for their accomplishments—the things they have done despite their learning differences. Working through the challenges of figuring out how individuals are different and accepting those differences are the first two monumental steps that students with hidden disabilities must experience if they are going to grow up to become empowered and proud adults.

PATH TO DISABILITY PRIDE

The needs, challenges, and self-perception of people with hidden disabilities often change as they progress through life. After people with hidden disabilities confront the initial impairments associated with their disability, there seem to be a few key stages that many people with hidden disabilities experience as they begin to understand who they are, what they need, and how to live as people with a disability. A framework to visualize the key stages many people will experience as they develop and work to maintain a sense of disability pride has been created to help students, teachers, and families better understand this somewhat stochastic process of disability identity development.

The Path to Disability Pride framework separates the key stages of identity development into two paths: a path of acceptance that leads towards disability pride and a path of rejection that risks underachievement. When people with hidden disabilities understand and accept their disability, they will use supports and accommodations, self-advocate, and progress on their path to pride and success. However, when people with hidden disabilities reject their disability and the supports and accommodations that may assist them, they may experience disability shame and risk underachievement. Instead of identifying with a disability community that has achieved much, they may engage in maladaptive behaviors that compromise their ability to develop their potential.

CONCLUSION

The Path to Disability Pride is presented in depth in the next chapter. A number of case studies are presented in the remaining chapters to illustrate how the authors and others have progressed towards developing disability pride. This framework hopefully will help contextualize an inner journey that many people with hidden disabilities experience as they live and grow. The Path to Disability Pride will support the work of teachers, parents, and other personnel as they help students with hidden disabilities acknowledge their current stage of development and construct a plan to bring them closer to where they want to be in the future.

Margo has ADHD, so most of the time her brain is running in high gear, jumping from thought to thought. She does not like dealing with details, but she works hard at putting together teams of people who can help manage the details in her professional life. She has also learned to manage her ADHD by taking medication and having a support system in place that helps her accomplish her goals. LeDerick has a learning disability, so many of the words he tries to write are misspelled. He also has a difficult time solving basic math problems, but he is known as a poet and is involved in the creation and management of several businesses. He is able to accomplish these tasks by using AT such as a spellchecker on his laptop and a calculator application on his smartphone. Every student needs some degree of support, whether he or she has a disability or not. The right supports, combined with a shameless acceptance of their differences, and a meaningful connection to people who have similar experiences give students with hidden disabilities a strong foundation on which to build their lives. People develop disability pride by refusing to waste energy keeping their disability hidden from others, embracing their disability, and focusing on their assets, strengths, and talents to accomplish their goals.

The Path to Disability Pride

Assisting Students as They Dare to Dream

"People with disabilities have forged a group identity. We share a common history of oppression and a common bond of resilience. We generate art, music, literature, and other expressions of our lives and our culture, infused from our experience of disability. Most importantly, we are proud of ourselves as people with disabilities. We claim our disabilities with pride as part of our identity. We are who we are: We are people with disabilities."
—Steven E. Brown (2003, pp. 80–81)

The disability pride movement is active and growing across the United States and across the world, as evidenced by more than 50 million web sites that address disability culture, history, and pride (Brown, 2011). This movement gained momentum in the 1960s when Ed Roberts, a student who used a wheelchair equipped with a ventilator, enrolled at the University of California at Berkeley. President John F. Kennedy established the Committee on Mental Retardation and the National Institute of Child Health and Human Development (NICHD) in 1961 to address the plight of his sister, Rosemary, who remained institutionalized in Wisconsin (Larson, 2015). He signed disability legislation in 1963 to establish research centers at universities on disability, which was followed by the establishment of Developmental Disabilities Councils in 1970 (National Council on Disability [NCD], 2011). Protection and Advocacy for Developmental Disabilities (PADD) programs were created in the Developmental Disabilities Assistance and Bill of Rights Act of 1975 (PL 94-103), which established a disability network in every state of the union. University Centers provided research to identify successful community-based alternatives; Developmental Disabilities Councils promoted laws, regulations, and policies to implement research findings from the University Centers; and PADD used advocacy skills and legal avenues to enforce the laws (NCD, 2011). The disability pride movement, however, is primarily driven by people with physical and developmental disabilities and the advocates who support them. People with hidden disabilities, for the most part, are not at the forefront of the disability pride movement, and many are not aware that it exists.

The Education for All Handicapped Children Act of 1975 (PL 94-142) mandated that all children with disabilities have the right to a free appropriate public education (FAPE) in the least restrictive environment. The Individuals with Disabilities Education Act (IDEA) of 1990 (PL 101-476) required schools to provide transition services that were based on the student's needs, taking into account the student's preferences and interests. The transition mandate highlighted the need for student involvement in the IEP process and gave rise to the self-determination movement (Ward, 1996). A number of self-determination models and curricula have been developed since the mid-1990s and are designed to teach self-determination skills to students with disabilities. Shogren (2013) provided an excellent overview of the self-determination movement. Table 2.1 provides a list of resources to assess and teach self-determination and transition planning for students from middle school through college.

Field and Hoffman stated that self-determination is "one's ability to define and achieve goals based on a foundation of knowing and valuing oneself" (1994, p. 164). One of the most frequently cited definitions states that self-determination is "understanding one's strengths and limitations, together with a belief of oneself as capable and effective" (Field, Martin, Miller, Ward, & Wehmeyer, 1998, p. 2). Yet, the literature and the authors' experiences reveal that self-determination skills for a majority of high school students with disabilities are still emerging (Field & Hoffman, 1994; Izzo & Lamb, 2003; Sitlington & Clark, 2006).

Self-advocacy is a skill that people who are self-determined use to request the supports they need (Shogren, 2013). Test, Fowler, Wood, Brewer, and Eddy (2005) identified four components that can be taught to increase students' ability to self-advocate:

1. Knowledge of self

2. Knowledge of rights

3. Communication of one's knowledge of self and rights

4. Leadership

Students' actions lead to greater levels of self-determination when they have accurate perceptions of their strengths, limitations, and choices and advocate for appropriate goals, supports, and accommodations. "Self-advocates have the skills to take on leadership roles and go after the things they want in life. Students can use self-advocacy skills to advocate for their right to make choices, manage their own learning and behavior, and set goals" (Shogren, 2013, p. 75).

The transformation from being a person who has been labeled with a disability to a self-determined person who embraces his or her disability and is actively taking charge of his or her life is challenging. The goal of this chapter

Table 2.1. Self-determination and transition planning web sites and resources

Assessment	Target population	Description	Ordering information
Adolescent Self-Determination Scale-Short Form (Wehmeyer, Little, Lopez & Shogren, 2011) and the The Arc's Self-Determination Scale (Wehmeyer & Kelchner, 1995)[a]	High school students with cognitive and developmental disabilities	Measures autonomy, self-regulation, empowerment, and self-realization.	Available in Shogren, K.A. (2013). Self-Determination and Transition Planning. Baltimore, MD: Paul H. Brookes Publishing Co. http://www.thearc.org/document.doc?id=3670 or http://www.beachcenter.org or http://www.ou.edu/content/dam/Education/documents/miscellaneous/the-arc-self-determination-scale.pdf
The American Institutes for Research (AIR) Self-Determination Scale (Wolman, Campeau, Dubois, Mithaug, & Stolarski; 1994)	All school-age students with disabilities	Measures two constructs: 1. Capacity—students' knowledge, abilities, and perceptions that enable them to be self-determined. 2. Opportunity—students' chances to use their knowledge and abilities. Three versions are available: 1. Student Form 2. Parent Form 3. Educator Form	http://www.ou.edu/content/education/centers-and-partnerships/zarrow/self-determination-assessment-tools/air-self-determination-assessment.html
Self-Determination (SD) Assessments Internet (SDAi). Four different scales are available to measure an individual's SD from three perspectives: 1. SD Student Scale 2. SD Student Scale-Short Form 3. SD Parent Perception Scale 4. SD Advisor Perception Scale (Hoffman, Field Hoffman & Sawilowsky, 2015)	Students with disabilities from age 14 to 22 in either middle, high school, or college settings	The SDAi instruments focus on variables that promote self-determination and are within the individual's control making them potential targets for instructional intervention. The model contains five components: (1) Know Yourself and Your Context, (2) Value Yourself, (3) Plan, (4) Act, and (5) Experience Outcomes and Learn.	User manual available at no cost at: http://www.ealyeducation.com/SDAi_Users_Manual.pdf Volume discounts available. Complete information on ordering the SDAi is available from the following: Ealy Education Group, Inc. 1043 Maravista Drive Trinity, FL 34655 Phone: 727-487-1890 Email: service@ealyeducation.com Web: www.ealyeducation.com ©2015, Ealy Education Group, Inc.

Table 2.1. (continued)

Assessment	Target population	Description	Ordering information
ChoiceMaker Self-Determination Assessment (Martin, Huber Marshall & Wray, 2004)	Middle and secondary students with learning disabilities and emotional/behavioral disabilities	Measures choice making, decision making, problem solving, self-awareness, self-advocacy, goal setting, and planning	http://www.ou.edu/content/education/centers-and-partnerships/zarrow/self-determination-assessment-tools/

Curricula	Target population	Description	Ordering information
The 411 on Disability Disclosure: A Workbook for Youth with Disabilities (National Collaborative for Workforce and Disability for Youth, 2005)	Youth and adults with disabilities	This workbook, available in Microsoft Word, PDF, and audio version, provides information and worksheets for students with disabilities to increase their self-awareness and self-advocacy skills including when and how to disclose	http://www.ncwd-youth.info/411-on-disability-disclosure
I'm Determined.org	Elementary through high school students with disabilities	Web site provides free information and training materials for students, families, and teachers. Downloadable templates and tools that promote goal setting and attainment are available.	http://www.imdetermined.org
Me! Lessons for Teaching Self-Awareness and Self-Advocacy (Cantley, Little & Martin, 2010).	Adolescents with moderate to severe disabilities	These materials include activities to teach students to understand their disability and abilities, rights and responsibilities, and self-advocacy skills. Students develop portfolios that include critical information and documents to help them transition from high school to postsecondary settings.	http://www.ou.edu/content/education/centers-and-partnerships/zarrow/trasition-education-materials/me-lessons-for-teaching-self-awareness-and-self-advocacy.html
S.T.E.P. (Student Transition and Educational Planning) (Halpern, Herr, Wolf, Lawson, Doren, & Johnson, 1995).	Special education and general education students in high school, middle school, and some post–high school settings.	Students assess their transition knowledge and skills and then complete activities using a workbook format. The activities are designed to assist students to learn how to take charge of their own transition planning.	http://www.proedinc.com

34

Program (Citation)	Target Population	Description	Availability
The Ohio State University E-Mentoring Program (Izzo, Murray, Earley, McCarrell, & Yurick, 2014).	High school students with and without disabilities enrolled in inclusive general education classrooms and students with mild and moderate disabilities in special education classrooms.	The Electronic Mentoring Curricula consists of a 17-unit transition-focused online curriculum that is aligned with national standards in English Language Arts, technology, transition, and financial literacy. It also contains an online and face-to-face mentoring component.	http://www.ou.edu/content/education/centers-and-partnerships/zarrow/osu-emp.html iTunes University: A collaborative effort with the OSU Office of Distance Education and E-Learning (ODEE), the E-Mentoring course on iTunes University is a packaged downloadable course that is available for anyone who has a free iTunes account.
The Self-Advocacy Strategy (Van Reusen et al., 1994)	Students with intellectual disabilities	This curriculum includes seven instructional areas with lesson plans focused on teaching students to participate in IEP meetings	Available for purchase from Edge Enterprises, Edge Enterprises, Inc. Phone: 877-767-1487 (toll free) or 785-749-1473 Fax: 785-749-0207 E-mail: eeinfo@edgeenterprisesinc.com http://www.edgeenterprisesinc.com/
Self-Directed IEP, ChoiceMaker Self-Determination Transition Series (Martin, Marshall, Maxson, & Jerman, 1993)	Students with all types of disabilities in middle and high school.	These materials teach students how to lead and participate in their IEP meetings, including how to select their own postsecondary goals.	http://www.ou.edu/content/education/centers-and-partnerships/zarrow
Whose Future Is It Anyway?: A Student-Directed Transition Planning Process, Second Edition (Wehmeyer, Lawrence, Kelchner, Palmer, Garner, & Soukup, 2004).	Students with mild to moderate cognitive disabilities ages 14 to 21	Commercial product includes student reader, workbook, instructor guide, and software to introduce students to transition planning, including how to become an effective team member or self-advocate.	Attainment Company 800-327-4269 http://www.attainmentcompany.com/whose-future A free version is available at: http://www.education.ou.edu/zarrow http://www.ou.edu/content/education/centers-and-partnerships/zarrow/trasition-education-materials/whos-future-is-it-anyway.html

aThe Adolescent Self-Determination Scale-Short Form and the The Arc's Self-Determination Scale are designed for same target population and measure similar constructs.

is to use the authors' personal and professional experiences to build on the disability pride and self-determination literature to assist parents, teachers, administrators, transition specialists, and other support personnel to promote disability pride within schools and communities but, most important, within students with hidden disabilities. Hopefully the stories, and the framework that follows, can be used to create learning environments that embrace disability as a natural part of the school culture. The chapter begins by exploring the ways LeDerick, Margo, and Margo's daughter, Anna, came to terms with their disabilities and began developing their own self-advocacy skills.

LeDerick Shares How Disability was Discussed in High School versus College

High school: I grew up in a household and school system where disability was not discussed openly. When teachers needed to address our learning challenges, they used terms such as *special* or *slow* to describe those of us who were not able to perform on the same academic level as our nondisabled peers.

College: I had a meeting within the first week of my freshman year at Middlesex County College that completely changed my understanding of what it meant to be a person with a learning disability. The meeting only took about 45 minutes, but it prepared me to become the self-advocate that I am today. My disability counselor reviewed my documentation, explained how my learning disability affected my learning, and recommended accommodations and supports. Although my path to self-advocacy began when I was an 18-year-old college student, I have met a number of people with disabilities who have had similar experiences of self-knowledge at much earlier ages.

Margo's Experiences with Advocacy as a Parent and Self-Advocate

I have experienced self-advocacy from four points of view. I understand it first as a professor and researcher who has worked for decades at Ohio State University to improve transition services and supports for people with disabilities. My second perspective comes from that of a mom of a daughter who was diagnosed with ADHD and rebelled against the label and the supports. I have coached and encouraged Anna and have had the joy of seeing her develop into an independent woman who is proud of how her mind works. Third, I embrace advocacy as a person with ADHD who accepted the diagnosis as an adult. Finally, I developed an ankle injury that resulted in eligibility for accessible parking. I have learned to accept the benefits and challenges that come with my disabilities, as well as learn to advocate for myself in a variety of settings.

As coauthors and self-advocates, we know how our lives changed when we accepted that we have disabilities, increased our understanding of the nature of our specific disabilities, and made peace with who we are and our disabilities. In addition, we realized that we connect with others who have hidden disabilities and encourage them to celebrate and build on their strengths when we share our stories. We hope that people with hidden disabilities (and their parents, teachers, and peers) see that our disabilities give us unique perspectives that enrich our contributions. Stigma and shame waste human potential. Disability pride enhances self-determination and potential.

THE PATH TO DISABILITY PRIDE

Disability pride is often embodied by disability activists and debated within the field of disability studies, but rarely finds its way into practical conversations about preparing students for their transition to adulthood. This chapter describes a framework that provides insights to the pathway that many people with hidden disabilities take in order to develop and maintain disability pride. The framework is based on our own journeys as well as the journeys of the countless people with hidden disabilities who we have worked with over the course of our careers. The Path to Disability Pride displayed in Figure 2.1 illustrates many stages of identity development that people with hidden disabilities experience as they come to terms with who they are and how they are treated by the larger society.

The Path to Disability Pride has two sides showing stages associated with disability shame and disability pride. The two sides show the key stages that many people with hidden disabilities experience as they make the transition through life and develop their identity. Some students with hidden disabilities unfortunately will experience some, if not all, of the stages represented on the shame side of the path before they develop the knowledge, skills, and self-awareness that promote disability pride. The journey of identity development is highly individualized. Although some students with hidden disabilities will navigate the stages of the path in the order we have presented them in Figure 2.1, others will make dramatic bounces from stages on either side of the path, depending on the environment and supports they are experiencing. Even when people with hidden disabilities develop a firm sense of disability pride, they may still need to work to maintain that pride on a daily or weekly basis. For example, the athlete with a learning disability or ADHD may feel disability pride on the basketball court, where she can think agilely and effectively communicate with her teammates. The next day, however, she may experience disability shame in an academic setting due to her inability to read fluently or focus on the teacher's lecture.

The goal of the Path to Disability Pride is to assist students with disabilities to advocate for the services and supports they need to reach their self-determined goals, free of shame and embarrassment. The Path to Disability Pride figure is also designed to be used as a discussion tool for educators, parents, and support personnel to

1. Understand what students with hidden disabilities may experience

2. Help students with hidden disabilities become aware of the various stages that they and many other students experience

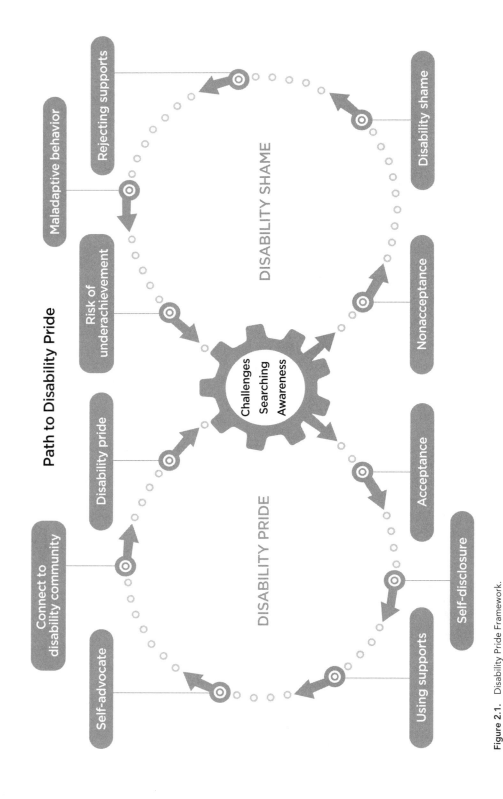

Figure 2.1. Disability Pride Framework.

Empowering Students with Hidden Disabilities: A Path to Pride and Success by Margo Vreeburg Izzo and LeDerick Horne.
Copyright © 2016 by Paul H. Brookes Publishing Co., Inc.

3. Help students develop their own identity as people with disabilities with a focus on their assets, strengths, and talents

4. Embrace who they are and navigate each day with disability pride

THE TRANSITION TO DISABILITY PRIDE

Each stage of the Path to Disability Pride is described, and case study examples are provided from LeDerick, Margo, or Anna's life. These case studies demonstrate the identity development that the authors and others with hidden disabilities experience as they make the transition from stage to stage. These examples are provided to assist students with hidden disabilities with their own identity development so they can transition with confidence and pride to their self-determined futures. Many people with hidden disabilities begin the path by experiencing challenges, searching for an explanation or a strategy to meet the challenge, and then, to some degree, becoming aware of their disability. Children and adults with hidden disabilities can either accept their disability and the supports and accommodations that they have a right to gain (see Figure 2.1), or they can experience nonacceptance of their disability and give up the supports and accommodations that would help them meet their challenges. These people may then experience denial, experience shame, or believe too many of the negative assumptions associated with their disability.

Challenges

The first stage of the Path to Disability Pride refers to the challenges that students or adults with hidden disabilities experience as they begin to struggle with communication, learning, social skills, organization, perception, or a multitude of other behaviors and abilities impaired by their disability. Students at this stage may not have received a diagnosis that properly explains why they have difficulty with some tasks, so they wrestle with feelings of isolation and loneliness that come from believing that they are the only person who has these sets of challenges. Performance at school and relationships with teachers, friends, and family might be difficult. This stage often occurs before adolescence for people who are born with a hidden disability. This stage may occur shortly after the incident that resulted in the disability for those who have acquired disabilities later on in life.

 ### LeDerick Encounters Challenges in Elementary School

The first 5 years of my life progressed without any indication that I had a disability. I was a very talkative child at home, and my mother believed that I was gifted, due to my ability to tell highly detailed stories that recounted my activities over the course of any given day. This talent for storytelling, combined with my ability to draw very well at an early age, gave my mother every indication that I would excel once I began going to school.

Kindergarten came and went with very little trouble, but it became apparent once I entered first grade that there was something very different about the way I learned. Reading and spelling seemed like skills that I would never be able to master. My classmates took their vocabulary list home at the start of the week and by Friday they had miraculously memorized the sequence of letters that made up each word. My spelling tests were never adorned with stars and smiley faces because I could not figure out how to spell even the most basic words, despite hours of studying with my mother right by my side. Reading out loud was an activity that I absolutely hated, and I would twist and squirm in my little desk, dreading the moment when I had to make sense of the words printed on the page in front of me.

Searching

Searching refers to the point in which students (and/or their families) begin searching to explain the challenges they have been facing. Because students do not have a disability that is easy to recognize, they might not use the word *disability* to represent the source of their impairments, but they are searching for a label that encompasses everything they know about the challenges they have been experiencing. Students may seek advice from their family, friends, teachers, and counselors at this stage. Their searching might eventually lead to a formal evaluation by medical doctors, psychologists, and/or learning experts. Students may become depressed, experience anxiety, or blame others for their challenges while they search for an explanation. They may begin to develop feelings of doubt or decide it is better to repress their questions about why they struggle.

Anna Experiences Challenges with Reading

Anna experienced reading difficulty in first grade and was referred to reading recovery in which she received small-group instruction. She received individualized reading instruction when she did not make adequate progress within her small-group. Anna liked the reading teacher and the way the teacher made practicing her letters fun. She compared it to playing games with the teacher. Anna had caught up with her peers by the end of first grade, but the school recommended additional accommodations for second grade to assist with reading fluency and comprehension. Anna had the option of listening to her books on tape instead of having to read them. She chose to listen to the majority of her books on tape until about fourth grade, when she said, "I'd rather read the books than listen to them."

LeDerick Receives an Evaluation

I needed to repeat the first grade due to my poor academic performance. After staying back that year, the staff at the private school I had been attending since kindergarten suggested that my parents withdraw me from the school so that I could begin the second grade in my district's public school. I still did not have a label at this time, no one had ever used the word *disability* to describe the challenges that I had in school, and I thought that I was just like every other kid. I could not do the same work as everyone else, however, and I had to stay back a grade. I began to have a growing feeling that there might be something wrong with me. I was able to pass the second grade, but it was clear to my third-grade teachers that I was way behind my classmates by most academic measures. My teacher suggested to my parents that I be evaluated by a learning specialist.

Awareness

The awareness stage in the Path to Disability Pride refers to the point when students or adults receive their disability diagnosis. A doctor, psychologist, or learning specialist assesses the student using standardized procedures to make a diagnosis and recommend accommodations, modifications, medications, and other types of support. This approach is often referred to as the *medical model*. The medical model treats disability as an impairment and deficit that must be fixed with treatment, accommodations, therapies, devices, and services (Smart, 2001). Many professionals fail to identify the student's assets or provide suggestions for structuring the environment to enhance a student's assets, thereby minimizing their deficits.

Smart (2001) identified two additional disability models—the functional model and the environmental model. The functional model of disability considers the person's ability to function at performing specific tasks, and the environmental model theorizes that a person's social and physical environment can cause, define, or exaggerate disability (Smart, 2001). For example, prior to the industrialization of a society, a person with learning disabilities could work on a farm without ever needing to read. The disability occurs at the intersection of environmental demands and the individual's ability to function to meet those demands. Teachers can create supportive classroom environments that build on students' assets by using small group instruction and evidenced-based strategies that minimize their deficits. For example, one small group of students is using technology to learn vocabulary words, another group is reading independently on self-selected high interest books, and another group is receiving direct instruction. Unfortunately, too many students experience stigma and prejudice because they need additional instruction or learning strategies to read. Stigma needlessly creates additional barriers for students who learn differently (Balcazar, Bradford, & Fawcett, 1988; Smart, 2001).

Depending on how the disability is presented, students may experience a sense of relief at this stage because of the clarity that comes from knowing why they struggle. Students may also experience grief or depression from learning they have a disability, or they may feel the full range of emotions moving from relief to anger. Professionals and parents can begin discussions with a focus on what the student does well, using an asset-based approach. By focusing on what students do well and acceptable strategies to work around the deficits during this stage of disability awareness, professionals can assist students and their families in accepting the disability. In addition, professionals and parents can introduce students to positive role models that students respect such as

Tom Cruise for a student with a learning disability who likes the movies that Cruise stars in, or Temple Grandin for a student with autism interested in animals (see Chapter 1, Text Box 1.4 for more role models).

Even if students are not made aware of their formal label/diagnosis, they may integrate their challenges into their identity. Drawing from the positive or negative social cues of teachers, parents, and their peers, as well as information they have received from the larger culture, these students will begin to construct an explanation of why they are not able to do the same things as other students. Although students may become aware of their disability, they may still struggle, particularly during adolescence, to fully incorporate disability into their existing self-concept.

The awareness stage is also the point of divergence in which students can move towards disability pride or towards disability shame. Every student has talents, strengths, and assets; and achievement naturally follows when teachers build on these talents and strengths (Clifton, Anderson, & Schriener, 2006). If awareness is developed within a supportive environment where disability is presented from an asset-based approach, then students are more likely to accept their disability. Parents, teachers, and diagnosticians can explain what the disability is and how it affects learning, with an emphasis on the students' assets and how modifying the environment can enhance learning outcomes. In addition, by providing a number of positive role models who have experienced success, students realize that many other people with similar disabilities reached positive outcomes. If this awareness is developed within an environment where disability is presented from a deficit-based approach, however, then students are more likely to deny their disability and begin to develop disability shame. Table 2.2 contrasts the asset-based versus deficit-based approaches to describing the impact of a disability on students' self-concept.

Table 2.2. A comparison of asset and deficit-based approaches to understanding disability

Asset-based approaches	Deficit-based approaches
Definitions	
Developing goals, strategies, and action plans by using a student's talents, strengths, skills, and abilities	Developing goals, strategies, and action plans by identifying a students' limitations, shortfalls, weaknesses, and discrepancies
Synonyms	
Synonyms: advantage, talent, strength, skill, ability, resource, benefit	Synonyms: shortfall, insufficiency, discrepancy, shortage
Examples	
Teachers/professionals explain disability to students as a natural part of the human experience; millions of students and adults have hidden disabilities	Teachers/professionals explain what students' deficits are, but do not balance the discussion with the students' strengths and assets
Teachers explain hidden disabilities, and positive examples of other adults with similar disabilities are shared	Students do not talk about disabilities and inaccurate information exists among teachers or students (e.g., stupid, lazy)
Teachers include and respect disability as part of the school's diversity initiatives and encourage students to disclose	Students are embarrassed and do not disclose their disabilities

LeDerick Receives His Diagnosis

The result of my first evaluation resulted in me being labeled as Neurologically Impaired (NI), and this impairment was explained as the cause of all the struggles I was having in school. I do not remember the test that I took during that first evaluation. But I know the diagnosis was never explained to me while I was a child.

Human beings love to look for patterns in the world around us, and even as a very small child, I was constantly trying to connect the dots that floated throughout my life. I drew a line to connect my bad spelling with the reason why I could barely read. I connected my trouble reading with the reason why some kids laughed at me when our teacher was not around. And, once I began to leave class each day to go to a teacher's storage closet that everyone tried to convince me was actually a Resource Room, I began to connect the feeling that there might be something wrong with me, to a belief that I was actually inferior. And after only a few weeks of getting help for my spelling and reading in a closet, the teachers decided that my struggles with learning were so severe, that I needed to be trans-ferred to a self-contained special education classroom.

My mother, who was my first advocate, was finishing up a bachelor's degree in Psychology when I was first diagnosed, so I am sure she understood on an intel-lectual level what the term 'Neurologically Impaired' meant. But for some reason my family, and my school, never thought to explain to me, in a meaningful way, what my disability was or how being in special education was going to help me. My parents were made aware of my diagnosis, and I began to form my own, more negative, opinion of what was happening to me.

Anna Receives a Diagnosis of Attention-Deficit/Hyperactivity Disorder

I took Anna to the pediatrician when she was in elementary school to determine if there were any medical issues that were affecting her ability to learn. The pediatri-cian reviewed some behavior rating forms completed by her teachers and parents and diagnosed Anna with ADHD. The pediatrician explained to Anna, "Your brain is just wired a little bit differently than other people's brains. We have some pills that you can take that will help your brain stay on track and learn better." Anna accepted this explanation and began to take medication for ADHD. The school completed an evaluation when she was in fourth grade, but her academic per-formance was not adversely affected by ADHD, so she did not qualify for special education services.

Anna would go through phases during the next few years in which she com-plained about the effects of her medication. We made a deal that if she could keep her grades up, then she did not have to take her medication. This started a cycle of not taking medication, her grades would slip, and we entered a power struggle on whether she should go back on her medication. Supporting Anna made me look more critically at my own challenges at work. I eventually decided to meet with a psychologist to determine if I had ADHD and whether medication would enhance my ability to manage my career and parenting responsibilities.

When I received my diagnosis and started taking medication, I could better share the positive and negative effects of having ADHD with Anna.

DISABILITY SHAME

Many parents, teachers, and schools unknowingly perpetuate a cultural stigma of disability, which directly affects healthy social-emotional functioning and development, as well as academic performance. Research and personal experiences show that teachers and parents are more likely to perceive disabilities negatively and hold lower expectations for personal and academic success for youth labeled with a learning disability or ADHD. In turn, these lower expectations contribute to the students' lowered expectations for themselves, creating a debilitating cycle of failure, depression, isolation, and behavior problems (Shifrer, 2013).

When parents become aware that their child has a disability, professionals need to assist the family members and the child in gaining a balanced and strength-based understanding of the disability. Saying nothing or using terms that the parents may not understand (i.e., *neurologically impaired*) generates confusion and promotes movement along the shame side of the path:

- Nonacceptance
- Disability shame
- Rejecting supports
- Maladaptive behaviors
- Risk of underachievement

Each stage of the shame side of the Path to Disability Pride is reviewed next, and case studies provide examples from the authors' lives.

Nonacceptance

Nonacceptance of the disability diagnosis is the first stage on the shame side of the Path to Disability Pride. Unless teachers, parents, or others help students with hidden disabilities gain an accurate understanding of their assets, students may focus entirely on the challenges that come from having a disability, and they may choose to reject the disability label. Students who are in denial about their disability may be reflecting the denial felt by their parents or teachers. Individuals with more apparent disabilities are not immune to this stage, but having a hidden disability can make denial a much more convenient option. Nonacceptance can also be experienced when a student is not given any information about his or her disability from authority figures such as teachers, parents, or doctors. Withholding a diagnosis is often done to save a student from the stigma associated with having a disability, but this lack of information may still result in feelings of shame, isolation, and inferiority.

LeDerick Realizes that Special Education = Disability

As a child, special education was a euphemism for disability. I did not refer to myself as a person with a disability because none of the adults in my life used the word *disability* to describe me. If I was asked what it meant to have a disability, my answer would have involved using a wheelchair or the inability to see. I did understand that I was a special education student. I began to accept that being a special education student meant that there was something wrong with me because my classroom was at the end of the hallway, I had to ride to school on a short bus, and I was unable to sit with other students in the cafeteria.

Disability Shame

This stage is the point in which students begin to feel shame related to having a disability. The trauma of bullying or being treated like second-class students can cause them to feel shame for being labeled with a disability. Many students in this stage may not want to attend special education classes or meet with the intervention specialists. Once students pass through the shame stage, these feelings of shame and inadequacy have the potential to influence their choices and self-image for many years after.

LeDerick's Scarlet Letter: *S* Is for Shame

My first special education teacher and her aide were both excellent educators who had high standards for all their students. I remember working hard every day with flashcards to help me master the spelling of simple words. I also was able to memorize some of the multiplication table, so math became easier. I still called myself things such as stupid, crazy, and dumb, despite the academic gains I made while in that first special education class.

  Once I moved into middle school, the shame that I felt about my challenges in school and being in special education manifested into a compulsion to hide the fact that I still could not read or spell as well as other students. Shame painted a scarlet letter on my chest, and that mark of inferiority attached itself to me at a time when I was trying to understand who I was within the context of the larger world. That feeling of shame has never completely left me, even as an adult. It still bleeds through sometimes when I begin to face challenges that are related to my disability.

Anna Qualifies for Special Education Services in High School

Anna did well in middle school due to a student-centered team approach in which her English, math, science, and history teachers met together to coordinate their content so that there was consistency for students and a lot of communication among the teaching team. Teachers coordinated when assignments were due, and tests were given so students could balance their workload. Teachers would share motivating strategies that worked well with particular students with the teaching team. Anna did well in middle school with the typical extra supports that many students receive: parent–student–teacher conferences, extra tutoring, and a lot of support from home. Anna passed the eighth-grade proficiency test and moved on to high school.

Instead of the student-centered programs that her middle school implemented, her high school expected students to manage their responsibilities for learning by staying organized and using time management and executive function skills. Anna had fallen behind by her sophomore year and was at risk for failing several courses her first semester. The guidance counselor suggested that we gain special education services so Anna would have an intervention specialist to manage the rigors of high school and provide extra tutoring and supports. We went through a second evaluation, and Anna qualified for special education services. When I told Anna that she would gain some extra help and have an intervention specialist that she could meet with, she said, "If you put me in special education classes, I will commit suicide." The school counselor and I assured her that she would not have to go into a special education classroom. Anna reluctantly agreed. We also referred Anna to counseling to address the shame Anna felt about gaining special education supports.

Rejecting Supports

At this stage students refuse assistance and/or supports such as medication, accommodations, technology, or specialized services that may help them work around the challenges associated with their disability. Students who reject supports may also reject the people who are trying to assist them, most often their parents and teachers. These students ultimately may reject the disability community as well as the benefits that come from being a member of this community.

LeDerick's Shame Turns to Anger

The shame of being in special education was turning into anger by the time I reached middle school. I did not know anything about the disability rights movement as a child, but my family had done a great job of helping me understand the Civil Rights movement and how African Americans were treated like second-class citizens. By the time I was 14 years old, I began to feel that my school was treating me and all my classmates in special education like second-class students. So I started a kind of protest. I would move to a desk in the back of the room, put my head down, and refuse to work whenever I felt like I was being openly disrespected by a teacher or I disagreed with the way a teacher was treating me.

Anna Refuses Intervention Supports

Ms. Smith walked into Anna's high school class while Anna was cramming for the quiz that was about to start. In front of the class, Ms. Smith asked, "Anna, are you sure you are ready for this test? Why don't you come with me to look over the material before you take the test?" Anna was totally embarrassed, burst into tears, and ran out of the room. She made her way to the nurse's office and was apparently too distraught to even tell the nurse why she was upset. The nurse called me and explained, "Anna is so upset that I think you should come to the school. I do not think she should drive herself home." When I asked the nurse what happened, she told me, "Apparently Ms. Smith was checking to see if Anna was prepared for the test. She embarrassed Anna by asking her if she needed extra help in front of the rest of the class."

I remember feeling my heart sink as tears filled my eyes. Dealing with ADHD and needing special education supports is tough enough. But being called out in front of peers can be difficult for a young person to endure, especially soon after he or she has been admitted to an ADHD club to which he or she does not want to belong. I know Ms. Smith was only trying to help Anna do her best on her math quiz, but discretion is critical regardless of how comfortable a student is with others knowing that he or she has a disability.

I knew as I drove to the school that it was time to have the conversation with Anna about accepting herself. Making peace with having a disability is essential to maximizing your potential and utilizing the supports that are available. Accepting yourself—the good, the bad, and the ugly—is critical. Anna needed to understand that it is difficult for her to maintain attention and focus, especially in content areas that require attention to detail, because she has ADHD. Extra support and extra time are common accommodations in grade school, high school, and college.

I picked up Anna at school, and we went home, had hot chocolate, and talked. We shared how embarrassing it is to admit having ADHD. We shared how challenging it is to discretely gain the extra supports needed. We cried together, and we laughed together. We celebrated how we loved how our ADHD minds could think out of the box. We often develop creative solutions to problems that others would never discover because our minds sort through a number of random thoughts. We both agreed that we would not trade our minds with anyone. Slowly, through multiple conversations, we both increased our acceptance, and we each took another step toward making peace with ourselves.

Many students do not have teachers or parents who provide the emotional support needed during times of confusion and embarrassment that LeDerick and Anna experienced. Many teachers and parents do not know what to say or do not have the time to help students increase their acceptance of their disability and the supports they need to learn. Teachers and parents can help students gain a more accurate perception of their strengths and limitations and embrace their disability as a part of themselves. They assist students to continue on the path of acceptance and pride versus the risk of moving towards maladaptive behaviors and shame.

Maladaptive Behavior

Students at this stage may find themselves searching for a peer group to find acceptance and a sense of belonging. These students sometimes become the class clown or have behavior problems like acting out and rebelling against the establishment. Self-medication to deal with shame, stigma, anger, and frustration can result in early sexual activity, alcohol and drug abuse, and ultimately may lead to addiction. Students are also at risk of bullying other students, dropping out of school, or committing crimes once they engage in these maladaptive behaviors (Sheff, 2013).

LeDerick: Ashamed, Embarrassed, and Frightened

My identity was at a crisis point by the time I reached high school. I had been in special education for years, but I still did not know exactly what my disability was or what was going to happen to me once I graduated. My academic skills were still way below my grade level and, as a result, I did not think that I was going to be able to go to college or have a career. I felt ashamed of my past, embarrassed by my present, and completely frightened by my future. I knew that I was going to graduate from high school. I knew they would push me across that stage and hand me a diploma. But then I had no idea what I was going to do. There was an abyss waiting for me on the other end of the graduation stage, and as the abyss grew closer, I was convinced that I did not have the skills needed to successfully cross over to the adult world. Anxiety, depression, and nervousness became as constant as the air I breathed.

My junior year of high school was the lowest point of my life. I was terrified by what was going to happen to me when I graduated, and I could no longer expend the emotional energy it took to pass for normal. I was in pain, and the pain drove me to a very dark place. I began to be haunted by suicidal thoughts that I kept to myself. My family had moved to an upper-class community where we were one of only a few African Americans. At one point I remember being in so much pain that I would walk through the streets in the middle of the night wearing a black hoodie and hoping someone would call the police. My goal was for the police to lock me up or perform an act of violence that would put me out of my misery. Luckily the police never came, and through equal parts of defiance and resiliency, I was able to begin imagining myself in a future that held the possibility of happiness.

While I was going through my own emotional breakdown, many of the students who had spent years with me in special education had already dropped out of school and were committing crimes, engaging in risky sexual behavior, and abusing drugs and alcohol. We were all expressing our hopelessness in different ways.

Anna's Trip to the Emergency Room

Anna was not having a good sophomore year. She had an intervention specialist, and she still was not doing well in geometry or Spanish. But she had a date to the homecoming dance. She schemed with her friends and they decided to smuggle in a bottle of vodka to the pre-dance dinner. She first drank a small shot of vodka. She did not feel anything. So she drank another shot, and then another, and another. She was so drunk when she arrived at the dance that the chaperones sent her to the principal's office. She became nonresponsive, so they called the emergency medical transport to take her to the hospital.

I was so scared I was going to lose my daughter. Was it the shame of being identified as ADHD, was it the impulsivity and risk taking that is associated with having ADHD, or was Anna just trying to be cool to impress her friends? Anna had her stomach pumped, she met with the doctor and psychologist, and we all had to agree to attend more family counseling and drug and alcohol education classes. We all learned how ADHD, school failure, and at-risk behaviors are intertwined.

Risk of Underachievement

Students compromise their educational achievement and begin to limit their options and choices for their future when they engage in maladaptive behaviors such as those described in the previous stage. Students at this stage could be prone to learned helplessness (Izzo & Lamb, 2003). For example, a student with dyscalculia who is not receiving support for his or her disability is repeatedly presented with math worksheets. Just seeing the worksheets eventually causes a sense of anxiety and distress because all of his or her previous attempts have resulted in poor outcomes no matter how hard he or she tries. This type of failure scenario can play havoc with one's self-esteem and can cause learned helplessness. A student may give up trying to do his or her best because he or she feels that failure is inevitable. Students who are not getting the support they need run the risk of increased alcohol and drug abuse. One third (33%) of young adults with emotional disturbances reported having used marijuana in the past 30 days, a rate more than twice that of young adults in the next highest category (learning disabilities; 16%) (Yu, Huang, & Newman, 2008). When examining school completion rates, students with emotional disturbances have the lowest school completion rates (56%) and the highest marijuana use rates (33%), whereas 75% of students with learning disabilities complete school. Although researchers cannot conclude that drug abuse leads to school dropout, a relationship between these two factors cannot be denied.

Going to prison is one of the poorest outcomes that can result from maladaptive behavior (see Chapter 1). Students with emotional and behavior disorders are twice as likely as other students with disabilities to live in a correctional facility, halfway house, drug treatment center, or on the street after leaving school (U.S. Department of Education, 2011). Approximately a third of young adults with learning disabilities (32%), other health impairments, ADHD (30%), and brain injury (35%) were arrested during the eight years after exiting high school (Newman et al., 2011). When comparing young adults with hidden disabilities to those with visible disabilities, such as hearing, vision, or orthopedic impairments, young adults with hidden disabilities reported more involvement with the criminal justice system (Newman et al., 2011). These findings suggest that young adults with hidden disabilities engage in maladaptive behavior at higher rates than their peers with visible disabilities.

DISABILITY PRIDE

Numerous catalysts can help students develop disability pride. The need for school personnel to provide meaningful explanations of each student's disability beginning with a discussion of the student's assets has been discussed. In addition, families and students need to be aware of others with similar disabilities within the school, the local community, and nationally, who have openly disclosed and are successful in their chosen career. In fact, many teachers and school staff who have hidden disabilities can serve as mentors to students (see Chapter 3). The school climate should be reflected in a staff that includes professionals who are open about having hidden disabilities and daily demonstrate how they competently work in a career area that is a great match to their strengths and assets.

Students and families need to be empowered to participate in the IEP process. Students are actively engaged with clear roles and responsibilities during the IEP meeting, and person-centered planning strategies are used (see Chapter 4). Teachers must understand how to provide accommodations so students are not stigmatized for using the accommodations. UDL principles can incorporate learning supports for all students that reduce the stigma associated with learning differences (see http://www.CAST.org). Effective co-teaching models can maximize the time students spend in general education settings while bringing interventions and supports into general education classrooms (see http://www.swiftschools.org). See Table 1.2 for web sites that provide additional resources on inclusion, co-teaching, and multitiered systems of support. Students can move from shame to pride with these supports. The pride side of the Path to Disability Pride consists of six stages:

1. Acceptance
2. Self-disclosure
3. Use supports
4. Self-advocacy
5. Connect to disability community
6. Disability pride

Most students and adults do not navigate these stages in a linear pattern, but they jump from Acceptance to Supports or Self-disclosure. At first, navigating through these stages might take a student several years, and then the student will need to work to maintain a positive self-concept as he or she faces daily challenges. Therefore, teachers and parents should review the Path to Disability Pride and accept where students are in their own journey while helping them set new goals with the supports they need.

Acceptance

At this stage students begin to accept the challenges that come with their hidden disability. They balance these challenges with their assets, talents, and abilities, some of which are a direct result of their disability. Students also begin to incorporate the label/diagnoses into their self-concept. Some students accept the limitations caused by their disability while choosing to focus on other aspects of their identity that they find more empowering. These students identify with the commonly used phrase, "I have a disability, but it does not define me."

Students at the acceptance stage begin to develop language that they feel best expresses their experiences. They either accept the formal diagnosis of their disability, or they choose to redefine the way they have been labeled. This act of self-definition might lead them to adopt terms such as *learning difference, differently able,* or simply *different* when conceptualizing their disability. Students reach a point in which they accept disability into their life, to some degree, and add it to the complexity of how they describe themselves. This stage often encompasses an acceptance that other people, their school, and institutions are not perfect as it relates to supporting or even understanding disability. Students at this stage might also begin to be made aware that there are federal laws that protect the rights of people with disabilities within education and employment settings. These realizations help students take a more active role in advocating for the things they need. Accepting their disability also creates the foundation for their ability to form meaningful, equal, and symbiotic relationships with others.

LeDerick Learns About and Accepts Learning Disabilities

I met Sarah, my counselor, at her office during my first week as a college student. When we set up the time for this meeting, Sarah told me that we would be reviewing the documentation I used to identify myself to the college as a student who would benefit from disability support. This documentation was like a clinical diary of my life as a special education student. It began with the results from the very first psychological evaluation that was completed when I was 9 years old. Then there was page after page of old IEPs and assessment reports that my school had completed from the third grade until I graduated from high school. Sarah sat me down at her desk, closed her office door, and began to read aloud each page.

As Sarah read words such as *disability, delayed,* and *neurologically impaired,* I listened and tried not to get angry at the psychologist who had written that report back when cassette tapes were cutting-edge technology. When Sarah read words such as *exceptional, advanced,* and *gifted,* I listened and tried not to get angry at that same psychologist who had used such beautiful language to describe my mind but had never taken the time to say it to my face. Once Sarah finished the last page, she set the reports down on the top of her desk and then she began to summarize everything she had read.

Sarah was the first person to explain to me that I was not stupid and I was not crazy, but there were biological reasons why my brain worked differently than the brains of most people. She said that the research at the time defined *learning disabilities* as a discrepancy between a student's potential and his or her academic performance in the classroom. She also made a point to talk about all the really positive things that the testing had revealed. She talked about my extremely high scores on tests that attempted to measure my overall intelligence.

She explained that the artistic ability I had displayed throughout my life was most likely connected to the impairments I faced in reading, spelling, and math. I began to smile a smile that was filled with appreciation and approval. This meeting affirmed things I had felt were true but had never been articulated by someone in a position of authority.

If I can summarize what Sarah gave me on that day, then I would say she gave me a balanced look at how my mind works. As a little kid I spent most of my time feeling like I was broken—like there was something wrong with me. Sarah was the first person to respectfully explain to me exactly what it meant to have learning disabilities. She told me that my problems in school were due to the way my brain worked and it had nothing to do with me being stupid or dumb. She helped me understand that I could learn almost anything with the right supports. She let me know that having learning disabilities could even be a gift in many environments.

 ## Anna Shares Having Attention-Deficit/Hyperactivity Disorder

Anna was in her college psychology class, and the professor asked if any of the students knew anyone with a disability. Anna raised her hand and said, "I have ADHD and my mom has ADHD, and she is a professor at The Ohio State University." I realized that Anna had accepted having ADHD when she told me about this class.

Anna was very comfortable sharing that she had ADHD in college. She was not apologizing nor flaunting the fact. When you examine Anna's history, she was supported in elementary school with a reading recovery program that she enjoyed, used medication on and off throughout middle school, and then experienced school failure, maladaptive behaviors, and underachievement within the first two years of high school. Anna accepted her disability during her final year of high school and first year in college. She completed her college degree and entered her master's program. Anna has mostly good days. Her disability pride slips down, however, when she overcommits, does not get enough sleep, or is overwhelmed. But she quickly recoups and digs in to accomplish the work that needs to get done. See how Anna's Path To Disability Pride outlines these key events from elementary school though college in Figure 2.2.

Self-disclosure

The Self-disclosure stage embodies a host of ways that students with hidden disabilities begin to make their disability known to others. It may begin with disclosing to close friends or family members that they have a disability. Self-disclosure may be situational, in which students are comfortable talking about their disability in some environments with some people, but are reluctant to do so in other settings. For example, students may talk with their special education teachers but not with their general education teachers. As students become more comfortable disclosing their disability to people that they find supportive, the chance they will disclose to people outside their natural support system may also increase.

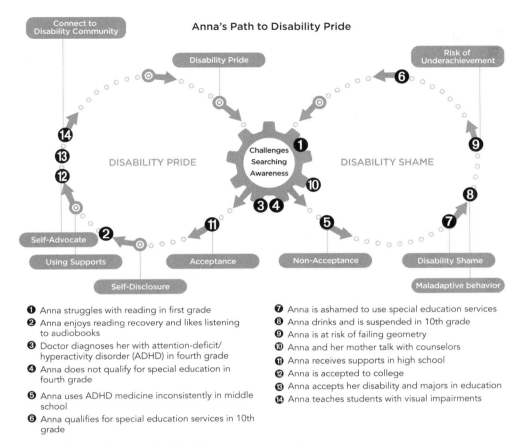

Anna's Path to Disability Pride

Connect to Disability Community

Disability Pride

Risk of Underachievement

DISABILITY PRIDE   DISABILITY SHAME

Challenges Searching Awareness

Self-Advocate

Using Supports

Self-Disclosure

Acceptance

Non-Acceptance

Disability Shame

Maladaptive behavior

❶ Anna struggles with reading in first grade
❷ Anna enjoys reading recovery and likes listening to audiobooks
❸ Doctor diagnoses her with attention-deficit/hyperactivity disorder (ADHD) in fourth grade
❹ Anna does not qualify for special education in fourth grade
❺ Anna uses ADHD medicine inconsistently in middle school
❻ Anna qualifies for special education services in 10th grade

❼ Anna is ashamed to use special education services
❽ Anna drinks and is suspended in 10th grade
❾ Anna is at risk of failing geometry
❿ Anna and her mother talk with counselors
⓫ Anna receives supports in high school
⓬ Anna is accepted to college
⓭ Anna accepts her disability and majors in education
⓮ Anna teaches students with visual impairments

Figure 2.2.   Anna's Path to Disability Pride.

Margo Discloses on a Disability Panel

After many years of designing interventions for people with disabilities and working with my daughter to accept her disability, I realized that I needed to embrace my own ADHD and help educate others about what it is like to live with ADHD by talking more openly about my own disability. I volunteered to participate on a self-advocacy panel hosted by the university. This very public panel was part of a series sponsored by the Disability Studies Program, and it would be the first time I had disclosed in a large forum. Three graduate students and two faculty members were on the panel. When the graduate students, many of them English majors, talked about their disability, they discussed how they were diagnosed with bipolar or obsessive compulsive disorder. After their very eloquent presentations on the impact of having a hidden disability on their college program, it was my turn to talk about having ADHD. It was easy as long as I stuck to facts about my professional life—when I received my doctoral degree and how my position and career progressed through the years. But I felt my voice crack and my eyes fill with tears when I started talking directly about having ADHD. "No," I shouted to myself.

These college students just disclosed much heavier types of disabilities. You only have ADHD. But it was too late. Everyone in the audience was silent—waiting for me to recover from my moment of embarrassment, my moment of public disclosure. I wanted to crawl under the table. I wanted to run out of the room. I identified with how my daughter felt when she was embarrassed by her intervention specialist. I pulled it together after an immeasurable silence and returned to talking about my career. Talking about ADHD was still too raw to share even though I had been using medication for more than a decade. Wow. I did not realize how scary disclosing can be. Since that panel, I have taken the opportunity to openly talk about my disability in a number of professional settings. It is not always easy, but I am much better at disclosing and sharing my story. Practice makes it easier to disclose.

Becoming comfortable disclosing to others takes time and practice. Students can become comfortable as early as elementary school if they are provided with the right tools, supports, and a respectful and welcoming class environment. And adults who are just beginning to practice self-disclosure might be surprised by their feelings as they share about the challenges associated with their disability. Margo's Path to Disability Pride started when she was a single parent, mom of two teenagers, and running a competitive grant program. She accepted the label and used medication, but did not disclose outside of her doctor–patient and family relationships for 10 years. Then, during one of her first large disability panel presentations, she is embarrassed by losing her composure as she discloses. Disclosing can catch someone off guard if he or she does not develop familiarity with the disclosure process.

Using Supports

Students and adults with hidden disabilities are open to using supports and accommodations at this stage on the Path to Disability Pride. They are not willing to let the challenges that come with their disability prevent them from completing tasks or reaching their goals. Medication, accommodations, technology, and supportive teachers and friends are integrated into a system of support, as needed. Some students will use approved accommodations offered by schools. Others develop natural supports that any student can use, such as study centers or groups, where teachers or peers will assist with homework or test preparation. Many students at this stage have reconciled the stigma that comes with their disability, so they can use supports and accommodations without feeling like they are cheating or seeking special treatment.

 ## LeDerick Uses the Entire Campus: Same Class, Different Teacher

As I began to mature as a college student, I realized that the entire college campus was at my disposal. I did not have to confine my learning to attending the classes I was registered for or just using the library as the place where I did my homework. A strategy that helped me get through precalculus is one of my best examples I have of using the entire campus.

Precalculus was a very difficult class for me, and I quickly realized that I was going to have to work extra hard if I wanted a decent grade. So, I went to every class, did every homework problem, got a tutor, and went to every one of my professor's office hours. But I also looked at my college's course catalog, and I found that there were a few precalculus classes that were being taught by different professors. On the days when my professor would present a concept that I did not understand, I would then ask one of the other precalculus professors if I could sit in on their class just so I could hear the same information presented in a different way. It was often very helpful to hear the same information taught by two completely different instructors. And, like many students with learning disabilities, I have always benefited by repetition, so attending multiple lectures on the same material really helped me to retain the information I was trying to learn.

 ## Margo Accepts Medication Support

I remember the day I filled my first prescription for medication. Before I put the first pill in my mouth I remember thinking, "Am I really ready to take this step?" "Am I ready to handle the stigma of taking medication?" and "I can always stop taking it if I do not like it." It has been 15 years since I filled my first prescription, and I can honestly say that my medication has helped me immensely. I take my medication every morning before I go to work. I love the ability to focus, even on tasks that are not my favorite things to do—the tasks that make my job feel like work. More recently, I attended a support group of adults with ADHD who learned and practiced cognitive-behavioral therapy. With these supports, I am focused, I am determined, I look over my to-do list, and I am ready to tackle the tasks that are scheduled for the day.

Supports come in many different forms and can range from formal accommodations and medication to natural supports such as friends and teachers. LeDerick discovered that attending multiple lectures on the same concept increased his knowledge of precalculus concepts. Margo discovered that medication and cognitive behavior therapy increased her productivity. As new supports and strategies emerge, people with hidden disabilities can continue to update and refine the supports they need.

Self-Advocate

Students have developed a meaningful command of the four components expressed in the self-advocacy framework by Test et al. (2005) at this stage on the Path to Disability Pride. They are aware of the benefits and challenges that come with their disability (knowledge of self). They have accepted their disability and, to some degree, have incorporated disability into their identity. They understand that as a person with a disability they are entitled to certain rights under the law (knowledge of rights). Students who self-advocate demonstrate that they have the skills to effectively communicate with others about what services and supports they need (communication). Finally, students who have reached this stage are willing and able to assert themselves in a variety of settings that may range from participating in their IEP meeting to advocating for accommodations in general education classes (leadership) (Test et al., 2005).

Students at this stage are often aware of the connection between environment and disability, so they actively seek to place themselves within supportive settings and around supportive people. Some students at this stage choose to pass for normal in some settings and not disclose, whereas they are open about having a disability and actively utilize services and supports in other settings. Being a self-advocate does not require someone to be out with his or her disability, but living a more open life can be less stressful and can help that person connect with a community of other people with disabilities (Brune & Wilson, 2013).

LeDerick Misses the Opportunity to Advocate at His Individualized Education Program Meeting

The first IEP meeting I remember being a part of was when I was in middle school. I was abruptly pulled out of class and sent to a conference room. The meeting moved very quickly, and I remember feeling like a bobble-head doll as I nodded "yes" to the myriad of questions that were asked by the members of the IEP team. It was an overwhelming experience, and every IEP meeting after that felt like the team had decided what was going to happen before I entered the room.

The IEP meeting is one of the biggest missed opportunities to teach students with disabilities the skills they will need to advocate and build a positive self-image. The IEP meeting in many school districts has been reduced to an annual ritual that is focused more on compliance and less on the development of a tool that can be used by the student and his or her teachers. Shifting to a meeting in which a student is expected to play a more active role is one way to improve the development and implementation of the IEP. By preparing your students to take a more active role in their IEP meetings, you will create an opportunity for them to gain a meaningful understanding of their disability and needs as a learner. The IEP meeting is also a safe environment for your students to practice the self-advocacy skills that will support them as they make the transition to a postsecondary setting.

Connect to Disability Community

Students understand that they are not alone at this stage on the Path to Disability Pride. They define themselves and identify with a community of others who have similar labels, have faced similar challenges, and celebrate similar achievements. This stage might express itself as a sense of community where people feel connected to historical figures or celebrities with the same disability. Or, they might connect with an actual community through mentors or disability support programs such as youth leadership forums, disability clubs, or students in their support classes. Connecting with a community of people with disabilities is an essential phase to gaining a full sense of disability pride.

◎ LeDerick Joins a Disability Community

The office that housed the support program I used at my community college became a safe place for students who learned differently. I remember a group of us would meet on Friday afternoons just to hang out with each other and celebrate surviving another week of school. We would eat pizza and play Pictionary, but we had to play with accommodations because no one could read the words on the cards. I really looked forward to the time we spent together laughing about what made us different, and I could feel myself becoming increasingly comfortable with having a learning disability during those hours filled with laughter and fellowship. I had finally found a group of people who had faced the same challenges I had faced and had come to the same conclusion: We were going to stop feeling ashamed of our disabilities and start taking control of our lives. See Figure 2.3 for many of the key events that LeDerick experienced on his Path to Disability Pride.

❶ LeDerick had difficulty in school starting in the first grade
❷ Third-grade teacher suggested that LeDerick get evaluated for a learning disability
❸ Labeled as neurologically impaired in third grade
❹ LeDerick's school and family did not tell him he had a learning disability, but he still felt different
❺ After becoming classified LeDerick began to feel shame about his challenges
❻ Started refusing to do work in middle school
❼ Suicidal thoughts and activity due to fear of graduating from high school

❽ Found learning disability support program at local county college
❾ College program trained students to self-disclose
❿ Started using adaptive technology, tutors, and other supports in college
⓫ Started speaking up for accommodations
⓬ Formed friendships with other college students who had learning disabilities
⓭ Began speaking and writing about his life to help others

Figure 2.3.   LeDerick's Path to Disability Pride.

Disability Pride

People with hidden disabilities are open to others with and without disabilities at this stage in the Path to Disability Pride. They feel confident sharing information about their life experiences as a person with a disability, and they feel connected to other people with disabilities. This feeling of pride might be expressed by showing solidarity for people who have a similar label to their own. Or, a person's expression of disability pride might extend to the larger community of people who have been labeled with some kind of a disability. People who reach this stage often feel compelled to advocate, mentor, and support other people with disabilities.

LeDerick Serves the Disability Community

The social group that I was a part of while attending community college eventually developed into a group focused on youth leadership. We might have started out playing games and eating junk food every Friday after class, but we eventually decided that we wanted to do something to help high school students who were in special education. Some of us reached out to teachers we knew at our old high schools, and we offered to speak with their current students with IEPs about what college life was like for students who learned differently. I got my start as an advocate by speaking to high school students about my journey. I became a proud member of this community once I was able to talk openly about my disability and when I was given the opportunity to help the next generation of students who were facing similar challenges.

MAINTAINING DISABILITY PRIDE

Just because a person with a hidden disability has experienced disability pride at some point in his or her life, he or she will still encounter challenges that will test his or her feelings of pride. This framework is presented as a path because maintaining disability pride is a journey that continues throughout a person's life. As people with hidden disabilities face new challenges, they should be encouraged to search for solutions, practice self-advocacy, and seek supports from members of their disability community as well as family and friends. Although the Path to Disability Pride is primarily a tool meant to support positive identity development, the stages can also be used to maintain pride on a daily basis.

Students with hidden disabilities face numerous personal or environmental challenges that can move them from disability pride toward stages such as disability shame, maladaptive behavior, or rejecting supports. The place where they find themselves on the path depends on many factors:

- Personal issues such as energy levels that may result from poor diet or sleep patterns

- Low expectations expressed by people in positions of authority

- Cultural views of disability that affect how their family provides support

- Not being well matched to a job or other task, so he or she needs an excessive number of accommodations and supports

Maintaining disability pride and a positive perception of one's self is important. Ask students to map their actions and consequences on the Path to Disability Pride figure on a regular basis to help them evaluate where they are on their path and the how their actions and behaviors influence their identity as a person with a disability. This will help students identify factors that are either promoting disability pride or disability shame. The remaining chapters provide practical ways for teachers and parents to support students to develop disability pride and maintain a positive self-concept.

Tips for Teaching

How to Get Started

Numerous suggestions are provided within the chapter and throughout the book that involve profound shifts in the policies, procedures, and culture that govern your school. Implementing new initiatives designed to improve your students' self-image and ability to self-advocate will take collaboration with administrators and other teachers, families, and students themselves. Here are some tips to begin the process of creating a culture of disability pride.

- Start small: Instead of beginning with a schoolwide shift in policy or practices, start with a small group of students to work with initially. It might be best to start with just a few students because of circumstances and resources.

- Select the right students: Look for students who will be willing to take part in these new initiatives. Select students who have a good relationship with school personnel, some degree of leadership skills, and an openness to learn about themselves.

- Gain family supports: Consider the support that student(s) will have at home and the relationship the family has with school staff.

CONCLUSION: AN EXPRESSION OF DISABILITY PRIDE

This chapter concludes with a poem that LeDerick wrote a year after he graduated from college and was working with the New Jersey Department of Education's Office of Special Education. He was the keynote speaker for a series of youth leadership conferences called Dare to Dream that the state of New Jersey organized to help build the self-advocacy and leadership skills for students with IEPs. This poem is an expression of the pride and potential that all students with disabilities should realize as they make the transition from school to adult life.

Text Box 2.1—Dare to Dream

We are gathered here today
to bear witness,
to bear witness to the union
of two beautiful people
Yes, today is the day that we merge
who you are
with who you want to be,
making the vision
and the reality—one
An integration
born of communication
and made tangible
by your commitment to yourself

Now, I know some of you might be afraid
but don't let cold feet
stop you from jumping the broom,
from taking the first step,
from beginning a journey
that will transform your life

Yes, I know some of you might be afraid,
But you see, it's my job
to show you that better days are coming

Yes, it's my job
to be Harriet Tubman like
with my movements and verse
So if I have to steal a way
just for us to make a way, well then Star
I'll be the first one with his hand in the cookie-jar
of self-advocacy,
I'll use these sticky fingers
to pick-pocket the pocket of
self-determination,
    And if I got to grand-theft-auto
    the Mercedes-Benz
    of a quality-education,
then they might as well leave the doors unlocked
and the keys in the ignition
'cause I'm gone in 60 seconds
and ain't NOTHING, and I mean NOTHING
standing in my way
You see, it's my job
to unlock doors

unshackle minds
break through glass ceilings
motivate, inspire, and challenge you,
I'm here to challenge you

And so I dare you,
I dare you to sit in your seat
and not feel moved
by the testimonies of these brave souls,
who come before you as examples of excellence

I dare you,
I dare you to look in the mirror
without imagining,
see yourself as yourself
A diamond, that might need a little polishing,
but whose beauty has always existed

I dare you,
I dare you to step,
bounce, and move to your own rhythm
excite minds
in time
we'll redefine the system
I write lines
designed to embrace and kiss,
plus supercharge like imports strapped with nitrous,
this is a revolution
a fight for inclusion
segregation is no solution
Brown vs. Ed is how I'm provin'
we deserve the best
nothin' more and nothin' less,
every child gets left behind
when all we focus on are tests

And so I dare you,
To judge yourselves by a different standard,
to lift as you climb,
to fight like gladiators
    to become master and commander
          of your own beautiful minds
But above all else,
I dare you to dream – dare to dream y'all

Following is the link to a video of LeDerick preforming "Dare to Dream:"
https://www.youtube.com/watch?v=HbOxNvuwabo

Mentoring

Guiding Students Toward
Disability Pride

3

"They just needed to hear a different message about
their potential. And they needed to hear it from someone
who wasn't their parents or who wasn't their teacher; from
someone who was relatable and close enough to their age,
and who they thought was cool. And that's what I could do
as an 18-year-old mentor [for these fourth and fifth grade
boys with learning disabilities]. So I just said:
'I am dyslexic, I have ADHD, and I'm in college.'"
—David Flink, Mentor and Founder
and CEO of Eye to Eye

Mentoring has traditionally been defined as a relationship between an experienced, wiser adult and a mentee, who is younger,
less experienced, and benefits from ongoing guidance, instruction, and encouragement that helps develop the competence and
character of the mentee (Sowers, Powers, & Shpigelman, 2012). Many
informal mentoring relationships occur naturally between teachers and students or coaches and athletes. Other mentoring relationships develop as part
of a more formal mentoring program. Some mentoring organizations (e.g., Eye
to Eye) pair college and high school students with LD/ADHD with elementary
and middle school students with LD/ADHD. Other mentoring programs connect college students and professionals with high school students, such as the
E-Mentoring Program. Teachers have developed peer mentoring programs to
support students' study strategies or short-term postsecondary plans and outcomes (Lee, Rojewski, Gregg & Jeong, 2015).

A mentor can play a key role in helping students develop disability pride.
The mentor–mentee relationship can serve as an opportunity to connect with a
community of people with disabilities. It can also provide students with a safe
space to help them become aware of their disability and learn to accept their
differences. This chapter will provide several examples of successful mentoring programs and discuss the benefits of mentoring. Margo and LeDerick have
both been involved with developing mentoring programs, and it is our hope

that more educators will consider mentoring as a support to help empower students with hidden disabilities.

MENTORS AS POSITIVE ROLE MODELS

Many mentoring relationships are informal, in which two people connect and develop an in-depth relationship that provides support and guidance that transcends the typical friendship or professional–student interactions. The presence of a supportive adult appears to be one of the strongest resilience factors for individuals with learning disabilities that is related to their success (Goldberg, Higgins, Raskind, & Herman, 2003). Many people say they benefited from positive role models who provided support and guidance during challenging times. These mentors may be family members, teachers, counselors, coaches, peers, or colleagues; a mentor is anyone with more experience who provides direction and contributes additional perspective to a life experience. Mentors provide encouragement, advice, and a listening ear during life's many transitions to help mentees reflect on their options and make good choices.

LeDerick Seeks out Several Informal Mentors

The college experience is as much a rite of passage as it is an educational opportunity. I remember being very excited by the opportunity to go to college but also terrified by all the new experiences and having to wrestle with a much heavier work load. There were different people that I turned to who helped me handle different aspects of my life. I was supported through this difficult time of self-discovery by a number of people who complimented the diverse aspects of my personality. I had Sarah, who was not only my academic counselor, but she also helped me understand what it meant to be a person with a learning disability. There were other African American staff who acted as cultural mentors who cultivated my identity as an African American student leader.

When I think about who helped me learn to like math, I have to acknowledge a relationship that I built with the last math teacher I had in high school. He was new to our school, and what I remember most are the conversations during the last few minutes of each class. There was something in the way his face lit up when he talked about his wife and daughter that impressed me. I knew he was an adult that I could trust. I could see that he was a great math teacher when he stepped to the blackboard, but it was his willingness to also show my class that he was a great human being that I really admired.

When I learned that I would have to take a placement test to get into MCC, I disclosed to my math instructor that I still struggled with long division and other basic math concepts. He offered to tutor me during the only time we both were available, which was lunch. We met in the teacher's lounge for several weeks, and he slowly built up my basic math skills. Although I still needed to take two semesters of remedial algebra when I got to college, I was able to test out of the lowest level math class that many students struggled to pass. I eventually made it to statistics and probability—a class that made me love math due to its ability to model the real world. My statistics and probability professor eventually suggested that I declare mathematics as my major. I followed that professor's advice and started studying math with the hope of eventually becoming a math teacher like the one I had during my senior year of high school.

Many times the word *mentoring* is never used, but the nods and words of encouragement provided during classes, practices, or games fall under the umbrella of mentoring. Many successful adults have acknowledged a mentor for helping them navigate an important life transition. Many times, a mentoring relationship occurs when a teacher, counselor, or advisor develops a trusted relationship with a student that extends beyond their role as the professional.

Margo Reflects on a Mentoring Relationship

I loved college and did everything that I could not do in high school, either because I did not have the supports or the guts to pursue my goals. I majored in psychology with certification in elementary and special education and minored in philosophy. The minor in philosophy happened by accident. I loved the philosophy courses, especially the courses taught by Dr. Jones. I would attend peace retreats in which groups of students would go away for the weekend with several faculty members, including Dr. Jones. We would explore the dichotomy of peace and conflict, both the conflicts within ourselves as well as the conflicts in our community and across the world.

   I met with Dr. Jones at the beginning of my senior year and expressed concern that I could not take any more of his courses due to schedule conflicts. Dr. Jones suggested I take an independent study, and I quickly agreed. We informally titled the course Philosophy of Self, and together we explored the type of person I wanted to become as I started my career as a special education teacher. We strategized the job search, and we figured out the best job match when I had two job offers. We discussed everything from relationships to teaching philosophies. As I look back, Dr. Jones was the mentor I needed to give me the confidence to accept a job in a new city where I did not know a soul and start my life as a professional with many dreams to fulfill.

MENTORING MODELS AND BENEFITS

The typical mentoring model consists of two people, a mentor and a mentee, who meet face-to-face and develop a relationship for a year or more. New models of mentoring are emerging, however, with the technological explosion of electronic communications such as Skype, FaceTime, Ning, Gaggle, listservs, discussion boards, and a variety of text messaging platforms. Some mentoring programs use a combination of face-to-face and electronic communications. Other mentoring programs use a combination of individual mentor pairs or group mentoring. The mentor–mentee pairs participate in joint activities or meetings in group mentoring and have relevant and supportive topical discussions. Mentees in group mentoring programs learn not only from their

Mentee benefits	Mentor benefits
Improve self-esteem	Enhance leadership skills
Expand positive relationships with caring adults	Establish proactive friendship with a mentee
	Develop an understanding of diversity
Increase reading and writing skills	Influence a mentee's direction in life
Increase academic motivation	Increase understanding of one's own values, priorities, and perspectives
Improve communication skills	
Increase support for future planning	Network with other volunteers and professionals

Family benefits	Teacher/counselor benefits
Connect with caring adults	Mentees improve reading and writing skills
Increase understanding of interpersonal relationships	Mentees gain a positive attitude about school, relationships, and future planning
Improve child's self-confidence and attitude about school and his or her future	Mentees more likely to graduate
	Mentees enhance relationships and communication skills with peers and adults
Increase communication between family members and child	Teachers and counselors gain assistance in reinforcing the needed academic skills

Figure 3.1.   Mentoring benefits. (From Izzo, M.V., Murray, A.J., Earley, J.A., McArrell, B., & Yurick, A.L. [2014]. The Ohio State University Nisonger Center e-mentoring program replication guide [2nd ed.]. G. Cirino & A. Regoli [Eds.]. Retrieved from http://go.osu.edu/ementoring. Work supported by grants from the Ohio Rehabilitation Services Commission [now known as Opportunities for Ohioans with Disabilities] [Grant Number GRT00001378] and grants from the Office of Special Education Programs, U.S. Department of Education [Grant Numbers H327A020037, H327A050103, H327A060066, and H327A090058]; adapted by permission.)

mentors but also from one another. These discussions assist the mentees in forming positive peer relationships and provide opportunities to mentor each other. In fact, research suggests that group mentoring promotes more positive peer interactions than one-to-one mentoring models (Dubois & Karcher, 2013; Herrera, Vang, & Gale, 2002; Sipe & Roder, 1999). Peers can provide some of the same benefits to mentees as adult mentors, such as offering advice, encouragement, and information.

Electronic mentorship programs have grown in popularity since the widespread popularity of online social networks (Burgstahler, Moore, & Crawford, 2011; Izzo, Earley, McArrell, & Yurick, 2012). Mentoring groups include peers, near-peers (individuals that are only a few years older than younger participants), and adult mentors. Mature college mentors are particularly powerful role models to high school mentees who have college goals. Both group mentoring and one-to-one mentor matches provide positive outcomes for mentees. Each model is briefly described next, and Figure 3.1 summarizes the benefits of mentoring for student/mentees, mentors, family, and school personnel (Izzo et al., 2014).

One-to-One Mentoring

Individually matched mentor–mentee pairs communicate face-to-face and/or through e-mail, using a secure system. Mentor–mentee pairs discuss achieving academic and/or career goals as well as building relationships and social skills. Program coordinators monitor all electronic communication. Online and face-to-face meetings address ideas, questions, and concerns about the transition process. Each mentee only has one mentor assigned to him or her.

Group

All mentoring participants (e.g., mentors, mentees, site coordinators, teachers) communicate together at mentoring events or through the listserv, discussion board, or social networking site. Participants post information and respond to questions from the entire group. The teacher or coordinator monitors all communications. Topical discussions can focus on achieving academic or career goals as well as building relationships and social skills. Weekly correspondence can include ideas about the mentees' progress in the program.

Electronic Mentoring

E-mail, discussion boards, listservs, or a dedicated online platform are the primary means of communication, with infrequent face-to-face encounters. Some programs promote the use of Skype or FaceTime for some visual connection, but the primary form of communication is electronic or virtual. E-mentoring can be implemented using either individual mentor–mentee pairs or the group format.

The advantage of one-to-one mentoring is that an in-depth relationship can result if a good match occurs and both the mentor and mentee are committed to sustaining the relationship. The disadvantage of one-to-one matches is that if either the mentor or mentee fails to maintain the relationship, then the mentoring match fails to provide positive outcomes and either the mentor or mentee may experience disappointment and be reluctant to engage in future mentoring relationships. From the perspective of the mentee, a disappointing relationship can cause more damage than not being involved in a mentoring program at all. Care must be taken to recruit mentors and mentees who choose to engage with the mentoring program for a minimum of 6 months to ensure that the pair collaborate during the initial relationship building stage of mentoring. If a mentor–mentee match is unsuccessful, then the mentor coordinator/teacher will need to rematch as quickly as possible. Poor mentor–mentee matches are less likely when group mentoring involves a number of mentors who engage in group activities that encourage both mentor–mentee and peer interactions that are supported by mentors. For example, three mentees and one mentor work together to complete either a school assignment or recreational activity. Deep relationships are less likely to form in group mentoring, but recruiting and matching mentors is less time consuming.

Whether mentors and mentees meet in person, electronically, in group settings, or in mentor–mentee pairs, the benefits of having another person value the choices and decisions that are made has a significant and positive impact on a mentee's future. After mentees reach the age of majority and are legal adults, they can reconnect with their mentor using the telephone and private e-mail accounts without the permission of the supervisors of the mentoring program.

POSITIVE OUTCOMES OF MENTORING: WHAT THE RESEARCH SAYS

Research confirms that successful mentoring programs improve self-esteem, social skills, academic achievement, and employment outcomes of youth who are at risk, and youth with disabilities. Numerous studies reported that positive relationships among mentors and mentees increase social, career, or academic outcomes of students (Battistich, Schaps, & Wilson, 2004; Berry & O'Conner, 2009; Gregory & Ripski, 2008; Rimm-Kaufman, 2014; Sowers et al., 2012). Although the majority of mentoring studies involved youth identified to be at risk for such problems as drugs and alcohol, dropping out of school, and involvement in the courts (Dubois & Karcher, 2013), mentoring programs involving youth with disabilities achieve positive outcomes as well (Sowers et al., 2012). Results of mentoring programs for youth who are at risk are presented because of the paucity of research on only youth with disabilities. Structured programs and naturally occurring mentoring relationships have powerful effects that provide young adults with positive and complementary benefits in a variety of personal, academic, and professional factors (Bruce & Bridgeland, 2014).

- Students who have mentors set higher educational goals and aspire to attend college versus youth who are at risk and do not have a mentor. Specifically, young adults who are at risk and have mentors are more likely to enroll in college (45% as opposed to 29% who do not have a mentor).

- Young adults who are at risk and have a mentor are more likely to participate in sports or extracurricular activities (67% as opposed to 37% who do not have a mentor).

- Young adults who are at risk and have a mentor are more likely to hold a leadership position in a club or sports team (51% as opposed to 22% who do not have a mentor).

In addition, youth satisfaction with mentoring relationships doubled when comparing relationships of more than a year to less than a year. Young adults with longer mentoring relationships report better outcomes than youth with shorter mentoring relationships in areas such as plans to enroll in college, participation in sports, and willingness to seek leadership positions (Bruce & Bridgeland, 2014). When examining the outcomes of structured mentoring programs versus informal mentoring relationships, structured mentoring programs provided more academic support, whereas naturally occurring informal relationships supported personal development (Bruce & Bridgeland, 2014).

Mentoring programs of varying lengths can positively affect outcomes such as increasing knowledge of perceived career options, including careers in science, technology, engineering, or math (STEM). Mentoring also increases confidence and engagement in STEM programs (Burgstahler & Chang, 2007; Sowers et al., 2012). Students involved in group mentoring using e-mail involving both peers and mentors reported that students enjoyed communicating with each other more than with mentors, and although students liked the convenience of communicating via e-mentoring with both peers and mentors, they felt it was difficult to express their feelings online and would have liked to meet face-to-face with their mentors (Burgstahler & Cronheim, 2001). Sowers et al. (2012) reported that mentoring programs that matched students with disabilities with mentors with or without disabilities, were more effective than a comparison group of students without mentors. Izzo, Murray, Priest, and McArrell (2011) reported that college students with disabilities majoring in STEM who were involved in peer mentoring through student learning communities, increased their self-advocacy skills and their persistence in their STEM degree programs. Numerous researchers recommend that mentoring programs deliver training to mentors before starting the mentoring process and provide coaching supports throughout the mentoring program (Axelrod, Campbell, & Holt, 2005; Sowers et al., 2012).

Mentoring programs that match students with hidden disabilities with young adults with similar disabilities improve self-confidence and self-advocacy skills of both mentees and mentors, according to reports issued by Eye to Eye's national offices (see http://www.eyetoeyenational.com). Survey results indicated that mentees reported improvements in self-esteem, hope for the future, self-advocacy skills, and academic empowerment. In addition, mentors reported that their self-confidence and self-esteem improved, as well as their ability to advocate for themselves. The Wyoming Department of Education conducted a separate evaluation study that compared three groups of students: 1) students with learning disabilities and ADHD (LD/ADHD) who participated in Eye to Eye mentoring, 2) students with LD/ADHD who did not participate in Eye to Eye, and 3) typical students without disabilities. The students with LD/ADHD who received mentorship through Eye to Eye scored as high or higher than the typical learners in reading and math on the state's standardized tests, as opposed to peer students with LD/ADHD who did not participate in mentoring (Flink, 2014).

Several studies examined the benefits of mentoring for employees in organizations that encourage them to mentor. Employees who served as mentors within their workplace reported greater job satisfaction and commitment to the organization compared with colleagues who did not mentor. In addition, higher quality relationships were associated with even greater benefits. Mentees reported greater satisfaction and a sense of affiliation, higher self-efficacy and health outcomes, and improvements in learning and socialization outcomes when mentors were matched to mentees based on deep-level similarities (e.g., values, personality, experience) rather than surface-level similarities (e.g., gender, race/ethnicity) (Eby et al., 2012).

MENTORS ASSIST STUDENTS IN NAVIGATING THE PATH TO DISABILITY PRIDE

Students with disabilities benefit from mentors who have accurate information about the effect a disability has on school performance. Text Box 3.1 illustrates how Dr. Bill Bauer, a college professor, mentors one of his students, Scott Nelson, through the Path to Disability Pride. Scott grew up believing that he was not very intelligent. He struggled to learn to read and hated reading out loud when he was in grade school. When his teacher announced to the class that everyone had to read a paragraph, he would count down to the paragraph that he had to read and practice all the words before it was his turn. Scott just figured he was not very smart. Dr. Bauer noticed that although Scott was talented and motivated, his writing and organizational skills kept tripping him up. Dr. Bauer suspected that Scott was a smart student that may have hidden disabilities that were not addressed.

> **Text Box 3.1—Scott Nelson**
> I was actually relieved to find out I had a disability and that I was not as dumb as I thought. I was more embarrassed thinking that I was dumb, than thinking that I had a disability. So, I just owned it very quickly and am very forthcoming with people about that.
>   Dr. Bill Bauer was very supportive. He explained, "This isn't your fault. I've actually embraced it myself by becoming involved in the disability field." Go to http://youtu.be/MIKKWl4E4kI to hear Scott tell his story.

Interview with Dr. Bill Bauer, Scott's Mentor

Margo Izzo: Why did you suspect Scott had a learning disability and perhaps ADHD or a traumatic brain injury [TBI]?

Bill: Several things. I befriended Scott while he was a student at Marietta College. Scott was an athlete at the college. He was a defensive back for our football team and a cheerleader for the basketball team. And so people told me I should meet this student. I was told he was a person with strong integrity. He was a friend to all and was not into drugs or alcohol, a rarity these days. As I got to know him I could certainly tell through observation and professional experience that he had all of the makings of a student who had some sort of learning difference. He would forget dates, times, and even forget things that I mentioned just a few minutes before. He would also use a lot of Post-it Notes to remind him to do things. He wasn't a bad kid but extraordinarily disorganized, which led me to believe that he might have had a brain injury. He mentioned that he wrestled and played football and many times he would get knocked out and would just get back into action at the urgency of his coach and/or father. He said he was knocked out multiple times both on the mat as a high school wrestler and on the field as a football player. He mentioned that his dad would tell him to toughen up and get back in the game after being knocked out.

Margo: How did you convince Scott to participate in disability testing?

Bill: I had him tell me his symptoms, and we developed a qualitative narrative life history. It wasn't hard to figure out after him telling me his life history that a learning disability in reading and ADHD were involved. I decided not to subject him to formal testing as his symptoms were very clear. "You clearly have ADHD. You have some memory loss. And I believe you have dyslexia." I explained that, "You're not dumb. You have some memory loss. A lot of these things you were born with, and some of these things are due to all your sport injuries." Scott had trouble with

- Reading comprehension: He mentioned that he started to notice this in elementary school, and reading became more of a hardship throughout his middle and high school years.

- Reading aloud: He was anxious when he had to read aloud.

- Spelling: He would spell the same word differently at different times in the same document.

- Poor organizational skills: He was constantly looking for his homework, and he stated that his bedroom was quite messy.

- Poor handwriting (his handwriting is sometimes illegible).

- Paying attention in class: Scott would often say that daydreaming was a common attribute of his. Oftentimes he would stare out the window or focus on things that were off track.

- Poor sense of direction: He would frequently get lost while driving.

- Short-term memory loss: This is one of his strongest attributes of his persona. I can remember we had Scott's video production company do a show for talented students at Marietta College. It was a spin-off of *America's Got Talent* but for college students. This major production required a lot of time for set up, and many expensive pieces of audio-visual equipment, lighting and sound equipment, and props had to be stationed 3–4 hours before production time. The production was underway, and, of course, Scott was responsible for the taping of the show from multiple television cameras. Upon conclusion of this 3-hour production, I asked Scott if everything was good. Scott smiled and gave me a "thumbs up." It was during the take down of the equipment and putting everything back into the trucks and trailers that Scott became immediately distraught. His usually sunny personality took a downturn to anxiety and concern. I asked Scott, "Hey, what's wrong, Bud?" He said, "Bill, I forgot to put tapes in all of the cameras." In other words, the entire show was not recorded.

- Short-term memory: Many times I would see him looking for his keys, his books, and his papers; sometimes he even lost his coat.

I discussed all of these issues with Scott. I asked Scott to tell me a little more about his educational and personal history and he stated, "All these years I thought I was dumb." He compensated by using his personality and seeing what he could get away with in school. Many times he would take the easiest route to task accomplishment even if it meant to just complete projects partially. He mentioned to me that upon talking about the symptoms and his current life situation that he felt a sigh of relief. Upon our discovery, you would often hear Scott say, "Now I know why I do the things I do."

Scott's Path to Disability Pride

Although Scott was not formally diagnosed with hidden disabilities until college, he experienced challenges in elementary school that made him question his intelligence. Scott was actually relieved to find out that the challenges he experienced were due to a combination of disabilities. Scott was at risk for underachievement because he had not learned critical organizational skills needed to navigate both school and his career.

Challenges   Scott felt he was different in elementary and middle school. He wondered why his classmates were "getting it" and he was struggling with reading and writing. Scott attended a prestigious private school that was exempt from formal testing, and he did not get special education services and supports.

Awareness   Scott knew there was something wrong. Academic supports were not offered to Scott. He simply maneuvered through the educational system the best he knew how. He compensated by using a variety of internal strategies (e.g., counting paragraphs, avoiding reading but looking at pictures, sitting in the back of the room to not get called on).

Disability Shame   Scott mentioned that he felt different and dumb before meeting Dr. Bauer. Scott did not receive a disability diagnosis before he went to college, and Dr. Bauer realized that Scott was embarrassed by his feelings of inadequacy caused by his disorganization, short-term memory loss, and challenges with reading and writing. Scott was not aware that these challenges resulted from his hidden disabilities. He was embarrassed and did not want others to find out that he could not keep up academically.

Connecting to a Disability Community   Dr. Bauer explained to Scott, "No one is to blame for having disabilities. Many people are born with hidden disabilities. Once you accept the fact that you have disabilities and learn to use accommodations and strategies to manage your daily tasks, then you don't have to waste the time it takes to hide your challenges." Dr. Bauer assisted Scott in making peace with his feelings of inadequacy and working on becoming an advocate with disability pride. Now Scott connects to the disability community both personally and professionally. Scott socializes with very diverse groups of people that range from university faculty to the Special Olympics basketball team.

Acceptance   Scott began to feel emancipated after Dr. Bauer explained the symptoms of reading disabilities, ADHD, and TBI. Scott realized that he was not dumb and that he had a lot to offer and just needed to accommodate his deficiencies. He also began to read about famous people with disabilities and began to relate to those stories. He immediately felt a feeling of relief and hope. Scott said the following to Dr. Bauer: "I wish I would have known this while I was still in school. I can't tell you how much easier it would have been for me."

Self-disclosure   After Dr. Bauer explained Scott's symptoms in a clear and concise way, he asked Scott if he would be interested in talking to his diverse learners class at Marietta College. Without hesitation, Scott said he would. Scott now gives lectures across the state about his story and is not afraid to tell his audience details of his history and his relationships with his teachers. Dr. Bauer also got him involved with the Ohio Youth Leadership Forum (YLF) as their videographer. This annual forum attracts area high school juniors and seniors with disabilities and brings them to the state capital to learn about disability rights, advocacy, self-determination, and self-disclosure. (See Chapter 4 for more about the YLF.) Scott became self-assured that he was not only helping himself but also helping others by disclosing his disability. Text Box 3.2 provides one student's reaction to Scott's lecture in his college class.

Using Supports   Scott now asks for help when needed. This is far from the person he was as a child in elementary and middle school. Scott now asks for printed copies of notes for meetings, or he audiotapes meetings using his iPad to help him remember names and items of interest. He uses sticky notes daily. He has paper and electronic sticky notes to remind him of important tasks. Then he transfers these tasks into his planner. Scott also asks his colleagues at work to look over his spelling on any important video projects. Scott

Text Box 3.2—Student's Reflection About Scott's Speech

I think that my favorite speaker was Scott Nelson because I can relate to his experience. Scott made it all the way to college without knowing that he had a learning disability and ADHD. He had problems all through school with being able to focus and learn what was being taught because he has ADHD. I went all through school without being diagnosed as dyslexic; yet, somehow still made it to college. I was diagnosed in college, just like Scott. Scott does not have an extreme form of ADHD; I do not have an extreme case of dyslexia. Scott had many concussions that have left him with some short-term memory loss. My short-term memory loss has gotten worse with every concussion. I think it is impressive that Scott chose to not take medication for his ADHD because he is able to work around it due to practice. I do not need accommodations for my dyslexia because I have just learned how to cope with it. And, if I have made it all the way to college, then I should be fine for the rest of my life.

is a technology guru. He relies heavily on technology, datebooks, and maps (e.g., GPS). He told Dr. Bauer that he would be totally lost without technology.

Self-advocate   As Scott became more aware of his strengths and weaknesses, he was able to ask for help and advocate for the services and supports at home and work. He is now able to say with confidence and pride that he is a person with a disability.

Disability Pride   Scott often advocates for others. It was not until the disclosure stage that Scott realized that there were so many other people like him. He likes to give back to others and listens to other people with hidden and nonhidden disabilities with empathy. Scott sees the positive benefits that his own story has on others when he shares the challenges he experiences with his own learning disability. Scott has come to realize that he likes and values who he is, especially when he helps another person with disabilities on his or her own Path to Disability Pride.

It is not hard to see how Scott moved through many of the stages of the Path to Disability Pride (see Figure 3.2). He is now a man with confidence and he knows who he is as a person. He asks for help when needed. Scott has learned the value of building community with others who have disabilities. He listens to others and offers advice to them, sometimes using his own story but also referring to others who may have gone through similar challenges as the ones in his life.

MENTORING PROGRAMS

The coauthors are involved with three mentoring programs that are specifically designed for mentoring students with disabilities. Eye to Eye is an art-based mentor program for students with learning disabilities and ADHD that recruits young adults with disabilities to mentor elementary or middle school

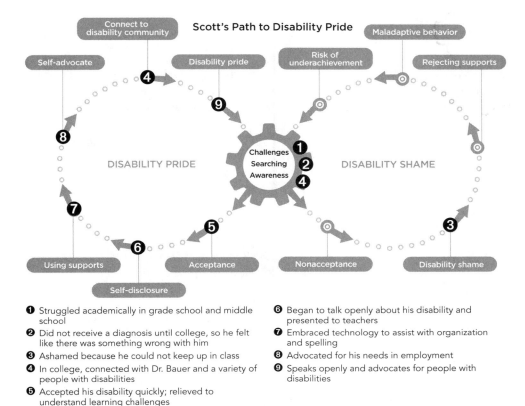

Figure 3.2. Scott's Path to Disability Pride.

1 Struggled academically in grade school and middle school
2 Did not receive a diagnosis until college, so he felt like there was something wrong with him
3 Ashamed because he could not keep up in class
4 In college, connected with Dr. Bauer and a variety of people with disabilities
5 Accepted his disability quickly; relieved to understand learning challenges
6 Began to talk openly about his disability and presented to teachers
7 Embraced technology to assist with organization and spelling
8 Advocated for his needs in employment
9 Speaks openly and advocates for people with disabilities

students with similar types of disabilities. The Ohio State University Electronic Mentoring Program recruits college students and professionals with and without disabilities to mentor high school students through monthly mentor mingles and weekly e-mail communications. The Ohio STEM Ability Alliance mentoring program uses a series of meetings to develop smaller learning communities of college students with disabilities who were majoring in STEM subjects. These STEM students support each other through challenging coursework under the guidance of an ability advisor, who many students referred to as their mentor.

Eye to Eye: A Mentoring Movement for Different Thinkers

In 1998, David Flink, a college student at Brown University, and four of his peers, all with learning disabilities and ADHD, began mentoring elementary school students with the same disabilities. The two groups worked together on art projects while the college student mentors helped the younger students better understand the way they learned, how to express their emotions and creativity, and how to build their self-esteem. Eye to Eye's web site explains, "they used art as their medium because it allowed for easier conversation about difficult topics, came with no right or wrong answers, and was just plain fun" (http://www.eyetoeyenational.org). After its start at Brown University, Eye to Eye has grown to a national nonprofit with a network of 50 chapters. In addition to their art activities, the mentors also receive training on how to talk about their learning differences to build awareness and LD/ADHD pride. LeDerick serves on Eye to Eye's board of directors and was the organization's first board chair. The following is an excerpt from an interview that LeDerick recorded with David Flink.

Interview with David Flink, Founder and Chief Empowerment Officer (CEO) of Eye to Eye and author of the book *Thinking Differently: An Inspiring Guide for Parents of Children with Learning Disabilities*

LeDerick: Can you tell me about Eye to Eye?

David: Eye to Eye is a mentoring program that matches college and high school students who have dyslexia, ADHD, and other learning disabilities with younger students who have similar learning differences or disabilities. Eye to Eye is the first ever movement for people who learn differently or think differently. So, when you think about learning disabilities, it's about 20% of the population. And we don't know each other because we're invisible. Eye to Eye deliberately asks young people to make that learning difference visible. Eye to Eye mentors are literally bearers of hope.

LeDerick: Tell me about one of your mentee-mentor relationships and what you learned from the experience.

David: Two of my early mentees stick out in my mind. They were very different students, Ricardo and Jim. Ricardo was incredibly talkative and extraverted; Jim was probably his polar opposite—very quiet, very reserved. Jim was a big kid who was kept back a grade, but he would have been a big kid regardless, but he was just big for his age. Ricardo was a tiny little kid, you know; it was so funny to me. I just kept looking at them. Okay, I'm going to take what I know and share with these two kids who just look so different and speak about our hidden disabilities. I mean, their personalities didn't matter, their cultural backgrounds didn't matter, they were relatively from the same social economic status, but honestly that did not matter. What mattered is that they both had constructed an entire identity about themselves that wasn't true. They had thought they weren't smart, and they thought they weren't smart because they had a language disability, and that message was confirmed in their mind because they were made fun of in school.

LeDerick: I know there are challenges that come with having any kind of disability like wrestling with the stigma. But are there some distinct challenges that people who have learning disabilities, ADHD, dyslexia, or any kind of hidden disability wrestle with?

David: Yeah, I think about the way that the individuals themselves experience success and how they make sense of it. So, when you have an invisible disability, like mine is a disability around language. As soon as I started to be successful, I oftentimes achieve that success by doing it in a different way. And then I begin to think, well, did the fact that I found this success differently mean it still is valid? So, it's like if all of a sudden, I decided, well here I am running this organization, and I have clearly had some measure of success. So, from now on I'm not going to have text messages read to me anymore. Like to really be a success would mean I could read everything that was put on my desk; like read it with my own eyes as opposed to listening to it in my ears. And I think that is inherent in the misinformation we provide young people with hidden disabilities.

The best mentors are those who are authentic and honest with their mentees. Note how honest David is as he shares how he still questions his success, years after he proved that his ideas have value. Remember that David Flink started mentoring when he was 18 years old as a college student at Brown University. He created Eye to Eye by building relationships with donors who have given millions of dollars, and he has motivated mentors with disabilities to donate thousands of hours of their time to support Eye to Eye's program. Figure 3.3 shows how David's identity as a person with a disability has developed from a young student who questioned his abilities to a nationally recognized leader who proudly shares what he has accomplished. At times, disability pride is held together by the thinnest thread. Other times, the strongest rope securely holds egos in place. The slogans in Text Box 3.3 have been used on Eye to Eye's web site (http://www.eyetoeyenational .org/) as part of their culture change work to provide encouragement to individuals when their LD and ADHD pride needs a boost.

> **Text Box 3.3—Own the Label**
>
> Got LD/ADHD? The first step to changing the world is accepting, owning, and celebrating your life and the way you learn. The second step is telling others.
>
> Our vision is simple, yet bold: To create a world in which people with LD/ADHD are fully accepted, valued, and respected, not just by society, but also by themselves.
>
> From Eye to Eye (2015). http://www .eyetoeyenational.org; reprinted by permission.

Electronic Mentoring

The E-Mentoring Program is an online curriculum in which students learn about information technology and transition skills with the support of mentors who are either college students or professionals. The curriculum includes activities in which students take self-assessments to help them determine their strengths,

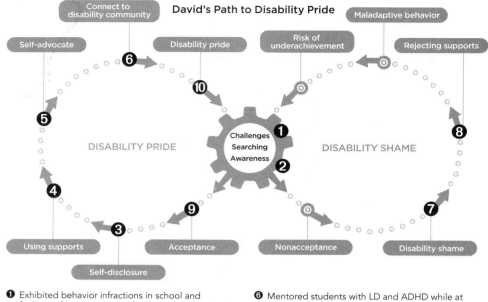

David's Path to Disability Pride

❶ Exhibited behavior infractions in school and feelings of loneliness amplified by regular removal from class
❷ Labeled in fifth grade with learning disabilities and attention-deficit/hyperactivity disorder (ADHD)
❸ Talked openly in middle school about having learning disabilities (LD/ADHD)
❹ Began using laptop and audiobooks in high school
❺ Enrolled at a university that fit his learning style

❻ Mentored students with LD and ADHD while at Brown University
❼ Went back into the LD/ADHD closet in first jobs after college
❽ Accepted a job that required reading applications as an admissions officer and didn't use accommodations
❾ Committed life's work to a career in the field of LD/ADHD after jobs in advertising and admissions
❿ Became Founder/CEO of Eye to Eye

Figure 3.3.   David's Path to Disability Pride.

learning styles, and interests to develop their transition plans to college and careers. Students explore postsecondary education programs and careers in which they are interested. Students create an individualized transition portfolio that summarizes the results of their transition assessments, the establishment of their postsecondary goals, and additional documents such as PowerPoint presentations, resumes, and college and career comparison charts. Throughout the curriculum, students communicate with their mentors using e-mail. Mentors provide guidance and feedback through e-mail and face-to-face mentor mingles.

The *E-Mentoring Program* is compliant with many of the transition services requirements of IDEA 2004, including the age-appropriate transition assessment and the establishment of measurable postsec-

Text Box 3.4—How Do I Find the E-Mentoring Curriculum and Resources?

The E-Mentoring Curriculum is available free at the Zarrow web site at http://www.ou.edu/content/education/centers-and-partnerships/zarrow/osu-emp.html.

To read more about the E-Mentoring Project, visit The Ohio State University Nisonger Center, http://nisonger.osu.edu/specialed-transition/ementoring.

ondary goals in employment, education or training, and independent living. Nine teachers and more than 500 students and mentors have piloted the curriculum and provided valuable suggestions to improve the content and activities. Based on this feedback, teachers and mentoring coordinators are encouraged to implement both electronic and face-to-face mentoring programs to support students with disabilities as they make the transition from classrooms to college and careers.

Using a quasi-experimental research design, it was found that high school students who completed the *E-Mentoring Program* compared with students who did not participate

- Significantly increased their information literacy gains using an information literacy curriculum-based measure

- Significantly increased their transition knowledge using a transition knowledge curriculum-based measure

- Maintained their AIMS web reading level as opposed to the comparison group, who experienced a drop in reading level from pretest to posttest administrations (Izzo, Murray, et al., 2014)

Margo Mentors a High School Student

I was working at Ohio State University and mentoring a sophomore high school student with a visual impairment who was completing the *E-Mentoring Program* in which mentors interacted via e-mail as well as in person. The high school students took interest and personality inventories to identify possible career goals. He ultimately combined two high-interest areas into one career goal: I will open a bookstore business that specializes in psychology books.

Matt shared the following when he returned to school for his junior year: "I've changed my career goal. I went to the web sites that I learned about in E-Mentoring and explored criminal justice and forensics. I realized that I have to go to college to qualify for both careers, so I searched for a college that offered both majors. I know that Ohio State offers both majors, so I've decided to apply to OSU and take courses in criminal justice and forensics." I helped Matt look up the entry requirements for admission to OSU, and he worked hard to raise his GPA and study for the SAT test so he could attend OSU.

The focus group results in Text Box 3.5 suggest that students who participated in the *E-Mentoring Program* have clearer and more focused transition goals and more confidence in expressing their transition goals. Gains in reading achievement were consistent for mentees with hearing, learning, and intellectual disabilities. The majority of students increased their internal locus of control, indicating that students are more academically competent, socially mature, and appear to engage in more self-motivated behavior. These results indicate that the *E-Mentoring Program* improves students' plans for their transition to college and careers. *The E-Mentoring Program* is available as an iTunes university course

Text Box 3.5—Focus Group Results from Students Who Participated in E-Mentoring Program

1. What are things you really liked and didn't like about the transition course?
    *   I've used the web sites in my portfolio to explore other careers that interest me.
    *   I created my transition portfolio in my sophomore year and then updated my resume in my junior year. Now that I'm a senior, I use my portfolio to help me with my college applications.
    *   I liked that you were able to research and explore careers, learn more about myself.
    *   I learned to compile my resume, and I liked seeing samples of college and job applications.
    *   It made me more confident in my skills and being prepared for college.
    *   The PowerPoint was fun. I liked that I could be creative. I sometimes do this in my other classes but not often.
    *   Being on the computers got old.
    *   I liked seeing what everyone else is planning on doing with their lives.
2. Do you feel your mentor has helped you plan for the future?
    *   My mentor definitely helped me to look into both of my career choices, helped me change my career focus.
    *   I had mostly a social relationship with Sarah, but it was more career and skills focused with Steve.
    *   My mentor helped me with the online course activities.
3. How do you feel this program helped prepare you for your future?
    *   Finding a good college match for my career choice.
    *   The program gave me the right questions to help me find the right school and kept me focused.
    *   The personality assessments helped me focus on the careers that were best suited for me.
    *   Sample college and job applications were helpful.
    *   The career research helped me find out the details about the career and find out what kind of education I needed.

Source: Izzo, M.V., Murray, A.J., Earley, J.A., McArrell, B., & Yurick, A.L. (2014).

or as an e-pub. Go to http://nisonger.osu.edu/specialed-transition/ementoring to access the links to review both versions of the program.

Ohio STEM Ability Alliance Program

The National Science Foundation (NSF) awarded grants to universities to establish alliances to improve the academic and career success of postsecondary students with disabilities in STEM disciplines. The unique challenges faced by students with disabilities in STEM are complex. Students face barriers to access in postsecondary education. Students must disclose having a disability and request accommodations—a process often laden with social stigma—in order to receive accommodations. Sevo (2011) observed that higher education institutions are willing to make physical accommodations for students with disabilities, but creating a welcoming climate, as evidenced by faculty who maintain high performance expectations while encouraging students with disabilities to use accommodations, has yet to follow suit. Students with disabilities often resist requesting accommodations due to poor societal perceptions of people with disabilities (May & Stone, 2010). Students are often met with negative attitudes from faculty and peers or are altogether discouraged from pursuing STEM degrees. In a study on the perceptions of parents and teachers on students with learning disabilities entering science and engineering fields, both parents and teachers had the perception that counselors, teachers, and parents do not encourage students with learning disabilities to take courses in science and engineering (Alston, Bell, & Hampton, 2002).

Many STEM students with disabilities participate in interventions such as student learning communities (SLCs), ability advising, mentoring, and internship programs to increase self-advocacy and self-determination skills. An SLC is a cohort of 8–15 students guided by an ability advisor. The students and advisor develop a social support network. The SLC can be implemented as a 1-week residential experience or a 10-week class on campus.

Ability advising is a customized form of academic, career, and self-advocacy counseling tailored to meet individual student needs. Students meet with their ability advisor to explore issues including but not limited to

- Disclosure (the process of revealing that one has a disability in order to obtain needed accommodations and supports)
- Effective communication with faculty about learning needs
- Academic goal setting and advising
- Effective use of learning tools and strategies (including AT)
- Career planning and development
- Access to needed resources (e.g., disability services, tutoring, financial aid)
- Effective utilization of disability services and the accommodations they can provide
- Perceptions of self, social identity, and societal stigma
- Mentoring, networking, and professional relationship building
- Effective stress and task management
- Assertiveness training
- Mental health and holistic wellness

Ability advisors develop authentic relationships with STEM students with disabilities that transcend beyond a typical advisor or faculty member when they plan and implement the SLC. The ability advisor teaches the essential skills previously listed to students in group settings and then works one-to-one through individual meetings with students who require additional practice. Many of the STEM students refer to the ability advisor, who has a hidden disability him- or herself, as their mentor. Andee, a STEM student with ADHD, shares her experience as she develops disability pride.

Andee Develops Disability Pride as a Graduate Student in College

Margo: Andee, please share your major and how you became aware that you had a disability.

Andee: I am working on my second BS degree as a computer science engineering major. I will be making the transition into the Ph.D. program in biomedical and informatics. I came to find out that I had ADHD when I was a sophomore in college the first time around. I was kicked out of my major for being overly disruptive in our small classes of six students that lasted for 2–3 hours at a stretch.

Margo: When did you learn about your learning style?

Andee: I did not learn about my learning style until I was a participant in the student learning community as a part of the Ohio STEM Ability Alliance program here at Ohio State. It was an NSF grant looking at interventions for students in STEM that had disabilities. One of the first things we were required to do was take an inventory of your learning style. I discovered that I was a multimodal learner. That made a lot of sense because as I started to adapt my learning style and as I started to do the things that are required for that, I was given an iPad. That was fantastic because I could download my PDF notes and my books and record the audio from my instructor. I could take notes at the same time on the PDF file while I was recording the audio. I could go back to my notes and click on my scribe pen and hear what was said. I was trying to draw and get the diagram and get everything down from the diagram. But while I am trying to focus on the diagram, I can't listen to what is being said, and while I am listening to what is being said, I am not getting all the parts of the diagram correct. It was really wonderful to be able to put all those pieces together by using technology that didn't exist when I was an undergraduate. It was completely different.

Margo: Excellent. Can you share a little bit about your self-advocacy plan?

Andee: My self-advocacy plan really started out with understanding what ADHD is. Not only what is ADHD on a broad, academic level, but what is ADHD for me, what traits really run strong in me, what traits don't run quite so strong, and really figure out how the disability affects me, what does it change in my daily life, what does it do in terms of changing my brain. Once I was able to understand that, my self-advocacy plan started to develop to include asking people what they need of me instead of presuming that I know. It also helps me be honest with people. Instead of making a joke, I say, "I have ADHD. This is how I am, this is how I need things communicated to me, this is the type of support that I need, this is the type of support that I can give you, what other types of interventions are needed, what other types of accommodations are needed." Not only do I advocate for myself in the classroom, but I advocate for myself in my relationships, and I advocate for myself in my career and internships. But really being able to be comfortable with my brand of ADHD and what it means to me and then being able to articulate that to be able to have my needs met as well as meet the needs of others.

Margo: Very well stated. Can you describe any mentoring relationships that you have had that have helped you embrace your disability and embrace your self-advocacy plan and the accommodations that you are now finding so successful?

Andee: Yes. There have been several. The first relationship that I had was with one of my class instructors. She met with me after my first exam: "There is something going on here. Take care of it. I know that you know this stuff in and out. Go talk with someone at the Office of Disability Services and see how they can help you. See what you need. This is a new ballgame. It is not the way that it was when you were an undergrad the first time." The fact that there was enough of a connection with her to see me as a student and recognize that there was something going on was very important because I think there are a lot of instructors that don't necessarily take the time to know their students that well, or really realize that their students are struggling more than just conceptually with understanding the information. That was wonderful. She and I continue to maintain a relationship and she has, in doing so, opened a lot of doors for me.

Also, Victor, who was the Ohio STEM Ability Alliance Program Coordinator here at Ohio State, has been a huge source of emotional and social support that I did not really experience prior to coming to Ohio State. Whether that was in other academic programs with other advisors or even from my mom, who will still tell you that I am not good at math and science and that I should just grow up and get a big girl job, to be able to have that type of guidance and someone who is willing to direct you in one particular way or another and say, "Hey, there is something that you should maybe think about doing. We have a new student organization that you should consider being a part of or we are doing mock interviews, that might be a good opportunity for you to shake off the cobwebs from previous careers and see where your feet land today." That type of encouragement landed me my current internship with Battelle. And I have wonderful mentors at the Battelle Able Alliance, which is their employee resource group specifically for individuals with disabilities, all sorts of different types, whether they are visible or invisible. And being able to work with other individuals who have disabilities and having their professional success as a foundational groundwork and something you can follow because you are able to see that success can be had, is really quite priceless in terms of bolstering pride and bolstering confidence, knowing that you don't have to be quiet about your disability. You can say what you need, and say what you have, and people don't run away.

Andee's disability pride was bolstered by faculty members who took the time to encourage her to meet with a disability counselor at the Office of Disability Services. Andee had success in challenging STEM classes once she became aware of how having ADHD affected her learning and embraced her accommodations. She utilized technology, mentors, and resources offered by her employer to support her in school and work. Andee learned that having ADHD is not something that she has to keep hidden, but it is an asset that has opened doors on her path to employment. Figure 3.4 illustrates Andee's Path to Disability Pride.

McKlin, Engelman, and Ranade (2013) concluded that nurturing mentoring relationships between trained and compassionate mentors and college students with disabilities are critical to program success for three reasons.

1. Mentors are invested in the students' maturation and psychosocial development and take a holistic approach toward the students' needs. Whereas the academic advisor is concerned with the students' course load and grades, and the disability services counselor is concerned with providing the right services and accommodations, the mentor responds to the students' needs and trajectories.

2. Mentors provide scaffolding to deliver the supports needed by students. A freshman student who is struggling to adjust to campus life may need assistance in terms of stress and time management as opposed to finding an internship. Yet, a senior student who is hoping to move on to a job after he or she graduates may benefit from having an internship to build his or her résumé and professional skills.

3. Mentors lead to increases in students' self-advocacy, self-determination, and personal responsibility. Students learn to define and come to terms with their disability, which in turn enables them to disclose their disability in necessary situations. The confidence that comes with self-advocacy leads to increased personal responsibility and self-determination because students feel that they can achieve what they want despite their disability.

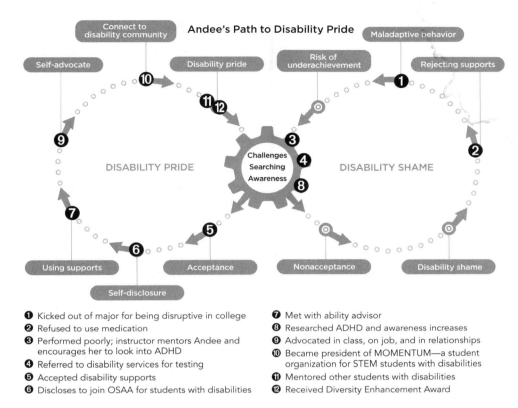

Figure 3.4.   Andee's Path to Disability Pride.

❶ Kicked out of major for being disruptive in college
❷ Refused to use medication
❸ Performed poorly; instructor mentors Andee and encourages her to look into ADHD
❹ Referred to disability services for testing
❺ Accepted disability supports
❻ Discloses to join OSAA for students with disabilities

❼ Met with ability advisor
❽ Researched ADHD and awareness increases
❾ Advocated in class, on job, and in relationships
❿ Became president of MOMENTUM—a student organization for STEM students with disabilities
⓫ Mentored other students with disabilities
⓬ Received Diversity Enhancement Award

Thus, nurturing is an essential quality in a good mentor. Consequently, it is a construct of mentoring that can be developed and assessed (McKlin et al., 2013).

CONCLUSION: MENTORING WORKS

The evidence on mentoring programs strongly suggests that many students benefit from both group and individual mentoring programs. It is important, however, to stress the value of teaching students to proactively seek out mentors to guide them in their quest for disability pride. The chapter closes with an excerpt from David Flink's interview in which he shares with LeDerick how Eye to Eye started when he was a college student at Brown University. David met with the Director of Brown University's Community Services Projects, to gain university support to start Eye to Eye. Not only did he gain support to start his mentoring project, but he also gained a mentor. David and LeDerick end the interview by sharing how much they have learned by being mentors. Mentors get as much, if not more, from the mentoring relationship. Mentoring is a win-win for both mentors and the mentees.

David Flink Advocates to Start Eye to Eye

Peter has a very old soul. He is as knowledgeable as the oldest person I know and is young and spirited. [He is as] willing to take on revolutionary ideas as the youngest person I know. And I didn't really care; I wasn't looking for some Yoda master. But I remember I met Peter because I had the idea of Eye to Eye. I knew I needed some kind of institutional backing in community service, so I started at the bottom. I didn't know the right language to use, so I just worked my way up to the top, which was Peter. I knew if I didn't get Peter on my side the idea was going to be done. I went in there to explain my idea.

I think I came in with a lot of anger. My message was: "I wasn't treated well in school, so I want to go in there and teach those teachers how we should be treated through a mentoring program." Peter took a minute and let some space fill into the room, and he said, "Why are you doing this? What do you hope to accomplish? Can we talk about this for a minute?"

And he just, he listened to me, more than anything else, he listened to me. He said, "You're doing this to help a part of you, to maybe heal a part of yourself, is that right?" I said, "Yeah." Peter said, "You've got to leave that before you walk into that school."

Peter continued, "Who do you need to help? You're angry because some teachers didn't treat you the way you wanted to be treated? And was that all of them, some of them or one of them?" And I was like, "It was probably just two [teachers] actually." Peter said, "You probably can teach these current teachers something, but they're your partners, and you want to build a movement." I never thought of this as a movement. So he took the time to ask questions to help me. What I liked about him was that he never made me feel like he knew everything, but he always made me feel like I might know something of value. I think the best mentors are humble.

I would say in fast forwarding and thinking about my role now as a mentor, I always have a handful of people I'm working with; and my greatest joy is watching them not need me anymore. I learned more from my mentee than I ever thought possible. I learned more about empathy and selflessness than I ever thought possible.

LeDerick: I think it's something that all of us benefit from. I also really appreciate you mentioning the value that the mentor gets from the mentee and how it can help you in your own journey. Oftentimes, we just think about older people working with younger kids. But I know, very much like you, from the times I've been able to mentor people, you get as much if not more from the experience yourself.

David: The insight I've learned most in life is that I'm actually gifted with paying attention. I went into that relationship dead set that I was going to teach Jim, my first mentee, these things. But my mentee taught me. When he advocated, and it worked, that reminded me that I need to keep advocating too. So as you try and teach students; often they teach you back.

Resources on Mentoring

Best Practices Guide on Mentoring Youth with Disabilities
Free tool to help create or expand a mentoring program for youth with disabilities. It includes topics such as mentoring models, e-mentoring, sustaining a program, and evaluating a program.
http://www.pyd.org/editor/images/resources-best-practices-for-mentoring-youth-with-disabilities.pdf.pdf

DO-IT Mentors, The University of Washington
The DO-IT program provides a mentoring guide titled *Helping Young People Prepare for Their Future,* which can be downloaded for free.
http://www.washington.edu/doit/Brochures/Programs/mentoring.html

E-Mentoring Program, The Ohio State University
This e-mentoring course is offered free of charge through the Zarrow Center and consists of 17 units, with each unit containing quizzes, guided notes, and activities.
https://itunes.apple.com/us/course/e-mentoring/id850432378

Eye to Eye
This mentoring program has more than 50 chapters and follows a straightforward model that is focused on individuals with different learning disabilities and attention-deficit/hyperactivity disorder.
http://eyetoeyenational.org/programs/mentoring.html

Foundations of Successful Youth Mentoring
This is a free guidebook that discusses the critical foundations of creating a long-term successful mentoring program. It includes assessments, key resources, checklists, and timelines.
http://educationnorthwest.org/sites/default/files/resources/foundations.pdf

National Mentoring Partnership
This provides resources on how to start a mentoring program, coordinates a National Mentoring Summit, and coordinates the Center for Evidence-Based Mentoring.
http://www.mentoring.org/start_a_program

The E-Mentoring Program—Nisonger Center
This program matches students with disabilities with mentors who have college and/or career experience. All communication is done via e-mail, and two models are used—group e-mail listerv and one-to-one mentor match. Information about the project is described at:
http://nisonger.osu.edu/transition/ementoring.htm

The E-Mentoring Program Curriculum and Resources is included at:
http://www.ou.edu/content/education/centers-and-partnerships/zarrow/osu-emp.html

Transition

Planning for College and Careers

4

The transition from high school to college and careers represents a period of changing roles and responsibilities for nearly all students and can pose even more of a challenge for students with hidden disabilities. Students in middle and high school attend school for about 5 hours each day and often have limited choices in what classes they must take. Students in many schools do not have the choice of whether they take classes with their peers without disabilities or are assigned to a class for students with disabilities.

In contrast, young adults are expected to make responsible choices about their college majors and career paths when they enter college or begin employment. College students often have the opportunity to schedule classes in the morning, afternoon, or evening. They also have large gaps between classes in which they can choose to study, work out, or take a nap. Young adults have choices about whether to apply for jobs, what jobs they choose to apply for, and how engaged they want to be in their work. How do students with hidden disabilities learn to become productive adults? What do teachers and parents need to do to assist and support these students during transition so they gain the skills needed to become responsible adults? How can students with hidden disabilities navigate the transition from high school to college and careers?

Strategies that promote successful transitions to college and careers will be shared and demonstrated through the lens of self-determination. Helping all youth gain the knowledge, skills, and attitudes needed to assume meaningful adult roles is the primary goal of federal and state legislation and is reflected in the majority of mission and vision statements of schools. Yet, given the disappointing outcomes reported by numerous researchers, more must be done during the transition years to adequately prepare students with hidden disabilities for the productive future they deserve.

FEDERAL DEFINITION OF TRANSITION SERVICES

Transition services is defined in IDEA 2004 as a coordinated set of activities for a student with a disability that

> is designed with a results-oriented process, that is focused on improving the academic and functional achievement of the child with a disability to facilitate the child's movement from school to post-school activities, including post-secondary education, vocational education, integrated employment (including supported employment), continuing and adult education, adult services, independent living, or community participation. (Sec.602, H.R. 1350)

In addition, IDEA requires that school personnel help students develop measurable postsecondary goals based on age-appropriate transition assessments related to training, education, employment, and, where appropriate, independent living. Finally, school personnel must identify the specific transition services to assist students in reaching their postsecondary goals. IDEA requires school personnel to invite students with disabilities to their IEP meeting to discuss their plans after high school, as well as what transition services will assist them to reach their college and career postschool goals. Transition services mandates are clearly designed to facilitate a multiyear planning process involving students, parents, school personnel, and other agency personnel who work together to support students in reaching their desired postsecondary goals.

Students with disabilities still graduate from high school unprepared for the challenges of adulthood, even with federal mandates to actively involve students in transition assessment and planning activities, as evidenced by lower rates of engagement in college and employment compared with their typically developing peers (Newman et al., 2011). The limited participation that students with disabilities are expected and encouraged to play in their own transition planning is one of the factors that may contribute to these poor outcomes. Do students walk into their IEP meeting with a good understanding of their strengths and challenges? Can students disclose their disability and their dreams to their IEP teams and describe what they need to reach their goals?

A number of evidence-based predictors, practices, and curricula are available for educators to assist students in learning to take a more active role in preparing for life after graduation (Izzo, Yurick, Nagaraja,& Novak, 2010; Test et al., 2009; Test, Fowler, & Kohler, 2013). Many of these practices are summarized within the web sites, resources, and curricula described in Text Box 4.1. Other suggestions to implement these practices are provided through this chapter's Tips for Teaching, personal vignettes, and disability pride fundamentals.

Text Box 4.1—Web Sites and Resources for Transition Planning

Career One Stop
  Developed by the U.S. Department of Labor, this site provides resources and tools for job seekers, students, businesses, and professionals.
  http://www.careeronestop.org

College Navigator
  Students, parents, and professionals use College Navigator to search for postsecondary programs that provide certificates or degrees for a variety of programs and majors. Students can search a college database by state, region, program/majors, types of degree, and institutional characteristics.
  http://www.nces.ed.gov/collegenavigator

IRIS Center
  The IRIS Center is a national center dedicated to improving educational outcomes for all children, especially those with disabilities, birth through 21 years, through the use of effective evidence-based practices and interventions.
  http://www.iris.peabody.vanderbilt.edu

The Job Accommodation Network (JAN)
  The JAN web site assists professionals and others on workplace accommodations and disability employment issues.
  http://www.askjan.org

National Collaborative on Workforce and Disability/Youth
  This site provides information about employment and youth with disabilities. Curricula materials are available at no cost.
  http://www.ncwd-youth.info

National Technical Assistance Center on Transition
  NTACT's purpose is to assist State Education Agencies, Local Education Agencies, State VR agencies, and VR service providers in implementing evidence-based and promising practices ensuring students with disabilities, including those with significant disabilities, graduate prepared for success in postsecondary education and employment. NTACT is funded from January 1, 2015 until December 31, 2019.
  http://www.transitionta.org

OCALI Transition to Adulthood Guidelines
  Resources including online booklets and modules on transition for students with autism or other low incidence disabilities.
  http://www.ocali.org/project/transition_to_adulthood_guidelines

Ohio Employment First Transition Planning
  A variety of resources for job seekers, families, and professionals that support the transition from school to employment for youth with developmental disabilities.
  http://www.ohioemploymentfirst.org

(continued)

Web Sites and Resources for Transition Planning *(continued)*

People First Language Resources
Kathie Snow's article, *To Ensure Inclusion, Freedom, and Respect for People with Disabilities, We Must Use People First Language,* can be found at this site.
http://disabilityisnatural.com

Person-Centered Planning
Professionals gain an overview of person-centered planning by completing a course, reading articles, and downloading a number of free resources through this course developed by Cornell University.
http://www.personcenteredplanning.org

Soft Skills to Pay the Bills: Mastering Soft Skills for Workplace Success
The Office on Disability Employment Policy developed this curriculum to teach workforce readiness skills.
http://www.dol.gov/odep/topics/youth/softskills

Transition to Independence Process Model
This web site describes the Transition to Independence Process Model to assist students with emotional and behavior difficulties through a transition planning process. The model engages youth in their own future planning process.
http://www.tipstars.org

Think College
A web site for students, families or professionals who are exploring college options for students with intellectual disabilities.
http://www.thinkcollege.net

Transition Assessment and Goal Generator
This web-based tool can be used by professionals, families, and transition-age students with disabilities to gain norm-based graphic profiles, present level of performance statements, lists of strengths and needs, and suggested individualized education program annual transition goals.
https://tagg.ou.edu/tagg

Youthhood
This web site is designed by and for students with disabilities to assist young adults plan for life after high school.
http://www.youthhood.org

Zarrow Center
The Zarrow Center provides numerous assessments and curricula on self-determination and transition planning.
http://www.ou.edu/content/education/centers-and-partnerships/zarrow.html

EVIDENCE-BASED PREDICTORS AND
PRACTICES TO IMPROVE TRANSITION PLANNING

The National Secondary Transition Technical Assistance Center (NSTTAC; 2009) identified 16 predictors of postschool success and 32 evidence-based practices in the areas of employment, education, and independent living. Researchers and practitioners continue to refine these predictors and practices ("Evidence Based Practices", 2015; "Evidence Based Predictors", 2015; Test et al., 2013; Test, Kemp-Inman, Diegelmann, Hitt, & Bethune, 2015). In an effort to make the information easier to navigate, the coauthors have clustered the predictors and practices into eight large categories that reflect activities, services, and supports that occur during the school years and are associated with higher rates of success in adulthood:

1. Self-determination, individual living skill instruction, and skill building

2. Inclusive practices and programs

3. Collaborative networks for student support

4. Individualized career development

5. Authentic community-based work experiences

6. Social and social-emotional instruction and skills

7. Academic, vocational, and occupational education/preparation

8. Supporting parental involvement and expectations

In addition to these predictors and practices, McConnell et al. (2013) identified nonacademic behaviors associated with successful postschool employment and education outcomes for students with mild and moderate disabilities, many of which are considered hidden disabilities:

1. Knowledge of their strengths and limitations

2. Actions related to strengths and limitations

3. Disability awareness

4. Persistence

5. Proactive involvement

6. Goal setting and attainment

7. Gaining paid employment experiences

8. Self-advocacy

9. Using informal supports (e.g., teachers/peers to clarify expectations) and formal resources and accomodations (e.g., tutoring centers and/or extended time on tests)

Having one or all of these predictors and behaviors will not guarantee students' success once they leave high school, but these predictors and behaviors, as well as the authors' own experiences, suggest that students with hidden disabilities who do well are often the ones who have many of these characteristics. Students achieve improved adult outcomes when teachers and parents have high expectations and teach the behaviors and skills identified above in inclusive settings. Students demonstrate these skills by setting goals that capitalize on their strengths and using accommodations and supports to compensate for their limitations.

LeDerick's Path to Success

Although phrased in many different ways, the one question I am asked more than any other goes something like, "Given everything you went through with your learning disability, what really helped you to be successful?" I often answer this question by talking about the advantages of growing up in a working-class household and the high expectations that my parents had. I describe the role that art and athletics had in nurturing my belief in my own abilities. I give credit to the handful of general education classes that I took before graduation from high school. I always give my IEP team credit for connecting me with a quality disability support program that was operating at a local county college. These are just a few of the many factors that I believe led to my success.

ESTABLISHING POSTSECONDARY GOALS BASED ON VALID TRANSITION ASSESSMENTS

The beginning of the transition process for students with and without disabilities often begins with one question: "What do you want to do when you grow up?" Many students will reply with an answer that is improbable, such as, "I want to play professional basketball" or "I want to be a fashion model." Students' ideas of what they would like to do once they graduate from high school will be formed by a number of factors, such as their skills, their interests, and what kind of exposure they have had to careers through school, family and the media. Students often are not systematically guided through a process that helps them discover their preferences, interests, needs, and strengths and then match these to potential careers. Many of the adults who work with students who express unrealistic goals quickly dismiss the student's career aspirations without seriously considering why they pick these larger-than-life goals.

Transition assessments are designed to assist students to develop realistic postsecondary goals and to determine what transition services and activities are needed to develop the skills and behaviors required for the student to reach his or her postsecondary goals. A number of formal and informal assessment methods are outlined in the "Age Appropriate Transition Assessment Toolkit" (Walker, Kortering, Fowler, Rowe, & Bethune, 2013), posted at the National Technical Assistance Center on Transition (NTACT, formerly known as

NSTTAC) web site. Schools can administer interest, learning style, personality, and aptitude surveys to help students discover their interests, strengths, and needs. Informal assessment methods are also valuable to validate career interests and skills. Students benefit from informal career exploration activities such as job shadows, job tryouts, career fairs, and interviews with workers who have jobs with similar interests. These types of activities will either validate or negate a specific career goal, and the earlier students determine a valid goal, the more time can be spent in school to deliver the skills needed to enter that career area.

Expand Career Assessment Activities

Both legislation and researchers emphasize the necessity of providing a strong foundation of career development experiences while students are still in middle and high school (Carter et al., 2010; Izzo et al., 2010; Mazzotti, Rowe, Cameto, Test, & Morningstar, 2013; Sitlington & Clark, 2006; Test et al., 2009; Wood, Sylvester, & Martin, 2010). Specifically, paid work experience within community employment while in high school is a predictor of paid employment as an adult (Test et al., 2013). Many transition frameworks include career development and job-specific employment skill training as an essential component (Kohler, 1996; Test et al., 2009). Shandra and Hogan (2008) reported that students who were enrolled in occupational programs of study were more likely to be engaged in full-time employment with benefits. Numerous researchers have reported positive benefits of career/technical education and vocational education programs in improving school retention and employment outcomes (Benz, Lindstrom, & Yovnoff, 2000; Repetto & Andrews, 2012). Teachers who integrate instruction on career exploration and transition planning with core content areas assist students in seeing the connection between academic content and career application. Therefore, facilitating self-directed transition planning assists all students in exploring their interests and skills, establishing college and career goals, and developing action plans to meet their goals.

Several self-determination and transition curricula that can be integrated into core classes are described in this chapter. The *EnVisionIT* curriculum was developed and refined by teams of teachers, parents, and professionals who the coauthors worked with over a number of years. *EnVisionIT* is an electronic curriculum for students with and without disabilities focused on developing key literacy and career skills needed for the 21st century workplace (see http://nisonger.osu.edu/envisionit). It is aligned with English/language arts Common Core State Standards (CCSS), college and career readiness standards, and technology and financial literacy standards. The curriculum has increased students' technology literacy skills, transition skills, and reading skills through numerous pilot studies (Izzo et al., 2010). More important, students prepare a presentation that they use at their IEP meeting to describe the results of their transition assessment process, their college and career goals, postsecondary goals, and the annual goals they need to accomplish during the current year. Margo is scaling up *EnVisionIT* in schools across numerous states with federal funding (2012–17). Project staff conducted focus groups with students at the end of the course to gain feedback on improving the course. Read what one student said about the *EnVisionIT* course in the following vignette.

EnVisionIT and Plan Your Future

I thought I wanted to be a school psychologist after college, or at least major in psychology, when this class first started. Now I do not want to do either. My career path has completely changed after researching careers and comparing colleges. I want to go to Ohio State and major in education with a minor in creative writing. Ohio State is not the only school where I could accomplish this—many other colleges, such as Ohio Northern University or Miami University, offer both education and creative writing as a major/minor combination. I feel that the goals I have set are going to be very good preparation for my future. I also have my résumé ready so I can apply for a job soon. My next steps are visiting more colleges, taking the ACT and the SAT, and applying to colleges.

THE IMPORTANCE OF THE INDIVIDUALIZED EDUCATION PROGRAM MEETING

The IEP meeting is one of the biggest missed opportunities to teach students with disabilities the skills they need to gain an understanding of their disability, strengths and needs, and how to work with others to plan their transition to college and careers. IEP meetings in many school districts have been reduced to annual rituals that are focused more on compliance and less on assisting students plan their transition to adult life. Shifting to a self-directed IEP meeting in which the student has an active role in leading the meeting is one way to improve the development and implementation of the IEP. Researchers reported that students who are taught self-determination skills and learn to lead their meetings have increased self-efficacy and transition knowledge (Test et al., 2009; Wood et al., 2010) and experience more positive postschool outcomes (Powers et al., 2012; Shogren, Wehmeyer, Palmer, Rifenback, & Little, 2015; Wehmeyer & Palmer, 2003; Wehmeyer & Schwartz, 1997).

Self-Directed Individualized Education Programs

The self-directed IEP materials are an evidence-based practice that is designed to assist teachers to prepare students to facilitate their own IEP meetings and to participate in a meaningful manner (Martin et al., 2006; Test, et al., 2013). The self-directed IEP curriculum consists of 11 lessons that teach students to take a more active role in their meetings (Martin, Marshall, Maxson, & Jermain, 1996). Opportunities are created for students to gain a meaningful understanding of their disability and needs when they take a more active role in their IEP meetings. The self-directed IEP meeting is also a safe environment for students to practice the self-advocacy skills that will support them as they make the transition to postsecondary settings.

Teachers can use the career exploration activities integrated throughout the curriculum to assist students in understanding that there are a vast array of jobs and courses of study that they might be interested in pursuing. It can also be useful to ask students questions such as, "What is it about that job that is interesting to you?" Or, if students are not at a point in which they can see themselves doing any kind of career, then teachers can ask them about the activities they enjoy doing now and help them determine if there are aspects of those activities that might be an indicator of what they want to do in the future.

LeDerick Demonstrates Career Interests as a Student Athlete

I was named captain of our cross country team as a sophomore in high school. I had been running distance since the seventh grade and was a quality athlete throughout high school, but I enjoyed being a part of a team more than the actual running. It was always fun to work out and joke around with my teammates. I also really enjoyed race days when I had to give "the speech" because I was the captain. This was a short motivational talk that I would give to the team to help them focus and perform at their best. I enjoyed running, but connecting and motivating my team were the best parts of being a student athlete. My professional life is now split between managing a number of businesses and working as an advocate for people with disabilities. A big part of my responsibility as a business owner is putting together teams of people who can work together to perform a task. I spend most of my time as an advocate delivering talks and workshops to help improve the outcomes of people with disabilities. Beyond going to college, I had no idea what I wanted to do after I graduated from high school. The talents and interests that I expressed in my early teens were strong indicators of what I eventually decided to do as a career.

HELPING STUDENTS SEE THE FUTURE

Many transition-age youth with hidden disabilities have a hard time articulating their transition goals, and they have an even harder time developing a plan to reach their goals. Why? Because their disability awareness and knowledge of their strengths and potential career choices are limited, resulting in a lack of self-determination. They have not had the opportunities to make choices. Ultimately, they do not dare to dream. Teachers, parents, and other support personnel need to provide numerous opportunities for students to make choices throughout their childhood. Text Box 4.2 provides an activity that can help students create a literal picture of their future that can be used to help them develop a series of transition goals to help that picture become a reality.

DISABILITY PRIDE FUNDAMENTALS

Graham Moore was awarded the Oscar for best adapted screenplay for the movie *Imitation Game* during the 2015 Academy Awards ceremony. Moore gave

Text Box 4.2—Your Future Self

- Draw a line down the middle of a piece of paper running up and down, and then draw a second line going from left to right. This will create four boxes on the page, dividing the paper into quadrants.

- Now imagine that you are 10 years older than you are now. You have graduated from high school, have gone on to college, and/or have started your career. With the picture of your future self still in your mind, draw a picture or write some words and phrases in each one of the boxes that describe the following four things:

  1. What you want to do for work in the next 10 years.
  2. What you are going to do for fun in the next 10 years.
  3. Who your friends will be in the next 10 years.
  4. What kind of home you want to have in the next 10 years.

You do not need to be an artist. Just do your best to fill each box with either a picture, or write some words with as much detail as you can. Will you work in an office or outside? Will you need to go somewhere special to have fun? What kind of jobs will your friends have? Will your home be in the country or in the city?

Now that you have a description of what your life will be like 10 years from today, turn your page around and answer the following questions that will help you make this picture a reality:

- What are three things you will need to do to make sure you have the career you want?

- What are three things you will need to do to make sure you can do the kind of things you want to do to have fun?

- What are three things you will need to do to make sure you can meet and spend time with the people you would like to be your friends?

- What are three things you will need to do to make sure you can get to live in the kind of home you want?

From New Jersey Department of Education, Division of Student Services (2004). *Connections: A guide to maximizing student potential.* New Jersey Department of Education, Division of Student Services, OSEP; adapted by permission.

a powerful testimony that can uplift young people who have felt different for any reason, in his acceptance speech. He said, "I tried to commit suicide at 16. And now I'm standing here. I would like for this moment to be for the kid out there who feels like he or she doesn't fit in anywhere. You do! Stay weird. Stay different, and when it's your turn and you are standing on this stage, please pass the same message along."

The following sections describe disability pride fundamentals that promote accepting disability and gaining confidence and self-awareness to successfully make the transition to college and careers.

- Normalize disability
- Provide supports and teach students how to use them
- Build awareness of students' disability, strengths, and limitations
- Teach self-determination, disclosure, and self-advocacy skills
- Build disability community to promote disability pride

Students who gain disability pride accept their disability as a natural part of the human experience. They do not let their disability completely define who they are as a person. They are self-determined and pursue their goals, making adjustments along the way as they self-regulate their progress to adjust their course.

Normalize Disability

Teachers need to reflect on their own attitudes and beliefs about disability and the language that they use with their students as they prepare students to successfully transition. Do they believe that their students have more ability than disability? Do teachers believe that students belong in the inclusive class-room? Some teachers may need to make some important shifts in language and perspective before the inclusive classroom becomes a nurturing environment where disabilities are accommodated as a normal component of the teaching and learning process. Teachers must be comfortable with talking about dis-ability in a way that will assist students in accepting their own disability. These shifts in perspectives help lay a firm foundation on which students will de-velop their pride and confidence to face the future.

 ## LeDerick Is Proud to Be in an Inclusive Honors Class

Mr. Taylor was one of my favorite teachers. He taught special education students, and he also taught an honors-level course designed to develop students' debat-ing skills. Based on Mr. Taylor's recommendation and his faith in my abilities, I was allowed into this debating class and was given the opportunity to go toe-to-toe with a room full of students that had been in honors classes for as long as I had been in special education. I passed the course and was able to leave high school with a transcript that showed I could perform outside of special education for at least one class.

Being educated in the inclusive classroom is a critical step to normalizing dis-ability. Mazzotti et al. (2013) reviewed the literature and cited numerous stud-ies that reported that students who received instruction in inclusive classrooms were more likely to participate in postsecondary education (Baer et al., 2003; Halpern, Yovanoff, Doren, & Benz, 1995) and employment after completing high school (Blackorby, Hancock, & Siegel, 1993; Halpern et al., 1995; Heal & Rusch, 1995). Yet, teaching the CCSS and the transition skills that students need within the inclusive setting is challenging teachers and administrators across this country. How do teachers ensure that students gain the skills needed to pass the high-stakes assessments that are required as well as the skills they need to make the transition to college and careers? Research-based methods such as coteaching (Murawski & Swanson, 2001; Villa, Thousand & Nevin, 2013) and UDL (Nelson, 2014; Rose & Meyers, 2002) continue to emerge as ex-emplary ways to deliver effective inclusive practices.

Commitment to Conversation   Committing to being open and honest about disability is an important step all educators have to take in order to help their students develop the skills needed to successfully transition. The preamble of IDEA 2004 states that "disability is a natural part of the human experience." Educators should always talk about disability in a way that makes it feel natural. The reality is that everyone's brain and body works a little different, and just about everyone requires supports to succeed or, at the very least, has preferences in how to gain access to information to have ideal learning experiences. For example,

- Many students with hidden disabilities have a hard time reading printed books but improve their reading comprehension by using text-to-speech technology. Other students improve their writing by using speech-to-text software programs (Anderson-Inman, & Horney, 2007; Leong, 1992; Lundberg & Olofsson, 1993; Parr, 2013; Silver-Pacuilla, Ruedel, & Mistrett, 2004).

- Many students, especially those with ADHD, benefit from direct instruction on executive function and organizational skills (Solanto, 2011).

Students must know what strategies and supports they will need to optimize their potential in future environments as they prepare to make the transition to college and careers. Many educators, and even parents, feel as if they will hurt students' feelings by discussing the unavoidable reality that disability will have a lasting effect and students will need to use accommodations and supports to optimize their experiences at school, work, and in personal settings. Despite the discomfort teachers and students might experience when they have these discussions, commit to using person-first language that explains each student's disability as well as strengths, challenges, and recommended learning accommodations and supports. Be compassionate but direct when talking with students. By giving students the clinical and social/political understanding of what their label means, you are also empowering them to think critically about that label, redefine it, and connect with a larger community of people who have shared their experience. See Kathie Snow's (n.d.) article *To Ensure Inclusion, Freedom, and Respect for People with Disabilities, We Must Use People First Language.* Review additional resources for transition planning in Text Box 4.1.

Anna's Journey

Anna did not want to be in special education. She did not want an IEP. She had more difficulty organizing her responsibilities and focusing on getting the work done correctly than actually doing the work because of her ADHD. Anna enrolled in the college-track classes because she wanted to go to college and they were the classes her friends were taking. She learned to seek out tutors and study tables to maintain her grades. She was challenged, but she learned more because she stayed in the tougher classes. Anna had an intervention specialist that she met with frequently who helped her organize and learn the content. She learned important study strategies that helped her in college.

Provide an Asset-Based Approach to Disability A student is not diagnosed with a disability because he or she has done something wrong. Failing to meet a prescribed standard is often the first step on the long journey toward being diagnosed with a disability. As a result of this inciting event and the challenges that follow, most of the conversations educators have regarding a student's disability tend to focus on what students cannot do. This deficit-based approach to disability puts all the emphasis on a student's limitations, and this approach can distort a student's self-concept and even destroy a person's potential to learn by limiting his or her belief in his or her own potential. Think of the kids who act out because they prefer to be kicked out of class than be embarrassed by reading out loud. Or worse yet, students who withdraw and are totally disengaged and become unwilling to even try to complete their assignments due to fear of failure. When students with disabilities approach life with a deficit model of their disability, additional challenges beyond what the disability presents are created because the student thinks he or she does not have what it takes to succeed. A student's postsecondary goals eventually are not based on pursuing a dream but are instead crafted to avoid feelings of failure.

When faced with the doubts of others, some people feel like they have to perform on a super human level. For example, Dr. Bill Bauer, professor of education at a small liberal arts college who also has a moderate-to-severe hearing loss, mentioned that he felt that his bachelor's and first master's degrees were completed to prove to his high school counselor that he could be a teacher. He stated,

> I got my bachelor's degree and first master's degree more so to prove to my high school guidance counselor that I could become a teacher. This guidance counselor suggested that I take the vocational route of education. I went to the vocational school because the majority of people with hearing impairments were counseled into data processing. I enjoyed my 2 years at the vocational school, and my self-esteem increased. When I graduated from high school, however, I knew that I wanted to make a difference in people's lives, not calculating numbers on a calculator. I got a bachelor's degree in education, became an elementary school teacher, and then got a master's degree in school administration, which I used to become a principal at a local school. Again, the whole time I am getting a quality education I am thinking that I am going to prove this guidance counselor wrong. It was not until I received my second master's degree in counseling and a doctorate degree in rehabilitation counseling that I felt I was going to school for me.

Focusing on students' abilities rather than their disabilities is a better approach to begin any conversation. This asset-based approach helps students think of themselves in terms of their strengths, and it can also help students expand what they believe they are capable of achieving. Educators should not ignore the impairments and challenges that come with students' particular disabilities. Teachers should, however, begin the conversation in a way that helps their students think of themselves in terms of what they have and not in terms of what they lack.

Tips for Teaching

Strengths, Limitations, and Disability Awareness

Help students gain knowledge and understanding of their strengths and limitations by

- Reading/listening to web content or watching movies about others with similar disabilities who talk about their strengths and limitations
- Listing and discussing their personal strengths and limitations
- Communicating their strengths and limitations to others
- Choosing courses and extracurricular activities based on their strengths and supports

Encourage students to take actions based on strengths and limitations by

- Seeking out situations that maximize strengths and minimize limitations
- Developing skills and strategies to compensate for limitations, such as sitting in front of class to reduce distractions, lip reading, mnemonics, and assistive technology
- Choosing employment and career goals based on their strengths
- Identifying/reflecting on situations in which they will be successful as well as unsuccessful
- Avoiding careers that require frequent use of their limitations

Discuss and reflect on students' disability awareness by

- Understanding their disability and how it affects them
- Discussing the challenges associated with their disability and learning how to face or avoid situations
- Explaining their disability to others to get accommodations and supports needed in any given situation
- Identifying mentors with the same disability and researching their career paths

Source: McConnell et al. (2013).

Provide Accommodations and Supports and Teach Students How to Use Them

Many students need and use supports that range from natural supports, such as meetings with peers for study groups, to legally prescribed accommodations and modifications as specified in students' IEPs, such as testing accommodations including extended time or alternate testing settings. Whereas 98% of students with disabilities reported receiving accommodations at the secondary level, only 24% received accommodations at the postsecondary level (Newman, Madaus, & Javitz, 2015). When postsecondary students who did not receive accommodations were asked if accommodations would have been helpful in college, 50% responded affirmatively (Newman et al., 2011), suggesting that many students are unaware of the differences in legal rights and responsibilities between high school and college and students lack the self-advocacy skills to properly disclose their disabilities and request accommodations.

Newman, Madaus, and Javitz (2015) underscored the importance of knowing how to find and use supports in a study of graduation rates of college students with learning disabilities and students who are deaf and hard of hearing. They reported that students with learning disabilities who used supports that were available to the general student population were twice as likely to graduate from 2- or 4-year colleges compared with students who did not use these supports. Seventy-two percent of students who are deaf and hard of hearing graduated from 2- or 4-year colleges if they used disability supports and accommodations versus a graduation rate of 26% of students who are deaf and hard of hearing who did not use disability supports and accommodations. Similar graduation rates were reported for students who are deaf and hard of hearing who used supports available to the general population. These studies highlight the need to teach high school students with disabilities how to request disability services as well as gain more universal supports available to the general population (Newman et al., 2015).

Anna Prefers Supports Available to All Students

Anna learned her freshman year in high school that she could sign up for peer tutoring at the guidance office for any subject she was taking. The school's National Honor Society members volunteered their time to help other students in math, science, or a foreign language. Anna enjoyed meeting with other students to study, rather than asking her teachers for assistance. She found that other students explained the concepts in terms that she could relate to better than her teachers' explanations.

Teaching students to use the appropriate supports at the appropriate time takes practice. Teachers play a pivotal role in assisting students to learn what supports they need and encouraging them to use those supports if and when appropriate. These critical conversations occur within IEP meetings as well as during classes. Teachers can model for students how to use supports and ensure that the classroom environment is respectful and safe so students will not hesitate to use their needed supports. Teachers should encourage students to use natural supports, mandated accommodations and modifications, and medication, if prescribed.

Technological Supports Numerous technological supports are available to all students with and without disabilities that include text-to-speech or speech-to-text software programs, spell/grammar checks, and mobile technology apps on smartphones and tablets to organize their time, assignments, or resources. For example, most smartphones have a voice-to-text feature

that is built into the opera-
tion system and can be used
to help students spell more ac-
curately. Scott Nelson used a
number of mobile apps to accommodate spelling and organizational issues related to his
hidden disability (see Chapter
3). Even though many schools

> **Text Box 4.3**
> Technology supports are available through
> a number of iPad apps. OCALI.org
> contains information about these emerging
> apps and lists the apps that can support
> people with a range of disabilities in a
> number of different settings.

look down on students using their smartphones in school, these devices can
be a powerful tool for many students with disabilities when they are used
responsibly.

Using the Right Support for Your Learning Style   Many learning style
assessments provide information on study strategies that are aligned with students' preferred learning styles. A number of tools are available that students,
educators, and family members can use to assess what learning style works best
for them. Margo used the VARK's questionnaire, which is available at no cost
at www.vark-learn.com, in her work with high school and college students.
This web-based tool can determine your learning style or modality by only asking 16 questions. The four learning styles outlined by VARK are visual, aural/
auditory, read/write, and kinesthetic. Many people learn by using a combination of styles depending on the material, setting, and how they process information. Students can use the VARK results to determine what learning strategies
are most effective for them and what potential careers may be a good match for
their preferred learning style. Teachers can use the learning style results as part
of students' age-appropriate transition assessments in their IEPs. Also, teachers
can provide a variety of assignments and projects for students to demonstrate
what they know about a topic area. For example, a student could develop a
poster, write a paper or a poem, or take a test to demonstrate his or her knowledge of a given topic. Helping students use their learning style strengths to
select projects that demonstrate what they have learned will enhance their motivation for learning and most likely increase their achievement.

Accommodations   An *accommodation* is defined as a device, practice, intervention, or procedure provided to a student that affords equal access to instruction or assessment. Accommodations change the manner in which content
or tests are presented, scheduled, or responded to; where the test is administered; or the type of special equipment used (Bolt & Thurlow, 2004; McLaughlin, 2012). Accommodations are often described as equalizers that level the
academic playing field so that students with disabilities can perform at their
fullest potential. Accommodations can also be thought of as supports that give
students access to materials and/or environments that would be unavailable to
them without accommodations. The use of accommodations does not change

the academic standards of a course, only how students gain access to the material and demonstrate acquisition of the standards. Many structural accommodations benefit people with and without disabilities, such as curb cuts on sidewalks and doors that open automatically. Teachers implement UDL when they build accommodations into a class that all students can use (Rose & Meyers, 2002). For example, when teachers give untimed tests and allow students to take as much time as they need to complete a test, they eliminate the need to provide accommodations and have universally designed the testing time frame (Izzo, Rissing, Andersen, Nasar, & Lissner, 2011).

Transition-age students should not only be using accommodations that are appropriate for their disability and will be approved within college settings, but they should also have a functional understanding of why they need certain accommodations. For example, students who receive extended time need to understand that they receive extended time because their brain processes information differently, and students who take tests in a distraction-free testing area need this accommodation because it is difficult for them to maintain their focus. Teachers and students can explore what accommodations students think they will need to use in their college or work settings. If students can complete the essential functions of a job without accommodations, then it may not be necessary to disclose their disability and seek accommodations.

Modifications Many middle and high school educators may make changes to tests or assignments given to students with hidden disabilities (e.g., asking fewer questions, allowing a shorter essay). Students with disabilities in a postsecondary education setting will be able to receive accommodations, but they will not be able to have their test and assignments modified. Therefore, it is a good idea to limit the amount of modifications students receive, especially if they plan to attend college.

Medication as a Support Medication assists students to maintain attention and manage anxiety or a number of other behaviors that students with hidden disabilities may possess. Although some people with disabilities have a strong aversion to using medication to treat the symptoms of their disability, medication can be a powerful support if used appropriately. The following are some important considerations when working with students who are prescribed medication:

- Understanding: A student should know what symptoms a medication is designed to treat, and he or she should take an active role in deciding what drugs, or combination of drugs, he or she needs to address those symptoms.

- Awareness: A student should understand the benefits and side effects of a drug.

- Control: A student might need to be medicated all the time, or he or she might want to cycle off during certain times of the day or school year.

Anna's Use of Medication

Anna used medication on and off during high school. She hated the side effects, so she would avoid taking her Adderall. Then she would get her interim grades and realize (with a little prompting from teachers and parents) that she needed to improve her grades. So, she would start taking her medication again. She experimented all through high school with how her medication supplemented her abilities to learn and succeed at school.

Chapter 2 presents the Path to Disability Pride to demonstrate how many youth and adults with hidden disabilities navigate the key stages as they incorporate disability into their identity. Each chapter provides case studies of how

---

Tips for Teaching

Persistence and Proactive Involvement

Persistence: Assist students to persist in completing rigorous course assignments and extracurricular activities in school or in their community by

- Finding alternate ways to reach their goals, so if studying with friends is not helpful, then meet with a tutor or prepare flashcards of key concepts
- Coming to terms with the idea that they may need to work harder and longer in some subjects than other students until they get into their career that maximizes their strengths
- Reminding students that learning persistence in high school will pay off when they get to college or career settings and know what strategies help them succeed

Proactive involvement: Encourage students to engage in activities that demonstrate their value and worth to a larger community by

- Interacting positively with others
- Taking advantage of their social network
- Getting actively involved in the world around them

Supports and resources: Assist students to schedule the supports and resources needed to reach their goals by

- Using all available support systems (e.g., teachers tutoring at study center, peer tutoring through study groups, study strategies aligned with their learning style)
- Utilizing advice and encouragement from significant others, including friends, family, faculty, and advisors
- Recognizing situations in which supports are needed and identifying individuals that can provide those supports
- Seeking people outside of their network to meet needs
- Seeking support from sources such as web sites, books, and the people around them.

Source: McConnell et al. (2013).

different people navigate the Path to Disability Pride. These case studies and figures are examples that students and teachers can discuss to see how others addressed specific challenges that arise in their lives. For LeDerick, graduating from high school and figuring out what would happen next was a challenging time.

 ## LeDerick Faces the Challenge of Transition

When I was in high school, I did not understand what my disability was or what options were available to me once I left school. This lack of information caused me to feel shame and to get very depressed. After an emotional breakdown, I eventually began to question many of the ideas I had come to believe about the potential of students in special education. I emerged from this depression with a strong desire to want to attend a four-year college. During my senior year, I began to search for ways to make this dream a reality. I talked about wanting to go to college and advocated for this goal during my last IEP meeting. Fortunately, my IEP team supported my goal. They explained that I could start college at a county college that had an excellent support program for students with hidden disabilities. (The path LeDerick took while facing his transition from high school to college is captured in Figure 4.1.)

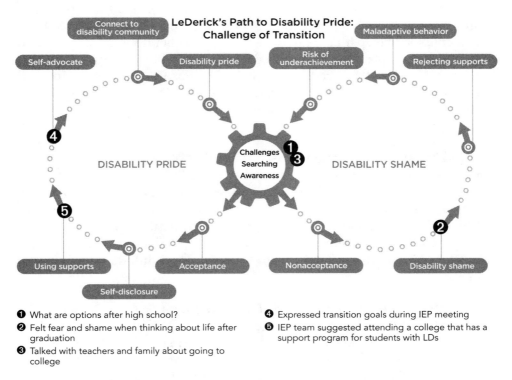

❶ What are options after high school?
❷ Felt fear and shame when thinking about life after graduation
❸ Talked with teachers and family about going to college
❹ Expressed transition goals during IEP meeting
❺ IEP team suggested attending a college that has a support program for students with LDs

Figure 4.1. LeDerick's Path to Disability Pride: Challenge of transition.

Build Awareness of Students' Disability, Strengths, and Limitations

"I wish that my experiences were no longer relevant, but the sad reality is that many
students with hidden disabilities graduate from high school after many years of
being on an IEP, and many of them still cannot tell you anything about their disability.
These students will find it hard to speak up for themselves and seek out the supports
they will need in the adult world without this basic degree of self-awareness."

—LeDerick

If a student is identified as having a disability, then somewhere in the
school there is a file with that student's name on it. That file might be locked
away in a drawer in the special education office or it might be vibrating in the
memory of your district's computer server, but that file exists, and this collection of documents can help students gain a greater understanding of who they
are as a person with a disability. Some students may not have the maturity
or desire to review their file, and respecting their choice is appropriate. But
explaining what their disability is in context of a larger community of successful people with similar disabilities may help students, parents, and siblings
increase their understanding of what it means to have a specific disability label.
The fact that Tom Cruise, Temple Grandin, and Whoopi Goldberg are all successful adults with disabilities may entice students to move towards feeling
disability pride versus the stigma of feeling "less able."

States are currently required to start planning their students' transition
from high school when the student is 14 or 16 years old. Reviewing a student's
documentation to help him or her understand his or her disability is a key part
of this transition planning. Many students with disabilities only know what
they cannot do, and they graduate lacking a functional understanding of their
strengths. Students have an opportunity to develop into individuals who are
proud of the unique way their body and mind works when they have a balanced understanding of their strengths and limitations.

Build System Navigation Skills   The IEP meeting is one of the first opportunities for many students with hidden disabilities to interact with a disability support system. Students making the transition to college and career
will find themselves in meetings with disability support professionals. They
will need to speak about how their disability affects their performance and
what supports and accommodations they will need. Learning to take an active
role during IEP meetings will help students navigate adult disability support
systems.

Exit Exam Requirements/High School Diploma Status   Students who
graduate from high school with a diploma versus a certificate are more likely to
participate in postsecondary education and engage in postschool employment.
Students need to understand the implications of receiving a certificate instead
of a diploma. The IEP meeting is the appropriate place to have these discussions with students and families.

LeDerick Encourages Students to Aim for the Regular Diploma

Far too many students with hidden disabilities have been tracked to leave high school with a certificate of attendance or a modified diploma. These alternatives to a conventional diploma should not be considered an option for students who, with accommodations, supports, or mild modifications, can perform the same work as their peers without disabilities. If a student has expressed the transition goals of postsecondary education, a career in the military, or postschool employment that requires technical training, then these students will need to present a standard high school diploma in most cases. Students without a standard diploma may not meet the educational requirements of certain branches of the military; postsecondary schools may determine that they do not meet the standards for acceptance; and if they are admitted to a postsecondary school, then they may not qualify for financial aid provided by the federal government.

Teach Self-Determination, Disclosure, and Self-Advocacy Skills

The ability to confidently disclose to others what their disability is and how it affects them in a variety of situations is one of the most important transition skills that all people with a hidden disability should master. Once a student graduates from high school and makes the transition to the adult world, services and supports will be offered if he or she personally takes the initiative to dis-

Tips for Teaching

Goal Setting and Attainment

Goal Setting: Use the individualized education program (IEP) to teach goal setting, monitoring, and attainment by

- Setting short- and long-term goals, then weekly or daily objectives that are monitored frequently
- Converting large goals into a number of small tasks that can be scheduled in the planner
- Encouraging students to set their own postsecondary goals
- Preparing students to take an active role in facilitating their IEP meeting

Explore college and career options by

- Completing informational interviews, job shadows, and Internet research to determine if the career area or related positions match students' interests and abilities
- Participating in work study, vocational education, career internships, or mentoring programs to validate career goals
- Visiting several colleges and participating in their college orientation programs
- Meeting with disability services counselors to determine the type of documentation their offices require to gain needed accommodations

close and ask for those supports. Given the confidence students gain by knowing they can effectively communicate an aspect of themselves that might not be obvious, all students with a hidden disability should learn how to disclose to teachers and faculty that they have a disability and request accommodations.

Simulation   Disclosing is not easy for anyone with a disability, but it can be even more difficult with a hidden disability. First, students need to realize that they do not have to disclose the type of disability they have; they only need to share that they have a disability that requires accommodations. If they choose to disclose their disability, however, then they should do so confidently. They need to describe how their disability affects them in a given setting (e.g., work, school, relationships). Finally, self-advocates should suggest accommodations that will improve their performance, such as extended time on tests, distraction-free testing settings, or notetakers.

Disclosure is more of an art than a science. Like all artistic expression, one can only get better through practice. Role playing is the best way to prepare students to successfully communicate information about their disabilities. Practicing different scenarios with peers and teachers and observing how other advocates disclose can help build confidence. Feel free to make up any scenario to role-play that will best prepare students to address the problems they will face in the present and when they make the transition to the adult world. It is also important to present a variety of realistic obstacles that students might face when advocating for themselves. Self-advocacy skills are ultimately mastered through real-world trial-and-error, but it can be helpful for students to practice

---

Tips for Teaching

Self-Advocacy Skills

Review the following tips with students, and discuss the various approaches to advocating. Practice by role playing various scenarios that students may encounter.

- *Communication.* Communicating what you need to another person is at the heart of all self-advocacy. Students have many choices when it comes to communication, so the first thing students should decide is the best mode of communication given the situation. Sometimes a face-to-face conversation is best, but it might be better to communicate via e-mail, printed letter, or over the telephone.

- *Best setting.* After students have picked a form of communication, it is important to determine the best setting to use when advocating. For example, students might be more successful if they talk one to one with their teacher after school or during a free period instead of in class. Determining the best time and the best place can really help leverage a self-advocate's ability to get what he or she wants in order to be successful.

(continued)

Tips for Teaching *(continued)*

- *Be polite/use social skills.* Once students have determined the best form of communication and an appropriate setting to advocate, the next thing to decide is how they will ask for what they need. Remind them that being polite when asking for anything is more than just good manners; it is also a proven tactic that can help influence a person to act in the students' favor. Starting a relationship on a positive note can make advocating much easier.

- *Use disability language.* Use language such as "because of my disability, I have trouble with..." or, "I have autism so I will need..." when it comes time for students to talk about how their disability will affect them in any given setting. Students convey how their disability affects them personally when they use the name of a diagnosed disability when asking for any support or accommodation. In addition, students with disabilities are protected by a host of laws against discrimination and exclusion. If they choose not to use the language of disability and instead use statements such as, "I'm not good at this part of my job" or "I get frustrated when I have to read out loud," then students are not being responsible self-advocates and might be mistaken as someone who is just lazy or uninterested.

- *Offer alternatives.* Students should offer alternatives after they have made it clear that they have a disability that might interfere with their performance in a given setting. Employers, educators, and people in general might not have the training or cultural competency to know exactly how to support them, so it is important for students to develop a list (written out or in their minds) of accommodations that will help them perform at their best. Creating this list in advance can help students sound more confident and competent as advocates. For example, "I have an auditory processing disorder so I can participate in discussions more effectively if I have a handout of key discussion questions" or "I have difficulty with reading so I use my laptop's text-to-speech technology to listen to the text."

speaking up for themselves by initially using a script like the one above in Tips for Teaching.

Build Disability Community to Promote Disability Pride

Many inclusive schools have organized the learning environment so students have a time to work with the intervention specialist to learn about their strengths and limitations, disability awareness, and self-determination/self-advocacy skills. Other schools provide adequate time for the intervention specialist to meet individually with students to learn self-advocacy skills. Still others integrate transition planning into inclusive classrooms for all students.

The need to help students develop these skills is so important that some states have organized youth leadership forums to provide training for student leaders from throughout their state. Many schools then replicate the training at regional, district, and school levels. Other schools organize self-advocacy training for students and staff at regional or local levels. Many of these activities provide training and support for parents so they can support the development of disability pride among their sons and daughters.

Youth Leadership Forums   Numerous community-building events are designed to teach self-determination and self-advocacy skills to students with disabilities. YLFs are one of the most notable events. The California Governor's Council for Employment of Disabled Persons developed the first YLF in 1992. The model has since been replicated by a number of states, which generally host their YLFs on an accessible college campus in or near their state's capital. Each YLF provides transition-age students the opportunity to serve as regional delegates and obtain training on leadership, self-advocacy, and civic engagement. For the first time, these transition-age students will learn about disability culture, explore meaningful relationships with mentors who have disabilities like them, and learn and create lifelong partnerships with people who share their common bond and experiences. The forum is the first time many of the delegates are able to spend meaningful time on a college campus. The YLF also serves as an excellent way for students to develop disability pride and build relationships with people who have a variety of disabilities.

Self-Advocacy Clubs   Some schools have created after-school clubs that offer support and community-building opportunities for students with disabilities. These clubs generally build awareness about disabilities, disability history and culture, and the IEP process. These clubs allow students an opportunity to organize around projects that help them meet a need within their school and community. Some clubs provide IEP support by pairing a more experienced self-advocate with a younger student who is attending his or her IEP meeting for the first time. These IEP coaches provide support for the student during his or her first few IEP meetings. Eye to Eye (see Chapter 3) is known primarily for its art based mentoring program, but they also allow college or high school students to serve as IEP coaches for elementary or middle school students.

Involving Parents and Raising Expectations   Parents who express high expectations for their children to learn the skills to become responsible students and adults are critical and, as such, are identified as one of the predictors of postsecondary success (Test et al., 2013). Parents must provide both the supports and expectations that their young adult has the ability to graduate from high school and make the transition to college or career.

LeDerick's Parental Involvement

Like many parents who have children with hidden disabilities, my mother's and father's understanding of my learning disability was informed by what they learned from school staff and from the reading they did on their own. They must have been concerned by how my lifelong impairments would adversely affect my quality of life once I left the relatively safe academic environment provided by special education classes. Disability was not a big topic in my household, and I do not recall any dinner conversation in which my problems in school became a topic of discussion. But, without being overly pushy, I remember my parents making me believe that I had the ability to grow up and become anything I wanted. Although no one provided them with a road map, my parents were convinced, and they convinced me, that I was going to college and that I would have an impressive career. I only remember my father attending one of my IEP meetings, but it was the very last meeting I had before graduation from high school. By then, I was an 18-year-old young adult, and I had already begun asserting myself in all aspects of my life and education. I had an idea of what I wanted to do once I left high school, but I have to think that having my father by my side helped me to feel more confident talking with my IEP team about my postschool goals.

CONCLUSION: THE VALUE OF QUALITY TRANSITION PLANNING

Federal legislation requires schools to deliver transition services within an IEP process that involves the student, their parents, and school and agency personnel. Postsecondary goals are developed based on transition assessments that reflect students' preferences, interests, strengths, and needs. Transition services are provided to help students reach their college and career goals, which drive the students' annual goals. Although IEPs for transition-age students indicate students' present levels of performance, the focus of services is to prepare students for college and career goals that maximize students' strengths. What do students need to learn that will prepare them to successfully enter college and careers? The focus shifts from remediating limitations, to building on strengths and assets that prepare students for productive roles as adult members of society. As the predictors and behaviors described in this chapter indicate, knowing one's strengths and limitations, and making self-determined decisions with these in mind, are associated with improved postschool outcomes. Students who are proud of their accomplishments, and do not feel ashamed of their disabilities, have self-directed and improved postschool outcomes.

College Life

Valuable Life Lessons in the Classroom and on Campus

5

"I believe students really need to come to terms with what their own disability is and what they need to be successful. You need to do some soul searching and you need to take the time to do the work and figure out what is your learning style and where are your weaknesses, where are your strengths, what do you need."
—Andee Peabody,
doctoral student in Bioinfomatics

More students with disabilities are attending college, and an increasing number of high school students with disabilities plan to attend college. In fact, postsecondary education is the most common postschool goal for 4 out of 5 high school students with disabilities who have transition plans (Cameto, Levine, & Wagner, 2004). There was a 17% increase from 1987 to 2003 in the number of students with disabilities attending college (Wagner, Newman, Cameto, & Levine, 2005). Students with learning disabilities constituted more than two thirds (69%) of college students with disabilities, and 36% of all college students with disabilities reported to have ADHD in addition to their primary diagnosis (Newman & Madaus, 2015). Obtaining a college degree is more important in the 21st century than ever before. The pay gap between college graduates with a 4-year college degree and people with some or no college credit continues to widen (Autor, 2014; Leonhardt, 2014). In 2007, young adults with a bachelor's degree earned 29% more than young adults who completed an associate's degree and 55% more than young adults who only earned a high school diploma (Planty et al., 2009).

Young adults with disabilities, however, are not enrolling in college at the same rate as their peers in the general population. For example, 67% of young adults in the general population had enrolled in postsecondary programs, yet only 60% of young adults with disabilities were reported to have enrolled in postsecondary education within 8 years of leaving high school (Newman et al., 2011). Young adults with disabilities were more likely to enroll in 2-year or community colleges after graduating from high school than enroll in adult vocational, business, or technical schools. Although young adults in the general population are most likely to enroll in 4-year colleges or universities, young adults with disabilities are least likely to enroll in 4-year colleges. In addition, students with disabilities are far less likely than their typically developing peers to complete a bachelor's degree (U.S. Government Accountability Office, 2003).

Although 11% of college students report having a disability (National Center for Education Statistics, 2009; Newman et al., 2011), the majority of these students remain hidden in the college classroom. Students with hidden disabilities are less likely to self-disclose their disability to college instructors; therefore, these students are less likely to receive needed accommodations (Barnard-Brak & Sulak, 2010; Dukes, Koorland, & Scott, 2009; Newman et al, 2015). According to a 2011 report from the National Longitudinal Transition Study–2 (NLTS–2),

> only 19 percent of postsecondary students who were identified as having a disability by their secondary schools were reported to receive accommodations or supports from their postsecondary school; in contrast, when these postsecondary students were in high school, 87 percent received some type of accommodation or support because of their disability. (Newman et al., 2011, p. 22)

Clearly, the majority of students with disabilities are not disclosing that they have a disability; therefore, they are not gaining access to the academic adjustments and accommodations that they need to succeed in college. These students may have experienced too much disability shame in high school to risk disclosing in college, or they may be unaware of how much their approved accommodations may enable their success in college. This chapter's goal is to provide teachers and support personnel with the knowledge and strategies they need to launch their high school students into college with enough disability pride to overcome the challenges that all college students experience.

High school students often do not have the opportunity to understand how their disability affects how they learn. Students in high school do not need to disclose their disability and need for accommodations to teachers to receive the supports they need; IDEA 2004 mandates that schools deliver an appropriate education, including the accommodations and supports that students need. Knowing when and how to disclose and request accommodations is an essential skill needed to navigate not only college but also employment and personal relationships. This chapter reviews the rights and responsibilities of college students with disabilities from a legal framework, followed by examples of strategies that successful college students use. In addition, examples of how students' disability pride affects their feelings and actions are discussed.

WHY IS COLLEGE IMPORTANT?

In addition to increasing earning potential, attending college provides opportunities for students to develop, practice, and refine the skills they will need in the future, as well as develop and refine their identity as an adult and professional. Students with hidden disabilities have intervention specialists, special education teachers, or content teachers in high school who provide the academic content, accommodations, and modifications that are needed. There are no special education teachers in college to ensure that students gain the accommodations and modifications they need to learn. Students with hidden disabilities must select classes based on their interests, skills, and requirements of their majors and negotiate accommodations with their instructors. If students want accommodations, then they must register with the disability support services office at the college or university, provide documentation, and request accommodations. If students do not want to disclose, then no one within the college setting can force them to disclose; however, these students give up the right to any accommodations and academic adjustments that may be available.

College becomes a rite of passage for students to assume the decision-making role in how much to disclose about their disability, what accommodations to access and how, and how often to meet with their instructors, advisors, and disability support counselors. Students must often negotiate with their disability services counselor and professors on how and when accommodations are accessed. If students want extended time to take a test, then they can negotiate with their professor to stay after class, or they can ask to take the examination in the testing center with a test proctor. If students want to negotiate course substitutions, then they have to know who decides if they can take a sign language class instead of French or Spanish. These are but a few examples that students may find themselves negotiating in college.

Students in college decide what classes to take, when to take them, and how hard they want to work for their grades. If students live on campus, then they decide when to go to bed, when to get up, and what to eat. These decisions and their consequences become critical learning opportunities to develop the study and work habits that will contribute to how successfully they perform in their future careers. How students organize and navigate college will, to some extent, provide important learning opportunities to figure out how to succeed in the future. Students with hidden disabilities can transform from compliant high school students to self-determined adults who know what they want and have the skills to negotiate and navigate their own path to successful adult lives.

WHAT ARE THE RIGHTS AND RESPONSIBILITIES OF STUDENTS WITH DISABILITIES?

Successful college students with disabilities can explain how their rights and responsibilities change from high school to college and what postsecondary institutions are required to provide. College students with disabilities are protected by Section 504 of the Rehabilitation Act of 1973 (PL 93-112) and Title II of the ADA, whereas educational access is dictated by IDEA 2004 throughout primary and secondary school. A number of differences exist between high school and college experiences for students (see Table 5.1; Grigal & Hart, 2010).

Table 5.1. Differences between high school and college

High school	College
Individuals with Disabilities Education Improvement Act (IDEA) of 2004 (PL 108-446)	Americans with Disabilities Act (ADA) of 1990 (PL 101-336) and Rehabilitation Act of 1973 (PL 93-112)
IDEA is about success.	ADA is about access.
Core modifications of classes and materials are required.	Modifications are not required—only accommodations.
School districts must identify disability.	Student must self-identify.
School district develops individualized education program (IEP) to determine the school's plan.	Student must identify needs and ask for services. No IEP exists, and IEP is not considered legal documentation.
School provides free assessments.	Student must obtain assessments at his or her own expense.
Student is helped by parents and teachers.	Student must seek help (as needed) from disability services.
School is responsible for arranging for accommodations.	Student must self-advocate and arrange for accommodations.
Personal care services are required.	Personal care services are not required.
Parent has access to student records.	Parent has no access to student records without student's written consent.
Parent advocates for student.	Student advocates for self.
School year runs from September to June.	School year is divided into two semesters: September to December and January to May.
Classes meet daily.	Classes meet 1, 2, 3, or 4 times a week.
Classes generally meet in the same building.	Classes are held in many different places on campus.
Average class length is 45–50 minutes.	Classes vary in length from 50 minutes to 3 hours.
Daily contact with teachers.	Classes meet less frequently, so instructors and teacher assistants are seen less frequently.
Student needs parent's permission to participate in most activities.	Student is an adult and gives own permission.
Guidance counselors and other staff schedule support services for student.	Student must schedule all support services.
Main office is center of activity for building.	The student is responsible for knowing where to go to get information and assistance.
Classes consist of about 30 students.	Classes may consist of about 100 students.
Teachers often remind student of assignments and due dates.	Professors expect student to read the course syllabus. They may not remind student of upcoming assignments and tests.
High school is free.	Student must pay for college.

From Grigal, M. & Hart, D., (2010). *Think College! Postsecondary Education Options for Students with Intellectual Disabilities.* Baltimore, MD: Paul Brookes Publishing Co.; adapted by permission.

Section 504 and the Americans with Disabilities Act

The U.S. Department of Education, Office for Civil Rights, enforces Section 504 of the Rehabilitation Act of 1973 and Title II of the ADA. Both of these federal laws prohibit discrimination on the basis of disability (U.S. Department of Education, 2011). Although Section 504 and the ADA prohibit discrimination across secondary and postsecondary institutions, the responsibilities of college programs differ greatly from the responsibilities of school districts, which must adhere to the requirements of IDEA 2004, which provide more prescriptive guidelines for ensuring that students with disabilities receive an appropriate education from K–12. It is important for students, as well as school personnel and parents, to become familiar with the requirements of Section 504 and the ADA, given that the rights and responsibilities of students significantly change as they make the transition from high school to college.

> **Text Box 5.1**
> Review *Students with Disabilities Preparing for Postsecondary Education: Know Your Rights and Responsibilities*, published by the U.S. Department of Education, Office of Civil Rights (2011) and is available at http://www2.ed.gov/about/offices/list/ocr/transition.html.

Although IDEA is an educational entitlement act, Section 504 and the ADA are designed to prohibit discrimination on the basis of disability. By law, professionals within a college's or university's disability support services (DSS) office must determine if a student's disability is current and substantially limits a major life activity such as walking, hearing, seeing, and learning. Some impairments are disabling for some college students but not for others, depending on the presence of other impairments or any number of other factors that combine to make the impairment disabling (Shaw, Madaus, & Dukes, 2010).

WHAT ARE POSTSECONDARY PROGRAMS REQUIRED TO PROVIDE?

Every postsecondary school who receives any form of federal funds is required to provide accommodations and academic adjustments, including auxiliary aids and services, to ensure postsecondary programs do not discriminate on the basis of disability. Postsecondary programs, whether it is an adult vocational and career school, a 2- or 4-year college, or a university, must employ qualified staff to review disability documentation, determine what accommodations are reasonable, and coordinate the delivery of these academic adjustments and accommodations.

> **Text Box 5.2**
> Many postsecondary institutions follow the documentation standards and guidelines published by the Association on Higher Education and Disability (AHEAD). See AHEAD's web site at http://www.ahead.org for more information.

Accommodations and academic adjustments are determined using an individualized process that is coordinated by DSS located on the college campus. The academic adjustments and accommodations are based on the student's disability and individual needs (Getzel & Webb, 2012). An accommodation can be a device, practice, intervention or procedure that does not change the content being taught, nor does it reduce learning or achievement expectations (McLaughlin, 2012).

The level of assistance to accommodate students with disabilities and provide the appropriate academic adjustments varies widely from 2- and 4-year college settings (Kochhar-Bryant, Bassett, & Webb, 2009). Although postsecondary institutions must provide academic adjustments by law, the type of adjustments they provide will vary across institutions. In fact, a recent meta-analysis of the literature published in the *Journal of Postsecondary Education and Disability* indicated that a very small percentage of rigorous studies have been conducted to evaluate what interventions improve learning and achievement for specific categories (e.g., learning disabilities, ADHD, autism spectrum disorder) of college students with disabilities (Madaus, Lalor, Gelbar, & Kowitt, 2014). Therefore, what works with students with disabilities is still a matter of trial and error,

> ### Text Box 5.3—Academic Adjustments and Accommodations
>
> Examples of academic adjustments include
>
> - Arranging for priority registration and reducing course loads
> - Providing extended time on tests
>
> Examples of academic accommodations include
>
> - Arranging distraction-free testing environments
> - Substituting one course for another
> - Providing notetakers, scribes, readers, or proctors
> - Using interpreters or Communication Access Real-Time Translation (CART) services
> - Equipping computer labs with text-to-speech and speech-to-text assistive technology software

which underscores the need for students themselves to understand how they learn and what strategies, interventions, and accommodations they need to successfully complete their college degree.

Postsecondary schools do not have to provide personal attendants, individually prescribed devices, readers for personal use or study, or other services such as specialized tutoring services that are often provided within the K–12 educational system (U.S. Department of Education, 2011). Some college programs offer these services as a part of their student's tuition, and some offer them for an extra cost. If students need these services, then they must identify and apply to a program that provides these services. Vocational rehabilitation services in some states will provide funding to purchase AT, tutoring services, or other supports. Vocational rehabilitation is a federal program administered by state offices to help people with disabilities gain employment. The college degree and any supports related to the disability must be related to students' employment goals for vocational rehabilitation to assist students.

Program modifications are an important difference between school districts and postsecondary institutions. Whereas the academic requirements in the K–12 system can be modified to ensure students' success, the focus in postsecondary settings is on providing students access to the content. Therefore, postsecondary programs do not modify the requirements for the courses needed to complete a certificate or degree program. The academic adjustments do not reduce the rigor of content within a certificate or degree program. The students within the postsecondary program are held to the same standards as students without disabilities who graduate.

The fear that the negative experiences in high school will continue in college is one of the biggest sources of anxiety for many students with hidden disabilities who are contemplating going to college. Parents, teachers, counselors, and students themselves must understand that special education services and supports are over once students receive their high school diploma. The laws change, and the way students are treated by teachers and counselors change. College students can be as open about their disability as they like, or they can choose to remain hidden and not disclose that they have a disability. According to the latest NLTS2 results, only 35% of college students with disabilities who received special education services in high school informed their postsecondary school of their disability and gained accommodations, as contrasted to the 19% reported in 2011 (Newman et al., 2015). Inviting college students with hidden disabilities to share the benefits of disclosing in college with current high school students may increase high school students' knowledge of the benefits of advocating for accommodations that will increase their college performance.

GETTING STARTED ON CAMPUS

Students with disabilities must provide documentation prepared by a qualified professional that verifies the presence of a disability to the DSS office. Most colleges will accept the documentation provided by school districts. Once the documentation is verified, students and DSS counselors discuss appropriate accommodations and academic adjustments that are needed to provide access to program content, college materials, and testing accommodations to ensure fair and equitable assessments of student mastery. DSS counselors also explain the recommended disclosure process students use to gain reasonable accommodations on their campus.

Provide Documentation to Disability Support Services

If students with disabilities want to use accommodations and academic adjustments such as extended time on tests or notetakers, then they must provide documentation to the DSS that substantiates their disability. The documentation must be prepared by a qualified professional, such as a medical doctor, psychologist, or other qualified diagnostician (U.S. Department of Education,

2011). Although disclosure of a disability is always voluntary, students will not gain access to the accommodations and academic adjustments they have a right to receive if they do not present their documentation to the DSS counselors. Students do not have to share any of their documentation with admissions counselors, faculty, or instructors.

If the documentation that students have does not meet DSS requirements, then students with disabilities may need to obtain a new evaluation at their own expense. The DSS counselor will often provide a list of acceptable diagnosticians that students can use to gain or update their disability documentation. Some colleges have these evaluations available on campus through either the student health services or psychology department. Students might also want to contact their state's vocational rehabilitation agency to see if they are eligible for vocational rehabilitation services, including comprehensive transition assessment and services. See http://rsa.ed.gov to find contact information for state vocational rehabilitation offices.

Determine Accommodations

Once this documentation is accepted, students meet with DSS counselors to identify appropriate accommodations. DSS staff will review the documentation and determine how learning is affected by the disability. For example, if a student has dyslexia, which reduces the rate of reading fluency, then extended time on tests is often a reasonable accommodation. Students should share what accommodations were effective in high school with their DSS counselor. The summary of performance, a document that high schools must provide for students prior to exiting high school, should provide an overview of the accommodations used in high school. The DSS counselor and the student should discuss how these accommodations are provided in college settings. Having a history of certain accommodations and knowing how these helped work around the challenges of a disability will help students and DSS counselors determine what is needed to succeed in college. When students submit their documentation prior to starting their first semester in college, it is more likely that reasonable accommodations will be available once they start college.

Colleges are not required to provide the accommodations that students request but can offer effective alternatives. For example, if students request a reader for course materials because that is what they used in high school, then the DSS counselor may provide course materials in digital format so students listen to the content using screen-reader software on computers. Determining the appropriate accommodations is an interactive process between students and their DSS counselors.

 ## LeDerick Transfers to a University with More Supports

I earned 65 credits after attending Middlesex County College for 5 years and was ready to transfer to a local university. I enrolled and I let the disability support office know that I had a disability and would need accommodations. I did not realize that a number of staff changes occurred just before I started my first semester at this new university and only one DSS counselor was available to provide support for all the students with disabilities on campus. After many weeks of not getting any accommodations and trying unsuccessfully to navigate the bureaucracy of a large school, I became frustrated, depressed, and afraid that I was going to fail my midterms because I had no support. I decided to drop out of this university just before my first midterm. I was emotionally crushed, and I felt defeated, despite all of my self-advocacy skills. After taking a few days to collect my thoughts, I began to realize that I still wanted a bachelor's degree, but I needed to find a smaller school with a supportive culture that had a quality program to help students with learning disabilities reach their academic goals. I eventually found my way to New Jersey City University, which was a great fit for me. The main campus was located on one city block, it had faculty and staff that went out of their way to support their students, and they offered a comprehensive support program designed for students with learning disabilities.

Disclose to Faculty and Instructors

Once the student and DSS counselor establish the accommodations the student will use, the student needs to disclose to faculty who are eligible to receive their approved accommodations. The procedures to obtain these accommodations vary from college to college. The DSS counselor at some colleges will obtain the student's permission and send a letter to faculty and instructors to introduce the student with disabilities and share the approved accommodations. Other DSS counselors will give the student a letter with a form attached that indicates what accommodations a student may use and how instructors should coordinate the approved academic accommodations. The student will give the letter and/or form to faculty as part of the disclosure process.

Disclosure is a personal decision, and the disclosure process can vary from person to person and from class to class. Students do not have to share what type of disability they have. Many students with hidden disabilities may choose not to disclose the specific information about their disability due to the negative biases that others may have toward people with hidden disabilities. Other students may choose to share the specifics of the nature of their disability so professors and instructors are better prepared to meet their accommodation requests and learning preferences. Still, other students may share more information with some faculty than others. Faculty and disability professionals employed at the DSS offices are not allowed to discuss a student's disability without the student's permission.

Students ultimately can decide if they want to disclose to faculty and course instructors to gain the approved accommodations in their classes. If students choose not to disclose, then they give up their rights to any accommodations or academic adjustments they are approved to receive (National Collaborative for Workforce and Disability for Youth, 2009; U.S. Department of Education, 2011). Professors and teaching instructors are far more likely to be understanding if students meet with them and disclose at the beginning of the class than if students show up at the middle or end of the semester with a failing grade and ask for lenience due to their hidden disability. Students must disclose in a respectful and assertive manner when requesting accommodations. Not every professor will know how to help a student with hidden disabilities, so students need to be prepared to suggest solutions that play to their strong points.

Sarah, a biology student, decided to disclose to professors and answer any questions that they had about her learning disability. Also, Sarah fought with herself to stay on the Path to Disability Pride when she found herself thinking she was stupid. She blamed herself when she encountered challenges, which chipped away at her self-esteem. However, Sarah was able to gain supports in college and learned to reinforce and strengthen her disability pride by connecting with other students with disabilities on campus.

 ## Sarah Works to Maintain Her Disability Pride

I took ownership of my disability in high school. Both my high school and college advisors offered to notify my professors directly, but I took it on myself to speak with each of them individually in order to explain my disability as well as answer any of their questions. Sometimes, though, I didn't always feel comfortable speaking with every professor; disclosing a disability is not always easy.

There are still those days when it seems as though nothing is clicking. I find myself thinking that I am stupid, just like I did when I was initially diagnosed. I no longer look at my educational roller coaster as a setback, but rather as an obstacle that I continue to overcome on a daily basis. Success takes longer for me than my peers and classmates because of my disability. The biggest support and source of strength for me was being able to connect with a community of other students who had disabilities. We shared stories, setbacks, and triumphs. We learned from one another's experiences, and learned to accept and be proud of who we are. (Figure 5.1 shows Sarah's Path to Disability Pride.)

The development of and ability to maintain disability pride is a fluid process in which people can bounce from accepting their disability and using supports to blaming themselves for being stupid. Sarah still has days when nothing is clicking and she feels stupid, just like she felt prior to being diagnosed with a learning disability. She knows that she is not stupid; she is in college, but she finds herself fighting off these old feelings of being stupid when she is challenged. When she is feeling this way, Sarah reminds herself that she is capable of meeting the challenges of college, and reaches out and talks to other students with disabilities who also learn differently.

The self-efficacy of students with hidden disabilities may be compromised when they experience challenges such as having their competence questioned. Some students experience feelings of disability shame during these challenges and need to find support in themselves and in their disability community. They must be aware of where to turn to find the supports they need to push through these challenges and avoid wasting time on doubting their competence and

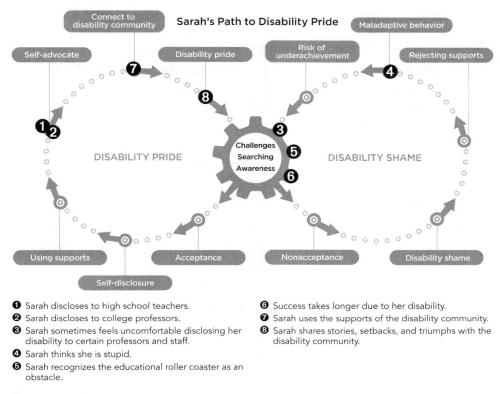

Sarah's Path to Disability Pride

❶ Sarah discloses to high school teachers.
❷ Sarah discloses to college professors.
❸ Sarah sometimes feels uncomfortable disclosing her disability to certain professors and staff.
❹ Sarah thinks she is stupid.
❺ Sarah recognizes the educational roller coaster as an obstacle.

❻ Success takes longer due to her disability.
❼ Sarah uses the supports of the disability community.
❽ Sarah shares stories, setbacks, and triumphs with the disability community.

Figure 5.1. Sarah's Path to Disability Pride.

denying themselves the opportunity to contribute to resolving the challenges they encounter.

STRATEGIES USED BY SUCCESSFUL COLLEGE STUDENTS

Thousands of students with hidden disabilities are successful in college every year. Many of these students start their journey to college long before they take their first college class. They become aware of their disability and how they learn best; they learn to advocate for appropriate accommodations while in high school; they select a college that offers the types of disability supports and services they need; and they use supports to work around their challenges. The next section presents strategies that successful college students plan and implement to ensure they reach their dream of graduating from college.

Develop a Self-Advocacy Plan

Information about disability disclosure as a federally guaranteed right and responsibility of college students with disabilities was previously presented. Doctoral student Andee Peabody's self-advocacy plan begins by understanding how ADHD affects how she learns and works.

> **Tips for Teaching**
>
> **Teaching Students How to Advocate with Confidence**
>
> 1. Prompt students to write a script (or at least bullet points) that indicates
>   - How much information they want to share about their disability
>   - What learning strategies they use to study and learn the content
>   - What academic adjustments and accommodations they need to learn the content
>   - What accommodations they use that improve their ability to learn and do well on class assignments and tests
> 2. Get students to practice with their teachers, disability support services counselor, parents, and friends.
> 3. Tell students to make an appointment with professors during office hours.
> 4. Instruct students that they should introduce themselves and share a few interesting facts about their background, major, and/or career goals.
> 5. Have your students review the information they prepared in their script.
> 6. Practice until they can disclose with confidence and without apologizing.

Andee Develops Her Self-Advocacy Plan

My self-advocacy plan really started out with understanding what ADHD is, not only on a broad, academic level, but also what it means for me. What traits really run strong in me? What traits do not run quite so strong? What does it change in my daily life? What does it do in terms of changing my brain? My self-advocacy plan started to develop once I was able to answer these questions. I learned that I needed to ask people what they need from me instead of presuming that I know. I also need to be honest with people, saying, "I have ADHD. This is how I am. This is how I need things communicated to me. This is the type of support that I need. This is the type of support that I can give you. What other types of interventions are needed? What other types of accommodations are needed?" I need to be comfortable with my brand of ADHD and what it means to me. I need to articulate that in order to have my needs met as well as meet the needs of others.

Select Majors and Careers that Maximize Strengths and Minimize Limitations

The NSTTAC conducted a meta-analysis of research to identify evidence-based predictors of postschool success for students with disabilities (Test, Fowler, & Kohler, 2012; Test et al., 2009). Test et al. (2009) reported that students who possessed career awareness, community experiences, paid employment, and self-determination skills were more likely to be successful within postsecondary education. McConnell et al. (2012) conducted a meta-analysis of the research literature to develop constructs defining student behaviors associated with positive outcomes in employment and postsecondary education after high school. McConnell et al. reported that knowledge of and actions to maximize strengths and minimize limitations are associated with gaining postschool employment and education. In addition to pursuing postschool goals that maximize strengths and minimize limitations, McConnell identified six additional behaviors—persistence, proactive involvement, goal setting and attainment, self-advocacy, employment, and using supports and resources.

Researchers repeatedly report the importance of self-awareness, career awareness, and self-determination skills in context of how students' strengths and limitations will affect their performance in postsecondary education and careers. Students who gain a comprehensive understanding of their disability, preferences, interests, needs, and strengths are better prepared to select careers that maximize their strengths and minimize their limitations. In addition to understanding their own strengths and limitations, students must understand the requirements of their chosen major and career area to make a good match. The career exploration and matching process needs to begin in middle school and continue until students select a career that maximizes strengths and minimizes limitations. Margo selected her major and courses following this process.

Margo Negotiates an Individualized Course of Study

I grew more excited about starting college when I looked over the course catalog of all the college courses that were offered. There were so many courses I wanted to take. I was willing to work hard to learn the things required to be a qualified teacher. I wanted to learn as much psychology and philosophy as possible but still find a teaching job after graduation. Therefore, combining psychology with teaching certification provided an interesting and employment-focused college program. I was willing to work hard and take more credits per semester than recommended as long as I got to choose what classes to take. I negotiated with the psychology department chair to waive my language requirements so I could take more philosophy and psychology courses. I excelled at the psychology, philosophy, and education courses because I wanted to learn about these topics. I graduated from college with a major in psychology and certification in elementary and special education. I also minored in philosophy and peace studies. I believe that we are more likely to succeed in learning what is important to us when we have the opportunity to have choices.

The ability to negotiate changes to a course of study can depend on the requirements of your major, the size of your college, and/or the disability documentation that indicates the need for an accommodation. Many colleges will approve a course substitution such as taking sign language instead of a traditional foreign language such as Spanish or French. Talk to an academic advisor or DSS counselor to find out more about the requirements of a program.

Successful students with disabilities schedule appointments to meet privately with professors during their posted office hours. It is recommended

Text Box 5.4

"Since so many learning differences are hidden, making them visible can be a positive step, despite the awkwardness. Being out in the open enables students to locate their LD peers and see that they are not alone. It also makes learning differences seem less mysterious, which in turn can boost students' self-esteem as they recognize that their differences don't mean they are weird or stupid, but part of a valuable and important minority."

—David Flink, 2014, p. 154

that students discuss the specific class requirements and what they do to maximize their own learning. Students should then discuss the accommodations and supports that they will use to complete the class assignments and assessments. These meetings are an excellent time to establish rapport with the professor and ask what other successful students do in the class to maximize learning. The professor may have several suggestions of supports that are available in this class that are not publically available through the syllabus or course web site.

Join Student Learning Communities

SLCs are defined as a group of students with common interests who create a social network and complete a collection of activities organized by common goals (Swaner & Brownell, 2008). SLCs have produced positive results for college students with disabilities, including increased academic performance, engagement in educational activities (Zhao & Kuh, 2004), and growth in self-advocacy skills (Burgstahler, 2003; Izzo, Murray, Priest, & McArrell, 2011). Izzo et al. used the SLC model to assist college students with disabilities who were majoring in STEM and participating in a National Science Foundation funded grant program. Students reported that learning about academic assistance, DSS, self-advocacy skills, and building relationships with other students with disabilities majoring in STEM were highly rated activities of the SLC (Izzo et al., 2011).

Jeff, a mechanical engineering major involved in an SLC, presented on what it was like to live with ADHD and developed his own self-advocacy plan.

Jeff Deepens Understanding of Attention-Deficit/Hyperactivity Disorder

Today, most people have no idea that I have ADHD unless I disclose to them, but the disorder was more obvious when I was younger. I really struggled then. When you are a child, it's hard to understand why you don't learn as quickly as the other kids. Your mind wants to keep up, but something is going on neurologically so that you can't. As I have gotten older, though, I have learned what I need to do to succeed academically, and I now know how to work with my ADHD. Here are my personal steps for success:

1. Utilize the appropriate accommodations

2. Take my medication

3. Stay positive and determined

Meet with a Disability Support Services Counselor Each Semester

Students may want to submit their documentation prior to their first semester to ensure that needed accommodations are available when the students start classes. Since postsecondary institutions have different requirements for the documentation they will accept, such as types, sources and recency of evaluation reports, high school students need to ask what documentation is accepted at the college they plan to attend (Madaus, Benerjee, & Hamblet, 2010). The Association on Higher Education and Disability (AHEAD) published guidance on documentation practices for substantiating a student's disability and request for accommodations (AHEAD, 2012). AHEAD suggests

(a) Primary documentation: Student's Self-report: An interview with a student regarding his or her experience of disability, barriers, and effective and ineffective accommodations may be sufficient for establishing disability and a need for accommodations.

(b) Secondary documentation: Observation and Interaction: The impressions and conclusions formed by higher education disability professionals during interviews with students are acceptable forms of documentation.

(c) Tertiary documentation: Information from external or third parties: Documentation may include educational or medical records, reports, or assessments created by health care providers or school psychologists or teachers (AHEAD, 2012).

Even if students initially decide not to use accommodations in their classes, having the registration process complete will ensure that approved accommodations will be available, if needed. Students can practice disclosing their disability and the impact it has had on their ability to learn. In addition, students can explain how specific accommodations either eliminated barriers or enhanced learning by leveling the playing field. For example, if a student has dyslexia and reads with difficulty, having extra time on tests will give the student the time he or she needs to complete the test at a slower pace.

Anna Registers with the Disability Support Services Office

Anna was excited to move into her dorm room and meet her roommate. The last thing she wanted to do was register with the college's DSS office. As her mom, I insisted. We found the building where the DSS office was located, and Anna introduced herself and me. We reviewed the documentation that the high school psychologist had prepared to gain accommodations on the ACT college entrance test during her senior year of high school.

On reviewing the folder, the DSS director indicated that the documentation was fine and Anna was eligible to receive extended time and distraction-free testing settings if Anna decided to use these accommodations. Anna said that she wanted to try taking her classes without accommodations. Also, Anna was a student athlete, so she had mandatory study classes with tutors that are provided for all entering student athletes. The DSS director indicated that the college's athletic program provided excellent supports for their college athletes. She also pointed out that all student athletes are required to sit in the front of their classes. We all agreed that Anna would come to the DSS office first before calling home for assistance if she ran into any challenges that exceeded the assistance of the athletic tutors. Anna used the supports from the athletic office and her peers, but she did not use extended time or distraction-free testing centers because she could maintain her grades without these supports (and she did not call home for help either).

Once registered with the DSS office, students should meet with their DSS counselor at least once per semester, and more often, if needed. For example, if students' grades fall below a *B* average, then it may be time to review the schedule and study habits to determine if there are accommodations or study strategies that may help students improve their grades. Students can ask the DSS counselor about specific accommodations or supports that may be available on campus, including the following.

- Where are the distraction-free testing areas located?
- If I am eligible for extended time for testing, who monitors the extra time provided?
- Are classes or learning communities available so I can gain more skills in understanding my disability or learning to use additional study strategies that will help me succeed?
- If there are several instructors who teach the same course, can you recommend an instructor that has a record of providing a welcoming class environment for students with disabilities?

Enroll in Study Skills Classes

Attending college as a student with hidden disabilities presents unique challenges. College coursework often requires students to use time management skills to organize their schedules; schedules that may start at noon and end at 9 P.M. in the evening. Also, college coursework can be more challenging with fewer prompts from instructors to determine if students are mastering the course content. Many college courses have two examinations that determine how well students have mastered the content, whether students have passed or failed the course, and what grades they have earned. If students do not do well on the midterm examination, then it is difficult to pull up their grade and/or pass the course in the rest of the semester.

Plenty of strategies and supports are available that students can acquire and access to make the most of their academic potential. With a little prep work and a lot of dedication, college can be a successful step toward the career that students have dreamed and planned to enter.

 LeDerick Takes a Study Skills Class

I was required to take a studies skills class called Becoming a Master Student (Ellis, 2002) as part of my first semester as a Project Connection student. Becoming a

Master Student was an elective that was available to every student on campus, but the staff of Project Connection required all of their new students to sign up for a section of the class that never appeared in any course catalog and was reserved for students with learning disabilities. We learned skills such as surveying our textbooks, using a calendar to manage time, and dividing large projects into more manageable pieces. The class transformed my study habits because every conversation about studying was presented with a learning disabilities slant. Because every student in the room had a learning disability of some kind, our shared experience brought a new dimension to each lesson.

Overall, I believe it is best to teach study skills to students in an inclusive setting—taking into account that within any class you will be faced with a full spectrum of abilities and learning styles. There is also an advantage, however, to creating a safe space within your school where students can learn valuable lessons with other students who face similar challenges. Knowing what models work best for students depends on the culture of your school and the level of acceptance that students have for their disabilities.

Use Technology Tools, Apps, and Devices

Technology offers many solutions for college students with hidden disabilities. For example, students who have trouble taking notes or following a lecture may use a notetaker or bring a computer, tablet, or voice recorder into the classroom as a way to capture the content and information they need. With permission of the professor or course instructor, they might use an iPad, phone, or other device to take pictures of information on the board or video tape lectures. This can be particularly effective for students with learning disabilities or ADHD, who might have trouble maintaining concentration for the duration of the class period. It is important that students with hidden disabilities learn how to advocate for what they need and think of creative solutions for success.

Address Challenges with Persistence and the Use of Supports

According to the NLTS–2, students with disabilities were more likely to give high ratings to their ability to handle challenges than to having a sense of humor, being sensitive to the feelings of others, or being well organized (Wagner, Newman, Cameto, Levine, & Marder, 2007). Many people with hid-

> ### Text Box 5.5—PSST: Here Is a Secret
>
> Having access to the disability safe list is one of the many benefits that come from disclosing a disability in college. This list is known by many different names, and it is not always written down on paper, but there is usually a list of professors who are are known for being more understanding of the needs of students with disabilities. This list is one of the most valuable cultural artifacts that students with disabilities can use to help them navigate through college. College students may have a number of instructors to choose from for many of their classes. Encourage students to identify professors who work well with students with disabilities so they can focus on passing the class without worrying about receiving their accommodations.

den disabilities take pride in their ability to think outside of the box, given that they have faced numerous challenges associated with their disability from a young age. Successful students with hidden disabilities have learned to persist and seek out the supports and resources that are available within their school or community to complete their degrees.

If students are enrolled in a class in which they are not doing well, then withdraw prior to the deadline or switch to another class on an audit basis. Some students will take a class on an audit basis prior to enrolling in the class for a grade. LeDerick used this strategy to fail successfully.

 ## LeDerick Fails Successfully

I had to take an elective to learn the computer language C++ because I was a mathematics major. I had no experience in programming, and I had a really hard time grasping the concepts the professor was teaching. I realized I was in danger of failing the class after poor performances on my first few tests. I had a meeting with my professor, and I asked her if I could withdraw from her class and audit it the remainder of the semester so I could spend more time learning the coding content without having to worry about passing the tests and quizzes. The professor agreed, and I came to every lecture and just absorbed the information. The following semester I enrolled in the same class with the same professor, but this time for a grade. The course was still challenging, but I came to enjoy writing programs and was able to pass the class.

CONCLUSION

Obtaining a college degree is a gateway to entering many careers. Many successful students with hidden disabilities have used the strategies presented in this chapter to complete their degrees and enter careers in which they excel. Even the best prepared student with a hidden disability will face challenges and even failure. It is important that these students are supported through these challenging times by giving them a strong sense of disability pride and the confidence to keep moving toward their goals. It is only failure if they do not learn a lesson from the experience. Part of the magic of college is that it is a time full of transformative experiences that offer countless opportunities for growth.

Daring for the Dream Career

Living a Life of Value

> You see, it's my job to motivate,
> inspire, and challenge you.
> Excerpt from *Dare to Dream*,
> —LeDerick Horne

LeDerick Dares to Dream

My career as an advocate began in college when I was asked to speak on a panel of college students with learning disabilities to high school students on IEPs. I began to understand the power of sharing my story after that first presentation, and I knew that I had to continue reaching out to students who were afraid to dream of a better future.

I now increase students' understanding of our shared journey toward disability pride. When I wrote the poem "Dare to Dream," I believed, and I still believe, that it is my calling to help students with disabilities

- "merge who you are / with who you want to be

- to unlock doors / unshackle minds / and break through glass ceilings

- to fight like gladiators / to become master and commander / of your own beautiful minds" (Horne, 2011)

I am working in a career in which my strengths and abilities are perfectly matched to my passion. My calling is affirmed every time a student tells me how I have helped him or her believe in him- or herself.

LeDerick's dream job entails motivating, inspiring, and challenging others with disabilities to dare to dream and become who they want to be. The coauthors consider their careers as a major defining component of their identities. Their careers are more than how they earn a living; they fulfill a part of their purpose for living through their work. Students with hidden disabilities can live a life of value by working with respect and disability pride whether they choose careers in the helping/serving professions, construction industries, or any other sector. Living a life of value brings an inner joy and peace that is priceless whether people with hidden disabilities serve others directly through their careers, donate a portion of their financial resources, or volunteer to enrich the lives of others. Helping students experience the positive energy generated from selecting valid career goals is one of the greatest joys teachers can experience.

Many people define who they are by their careers and feel as if they are productive members of society by working (Levinson & Palmer, 2005). If students with hidden disabilities are afraid to "merge who they are with who they want to be" (Horne, 2011), then they are at risk of underachieving in their career. These students must maximize their interests and skills while minimizing their limitations to make the transition to their dream career. A number of vignettes are presented in this chapter of employees with hidden disabilities who accept who they are and are successful in their careers.

CAREER EXPLORATION: FINDING ONE'S PASSION

Federal policies emphasize that the goal for America's education system is to ensure that every high school graduate is college and career ready (U.S. Department of Education, 2010). As a result, states developed standards and statewide accountability systems that collect and report academic achievement, graduation rates, college enrollment rates, and school climate variables (U.S. Department of Education, 2011). Students are college and career ready when they have the knowledge, skills, and academic preparation needed to enroll and succeed in introductory college courses within an associate's or bachelor's degree program without the need for remediation (Achieve, n.d.). Therefore, much of the data reported to evaluate students' progress on these college and career readiness standards focuses on academic achievement; career readiness is not defined (U.S. Department of Education, 2014). Career readiness involves three major skill areas:

1. Core academic skills and the ability to apply those skills to concrete situations in order to function in the workplace

2. Employability skills, such as critical thinking and responsibility

3. Technical, job-specific skills related to a career pathway (Association for Career and Technical Education, n.d.).

Students who are career ready possess the ability to enter a career pathway that provides their family a sustaining wage, as well as the ability to advance in their career by obtaining training. Measures of students' career readiness unfortunately are not reported in mandated accountability systems managed by state and federal departments of education.

Opportunities for career exploration have expanded in some schools to include annual career portfolios and individual learning plans for all students, including students with disabilities. Yet, many high schools resemble the high schools that the coauthors attended, with little attention to help students explore their preferences, interests, skills, and strengths and determine what career areas they should pursue. Some state leaders have implemented statewide initiatives in which every student takes interest surveys and explores careers of high interest. For example, a web site is available to middle and high school students in Ohio to explore their interests, develop career plans, and build résumés that they save in their online "backpack" (Ohio Means Jobs Guided Tour, n.d.). Using these resources, however, is often left to teacher discretion, and far too many students enter college without valid career goals.

Margo Explores Careers Through Middle and High School

My first recollection of developing a career goal was in eighth grade during our class Career Day. Our assignment involved researching a career and giving a speech in clothes that we would wear if we worked in that career. I dressed as a flight attendant and explained how I ensure the safety of the passengers.

We had little discussion about careers in high school. I remember being sent to talk to the guidance counselor, who provided little assistance. I thought about being a nun. I was not sure if I really felt called by God to serve or if this career was motivated by my love of the movie *The Sound of Music*. When it came to picking college majors, I knew that I was a curious person and wanted to help people. A college recruiter explained about a degree program at D'Youville College where I could major in psychology and gain teaching certificates in elementary education and special education. This degree provided many options that would ensure that I could find a job after college—a family requirement to gain support to go to college.

The following Tips for Teaching provide a variety of activities that any general or special education teacher can implement to help students find their career interests and passions.

Tips for Teaching

Help Students Discover Their Interests and Passions

- Ask students to complete either an online or paper personality assessment to determine personality styles and write research papers or complete career projects to explore careers related to their personality.
- Administer learning style surveys, and have students match various learning styles to specific career areas. Divide the class by learning styles, and have students generate a list of careers that would be a good match for each learning style (e.g., visual, aural, kinesthetic, multimodel).

(continued)

Tips for Teaching (continued)

- Require students to conduct visits to worksites and informational interviews with workers who are employed in areas of high career interest and complete an assignment that summarizes their interview (see Figure 6.1 for a sample worksheet).
- Coordinate a Career Day for the class (or school). Ask students to develop a presentation about their ideal career and why they think this career is a good match to their interests, strengths, and other personality or learning styles.
- Ask students to research what education and training certificates or degrees they will need to enter their career goal. Then, research education or training programs that offer the education they need, and have them compare and contrast two programs on costs, length of program, and availability of disability support services.
- Ask students to write about their interests, likes, and dislikes at the beginning of the year. Then, connect course content and assignments to their career preferences whenever possible.

WHAT ARE THE EMPLOYMENT OUTCOMES OF HIGH SCHOOL STUDENTS WITH DISABILITIES?

According to the NLTS–2, 60% of young adults with disabilities who had been out of high school for up to 8 years were employed at the time of the interview, and 91% had been employed at some point since leaving high school (Newman et al., 2011). Young adults with learning disabilities, speech-language impairments, or other health impairments were more likely to be employed than young adults with sensory or orthopedic impairments, autism, or intellectual or multiple disabilities (Newman et al., 2011). Students with learning disabilities and ADHD had the highest employment figures of any disability category across years. For example, 35% of students with learning disabilities and ADHD were employed 1 year after exiting high school; employment rates for people with learning disabilities reached a high of 79% employed 7 years after high school, whereas 68% of people with ADHD were employed 7 years after high school (Newman et al., 2011).

Young adults who had been employed had held about four jobs since leaving high school and had held their current job for 12 months or more, on average (Newman et al., 2011). Approximately two thirds of young adults with disabilities worked full time (35 or more hours per week), and they averaged 36 hours per week, which did not differ significantly from young adults of similar age in the general population (Newman et al., 2011).

Newman et al. reported on the types of jobs these young adults obtained: "Young adults with disabilities were significantly more likely to work in food preparation and serving-related occupations and sales and related occupations (13% and 12%, respectively) than in education, training, and library

Student name:	Business name:
Employer name being interviewed:	Length of time:

1. What is the mission of your business?

2. Could you describe a typical day?

3. How many people work here? Do you work in large groups, in teams, or one to one?

4. What are the different jobs in the business?

5. How are people trained in their jobs?

6. What are the prerequisites for working here (training/qualifications)?

7. How or where do your employees gain the experience required to work here?

8. What do you like best about this job? What is the hardest part of this job?

9. What personal characteristics do you look for in employees?

Be sure to thank the site for their assistance verbally or with a thank-you note.

Am I interested in this job field? (Check one box)   Yes ☐   No ☐   Maybe ☐

1. How has this interview helped clarify or redefine my career goal?

2. List two things you learned about this job:

Figure 6.1. Informational interview questions.

occupations (4%); computer, mathematical, architecture, engineering and science occupations (3%)" (2011, p. 62). Significant differences were not found across disability categories for most types of jobs obtained.

 ## Margo's First Teaching Position

After I graduated from college, I worked in a special education teaching position at a school for students with behavior disorders for 3 years. Although many of my students made progress, I was frustrated that I did not teach all of them the skills they needed to navigate employment and live independently. So, I pursued my master's degree in vocational special education. I worked several internships during my master's program—one as a vocational evaluator and the other at the U.S. Department of Education. I learned more about assessing students' vocational potential and about grant programs through my internships in order to research more effective strategies to educate and help students with disabilities make the transition to adult life. It was then that I knew I wanted to write grants and develop more effective transition programs.

Many students with hidden disabilities work a number of entry-level jobs throughout high school and college to acquire work experience and determine their interests and abilities. Many young adults develop the skills they need to enter careers of their choosing during these early work experiences. As the case studies demonstrate, people with hidden disabilities can make the transition to college and careers that match their interests and abilities. Career exploration, work experiences, self-determination, and mentoring provide the foundation for individuals with hidden disabilities to succeed in their dream careers. Working in an area of passion that students think is fulfilling their purpose can sometimes backfire. See how Margo's dream job turned into a poor job match.

 ## Margo's Employment Joy Factor

After I was recently divorced and raising two daughters, I decided that I needed a more stable job than my soft money grant position. Although I loved working on grants, I was concerned that I would be unemployed and a single mom with two small girls to support if there was a lapse in funding. So, I obtained a job at a large organization that had many procedures and guidelines—so many that even I had difficulty following all of them. There were times when I would work with a school and agree to assist them with some of their issues. When I shared what I was doing with a supervisor, expecting to be rewarded (or at least affirmed), I was chastised for offering technical assistance to teachers and parents without following company guidelines and procedures. I slowly lost my passion for the job and spent more time following procedures (or at least trying to) than doing what I really wanted to do, which was solving problems facing students with disabilities, parents, and teachers.

I heard a speaker later that year who spoke about the "employment joy factor." She was speaking to a room full of educators, and she said that if you do not experience joy at your job, then you should consider either changing your attitude or changing your job. If you dislike your job and are unhappy, then you are not bringing positive energy to your colleagues or the students you serve. You may be harming yourself because being unhappy brings you down from a psychological and health standpoint.

I thought long and hard about my joy factor. It took me about a year to plan my transition to a position in which I would be excited to go to work, share my ideas, and write grants to test new interventions for students with disabilities. I worked hard and planned for several potential positions, and I eventually accepted a position in which I could spend more of my time in my creative space— developing and testing new interventions for students with disabilities. Because I knew that I would still have to comply with the many procedural safeguards that are required (which is not a strength of mine), I learned to write a program manager position into the projects to manage these critical details. So, I learned to proactively increase my joy factor by playing to my strengths and knowing my limitations. Hiring people who find joy in managing project details is a win-win for me and my staff.

Many people in today's society spend more time at work than in any other single activity. Workers who enjoy their tasks, co-workers, or customers are more likely to feel valued and experience a higher joy factor. Some workers, however, may be in careers that are good matches, but they may struggle with organization, time management, or other emotional obstacles due to deficits in executive function skills. Employees with hidden disabilities can learn to increase their productivity and efficiency by gaining and improving their executive function skills.

EXECUTIVE FUNCTION SKILLS: CRITICAL FOR PROFESSIONAL SUCCESS

Many people with hidden disabilities, especially those with ADHD, have trouble with executive function skills such as time management, planning, and organization (Solanto, 2011). Deficits in executive functions may be attributed to problems with working memory, self-inhibition, distraction issues, attentional shifting, organizing, planning, self-monitoring, and time tracking (Barkley, 1997; Barkley, Murphy, & Bush, 2001). Several studies demonstrated that cognitive–behavioral treatment, delivered in individual or group sessions, can help to increase executive function in adults with ADHD (Safren et al., 2005; Solanto et al., 2010). The following case study shows how Margo improved her understanding of ADHD, her executive function skills, and her joy factor by joining a support group of professionals with ADHD.

 ### Margo Works on Her Executive Function Skills

I became aware of a support group for professionals with ADHD who wanted to improve their executive function skills. I was ready to try anything because I felt overwhelmed by several challenging projects and other commitments that increased my work week to more than 60 hours. The thought of spending 40 hours over 12 weeks in a support group was not a welcome thought, but I registered because I desperately wanted to improve my time management and organizational skills.

The psychologist that facilitated the support group used an excellent book by Mary V. Solanto (2011) titled *Cognitive-Behavioral Therapy for Adult ADHD: Targeting Executive Dysfunction.* Solanto stated, and the majority of my support group affirmed, that adults with ADHD have "trouble with executive functions of everyday life—time management, planning and organization" (p. 8). I want to share some of the highlights with personal applications of what I found valuable.

- *Acceptance.* I made peace with having ADHD years ago and experience more positive benefits than negative drawbacks of how my mind works. Yet, I realize that I need to manage my time better and be more realistic about what I can accomplish when I get overwhelmed and drive home exhausted after a 12-hour day. For example, I have learned to say "no" to additional work, whether it comes in the form of writing a grant or an article that must be completed within the next few months.

- *Procrastination.* I learned that if I am having trouble getting started on a task, the first step is too big. For example, I cannot put "write Chapter 6" on my to-do list. I need to break the task down into 2- or 3-hour chunks of work that can be accomplished in a given afternoon. I have also learned to reinforce myself for getting it done.

- *Time management.* People with ADHD are very poor at estimating how much time it will take to complete a task. I think I can write an article in a day, but, in reality, it takes me 3 days. I am learning to be more realistic by maintaining a time log.

- *Planning.* I practiced organizing a list of priorities and then scheduling each task in my planner with adequate time to complete it. I am still working on planning and scheduling my priorities, even though I practiced this skill for weeks. In the process of making my list of priorities, I typically jump in and start working on something that is due soon before I plan the entire week.

- *Reinforcement.* I have learned to take breaks and do something I enjoy after I complete a task. I do not try to work without breaks any longer. So, I stop and go for a walk or do a task I enjoy. I am amazed that this helps me stay focused, and I am setting more reasonable expectations for what I can get done.

There are a number of tasks that I have not mastered, primarily with organizing my desk. The messy desk does not mean an unproductive person; everyone works differently.

Margo was unaware of having ADHD for more than half of her career. As her responsibilities grew, so did the challenges. She had passion and vision, but

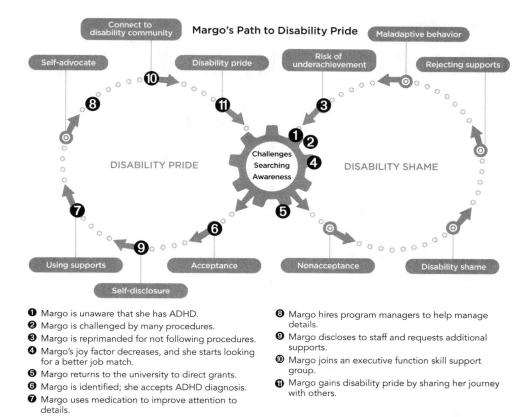

Figure 6.2. Margo's Path to Disability Pride.

❶ Margo is unaware that she has ADHD.
❷ Margo is challenged by many procedures.
❸ Margo is reprimanded for not following procedures.
❹ Margo's joy factor decreases, and she starts looking for a better job match.
❺ Margo returns to the university to direct grants.
❻ Margo is identified; she accepts ADHD diagnosis.
❼ Margo uses medication to improve attention to details.
❽ Margo hires program managers to help manage details.
❾ Margo discloses to staff and requests additional supports.
❿ Margo joins an executive function skill support group.
⓫ Margo gains disability pride by sharing her journey with others.

she did not have the skills to manage the grants she won. Once she acknowledged having ADHD, she began to take medication to improve her attention to detail. Even joining a support group of adults with ADHD who were all committed to improving executive function skills did not solve all of the challenges associated with managing grants. Improving planning, organization, and time management skills, however, reduces the challenges that Margo experiences in her life. Figure 6.2 illustrates Margo's Path to Disability Pride.

Chapter 1 provides Tips for Teaching on how to teach executive function skills to students with and without disabilities. Gaining instruction on these skills is often not enough for many students to become proficient. Many students need ongoing coaching throughout their school experience to acquire adequate executive function skills. Students can improve their executive function skills if teachers incorporate frequent practice and coaching sessions to assist students to break assignments into smaller chunks and then organize and schedule these smaller chunks, each with an estimated time allocation delineated on their calendars. Once these skills are acquired, students and adults with hidden disabilities will have the potential to improve their performance within academic, employment, and social settings.

ENTREPRENEURSHIP

Entrepreneurship is defined as the process of finding and evaluating opportunities and risks and developing and executing plans for translating those opportunities into financial self-sufficiency (Kaufmann & Stuart, 2007). Many high schools, colleges, and universities are recognizing the need to introduce students to the concept of entrepreneurship. These programs are teaching the skills needed to start businesses. A number of positive outcomes have been reported for involving youth with disabilities in vocational and entrepreneurial activities (Bronte-Tinkew & Redd, 2001, as cited in Kauffmann & Stuart, 2007), including:

- Improvements in attendance and academic performance

- Acquisition of practical skills such as problem solving, teamwork, money management, and public speaking

- Job readiness and social development

- Enhanced self-esteem and social psychological development

Logan (2009) reported that more than 35% of America's entrepreneurs are people with learning disabilities who scored higher on risk-taking measures than entrepreneurs without disabilities. Many people with learning disabilities compensate for their lack of academic skills by developing enhanced communication and negotiation skills, two skills that may explain why people with hidden disabilities tend to grow their companies more quickly than entrepreneurs in the general population (Logan, 2009). These skills are essential because entrepreneurs need to establish the vision and motivate others to build a successful company. The mission of the Yale University for Dyslexia & Creativity (see http://www.dyslexia.yale.edu) states, "With the Center's emphasis on strengths rather than failures, children and adults [with dyslexia] can become some of society's most creative and valued contributors. Dyslexia can also be a hidden source of great abilities and frequently unrecognized powers."

Many entrepreneurs with great abilities attest to the value of having mentors, parents, or both who believed in them, reinforced their abilities despite their learning challenges, and took a genuine interest in their success (Meinzen & Meinzen, 2013). The following case studies show how Chris and Scott identified their strengths, worked around their limitations, and started their own businesses. In addition, they both had mentors who believed in their abilities. Chris started a successful beauty salon in the DC Metro area. He not only supports his own family with a very comfortable lifestyle, he has mentored three budding entrepreneurs who provide massages, facials, and tattoos. He provides them with space, health insurance, and a clientele who enjoy having multiple services available at one location. When Chris found out about this book to assist people with hidden disabilities, he told Margo about his learning disability.

Chris: An Entrepreneur with Style

In elementary school, my second grade teacher told my mom that I had learning challenges and recommended that I be placed in a separate class for students with disabilities. My mom decided to teach me herself rather than have me experience the stigma of being separated from my peers. I saw my friends through my baseball and basketball teams, and they accepted the fact that my mom decided to teach me at home. Since I was a good athlete, it didn't matter to my coaches or friends. When I was a teenager, I wanted to go to high school and play basketball on the high school team, and my mom agreed. High school was painful. I sat in classes and did not understand much of what was being taught. My mom would reteach me almost everything that I was supposed to have learned at school.

I went to a cosmetology program for adults after high school and learned to cut and style hair. The academic components were hard, but I passed the state board exam and received my license. The first salon I worked at had a wonderful mentor who helped me expand my skills and develop my creative side of cutting hair. I opened my own salon after a few years. I hired full-time hairdressers, masseuses, nail technicians, and a tattoo artist—all who provide services to our clientele. I'm proud to say that I provide health care benefits to all my colleagues. I know what I am good at, and I love helping my clients find a look that they like. I enjoy cutting, coloring, and styling hair. I hire others to assist me in the tasks that I do not enjoy. As many business owners, I hire an accountant who keeps the books. I am proud that I pay all my taxes and give 10 other people an opportunity to work in an area in which their talents help my customers get the services they want and need. It doesn't matter to me if my colleagues have hidden disabilities or not. I'm sure some of them do. But they excel at their professions as artists. The world would be a very boring place if we didn't have diversity regarding our talents and passions. And bottom-line, my salon provides our customers with the best services in the DC area.

Successful entrepreneurs set the vision in motion and carve out the tasks that match their abilities, talents, and strengths and delegate the rest to their partners, colleagues, or employees.

Not everyone has to become actively engaged in a disability community to be successful. Not everyone needs a disability community to accept their disability. It doesn't matter that he struggled as a student. Chris doesn't share his story with many of his customers, but he gains self-confidence and satisfaction in knowing that he delivers quality hair care that keeps his customers coming back.

The following vignette shows how Scott started a business in video productions and had a variety of clients, including Ohio's Youth Leadership Forum (YLF) for young adults with disabilities. Scott's mentor, Bill Bauer, was the statewide coordinator of YLF and contracted Scott to produce a marketing video to recruit students with disabilities to participate in the annual YLF conference.

Scott Graduates and Starts a Business

Scott started a company called LimeLite Productions the semester before he graduated from Marietta College with a bachelor's degree in broadcast and communications. Scott was diagnosed with a learning disability and ADHD, and with the encouragement of his mentor, he began booking projects. One of his first projects was to produce a video promoting Ohio's Youth Leadership Forum. Scott served as a mentor to several of the young adults who participated as he filmed and developed the YLF video. Then he expanded to other clientele outside of the disability community. LimeLite Productions developed, marketed, and produced entertainment shows for college campuses. Numerous college campuses hosted performances by LimeLite Productions.

Scott relies on technology to do most of his work and provide the majority of his accommodations. He uses his cell phone and tablet to manage his calendar, allowing him to plan his projects in great detail. He stores his video footage on his computer and all of his finished projects on a private YouTube channel. He uses spellcheck and grammar programs to ensure that his e-mails and the titles and captions do not have errors. He often asks a colleague to proof his video projects because sometimes errors slip through spellcheck. He relies on directional maps with GPS to navigate from location to location. Scott doesn't share that he has hidden disabilities with his clientele, but his business partners are aware of his creative abilities and the areas where he needs support.

Many people with hidden disabilities start their own businesses and become entrepreneurs who set the vision in motion and hire people who provide the supports they need. Many benefits are gained by those who connect to a disability community, if only for a short period of time, just as Scott did. Knowing and understanding that others encounter similar challenges and sharing solutions that have resolved some of these challenges provide a level of support and acceptance that teachers, parents, or friends may not have the capacity to deliver.

Tips for Teaching

Assisting Students on Their Path to Disability Pride

Complete the following steps for students who are in denial and refuse to acknowledge their disability.

- Build a relationship with students by acknowledging their strengths in academic, athletic, or social areas.
- Reinforce the effort that students display, even if it is trying (e.g., "I am glad you completed your homework. Let's work on it together so I can explain some tips that might make it easier").
- As your relationship grows, share examples of others with similar strengths who also have a disability and are now successful in their chosen career.

(continued)

Tips for Teaching *(continued)*

- Have short class discussions using examples from current events to highlight the number of people who admit to having disabilities and working through the struggles of adolescence and now are fulfilling their dream career.

Complete the previous steps and the following steps for students who know they have a disability but do not want anyone else to know.

- Never publicly embarrass the students in front of peers by disclosing more than what is comfortable for the students.
- Bring in speakers who have hidden disabilities and who have interesting careers.
- Encourage all students to share their strengths, interests, and challenges, whether or not they have disabilities.
- Match students to mentors who are older students, alumni, or professionals with hidden disabilities.

Complete the following steps for parents of students with hidden disabilities.

- Meet often with parents and share their children's strengths from an asset-based approach, using the previous strategies.
- Provide workshops to describe how disability affects learning, with positive examples of the importance of choosing career paths that minimize students' limitations. Invite adults with hidden disabilities to disclose their path to disability pride and their dream career.
- Emphasize the importance of self-directed individualized education programs that include realistic and valid postsecondary goals for employment and further education and training.

TECHNOLOGY SUPPORTS

Scott's vignette and the ones you will hear from Adam and Anna show how they use technology to accommodate the challenges that their hidden disabilities create. Technology enhances numerous skills, from basic spelling and grammar to organizational skills, for many employees with and without disabilities. See how professionals with hidden disabilities use technology to work around some of the challenges caused by their disabilities.

An Interview with Adam the Designer

Margo: Can you tell me about your high school experiences?

Adam: High school was hard because there was a lot of reading and writing, and I made countless spelling errors because of my dyslexia. I was marked down in every class—history, science, and English. I took every art class I could in high school. My art teacher encouraged me to go to an art college. My college experience was much more positive than my high school experience because of the focus on art rather than academics. My major was painting and drawing, but I switched to industrial design because painting was fun but I could not make a living out of it. My grandfather would teach me how to make things, and I enjoyed that. Industrial design classes taught me how to think in 3D and be creative. I have been forced to find creative ways to approach problems because my brain does not work in a traditional way. It helps me in my job.

Margo: Why did you do so well, when so many other students with hidden disabilities fail to reach their potential?

Adam: My parents were very supportive; my mom worked in the disability field for years so she understood the impact of a disability. My parents forced me to do the things I did not want to do in school. I wanted to give up on school, and I felt totally inadequate. My mom would remind me that my intelligence had nothing to do with how I was being graded.

Margo: What do you want to tell teachers and students?

Adam: I do not know if it is the teachers' fault—it is the system. I mean everything we do, such as reading a menu, is all based on reading. I am an outlier, so I do not blame anyone. We live in a society that is dependent on reading and writing. We need to learn to read and try to get through it. And then find your niche—do not let schools define who you are.

Margo: Tell me about your career.

Adam: My first job after college was at an architectural design firm. I am not licensed [as an architect], but I do a lot of 3D modeling and drafting that include a lot of details, such as how materials fit together. We did a lot of renovation at the first firm I worked at. I did the detailing on the architectural drawings and recommended material choices. We worked on projects in groups at my firm, so it was easier for some of my co-workers to read the building code, and I would listen to them and then tell them how I would apply it in a renovation project.

We had AT (assistive technology) programs to catch spelling errors on the drawing's labels. During a slow period in my fourth year at this firm, my boss loaned me out to another firm to help out with one of their projects. They did not have my AT program installed on their computers, so I made a lot of spelling errors. My boss would say, "You are a crappy speller. Can't you fix that and spell correctly?" People just do not understand dyslexia and spelling errors. You would not tell a blind person to go look at a building; but bosses or co-workers will tell me to spell correctly. I had a

Figure 6.3. Adam's Path to Disability Pride.

❶ Adam accepts his learning disability in grade school.
❷ Adam advocates to gain technology supports on the job.
❸ Adam uses technology supports on the job to assist with spelling.
❹ Adam changes jobs to a firm in which colleagues value his strengths and do not criticize his spelling challenges.
❺ Adam does not flaunt having a learning disability, but he does not hide it either.

meeting with my boss and told her that I needed the AT program to help me with my spelling. After 5 years with the company, one of my co-workers who was laid off and got a job at a larger firm recruited me when there was a job opening. So, now I work at a different firm making more money and with colleagues who understand and appreciate what I bring to a project. (Figure 6.3 shows Adam's path to disability pride.)

Technology is also utilized frequently by Margo's daughter, Anna, who finished her master of education degree with licensure in hearing and vision impairments at The Ohio State University. Anna also works as a teacher for students with visual impairments, where she uses technology to teach students to read and write. She spends the majority of her day using technology to communicate with teachers and parents or teaching her students how to use technology to read, write, and access the general curricula.

ROLE OF NATURAL SUPPORTS

Natural supports are defined as assistance provided by people, procedures, or technology and equipment that are typically available within a workplace that leads to desired work or personal outcomes (Butterworth, Hagner, Kiernan,

& Schalock, 1996). As many of the vignettes demonstrate, successful people with hidden disabilities learn to use natural supports such as technology and co-workers to compensate for their deficits (Fitzgibbon & O'Connor, 2002). These strategies become transferable skills, often giving workers with hidden disabilities an edge in business (Logan, 2009). Many executives have assistants who implement the specific tasks of their projects. The coauthors use natural supports to accomplish their goals by organizing tasks to ensure that colleagues with the right skills complete tasks that are not a good match to their abilities. For example

- Margo designs projects and sets the vision, recruits the partners, and describes the scope of work and research questions in as much detail as a 40–70 page grant application allows. Once the project is funded, Margo delegates project management duties that include managing pilot sites, data collection, and analyses.

- LeDerick consults with state departments of education, local schools, and other organizations. He determines the topics of his workshops, writes his speeches, and develops plans to tell future clients about what he has to offer. He uses an agent to coordinate his schedule, make his travel arrangements, negotiate fees, and manage the billing process. He also utilizes recording studios to produce his poetry CDs, invest in fitness facilities, and manage several rental properties.

Both Margo and LeDerick pay others to complete tasks associated with their careers. But neither Margo nor LeDerick would be successful if their circle of colleagues and friends did not also provide natural supports. For example, Margo's colleagues provide prompts for upcoming deadlines and manage many of the details for upcoming events. LeDerick provided support for Margo during this writing project by assisting with managing time lines and priorities. Margo provided LeDerick with supports on editing, citations, and reference lists.

Margo Advocates for Additional Natural Supports on the Job

I remember working on several challenging projects to create 21st-century curricula that were aligned with English/language arts academic standards and taught students how to use the Internet to research their own transition plans. Students develop their own transition portfolios to guide their IEP based on online transition assessments and ongoing research to establish self-directed postsecondary goals for employment. My staff raised concerns and complained: "You keep changing your mind. You approved the outline and now you want more changes." I rationalized: "We know more about what is needed today than we did 6 months ago when the outline was approved. These projects are complex, and there are no easy answers. There is more than one way to do this."

    After several frustrating meetings, I decided to share that I have ADHD. I let them know that it was hard for me to keep project details organized. I explained that I was more of the visionary, the hunter, and the director of a project who designed these grants to solve some of the issues facing schools today. I also let them know that even though I designed the projects we were working on, I was not very good at the detail work that was necessary to bring them to completion. After much discussion, we realized that we needed to work as a team. My role is the visionary and hunter. I select the grant competitions that match our team's strengths and interests and then develop the conceptual design of the project. The project managers then deal with all the details to bring our vision to reality.

EMPOWERING STUDENTS TO OBTAIN THEIR DREAM CAREER GOAL

IDEA 2004 requires that students complete age-appropriate transition assessments and establish postsecondary employment goals on their IEP from age 16 through their exit from high school. If students do not gain information about their own strengths and limitations, then how can they establish employment goals? If students are not aware of how others with similar disabilities successfully entered a variety of career areas, then how can they see themselves as successful adults working in satisfying careers?

Teachers and parents must assist students with hidden disabilities to select career goals that maximize their strengths while minimizing their limitations. Too often teachers and parents lower their expectations for students with hidden disabilities. They discourage students who struggled with reading or spelling to attend college. They encourage these students to accept entry-level jobs that are beneath their potential. Students with disabilities can and will achieve when high expectations are set and they are taught to use the technology, resources and supports that are available for them. For example, students who use tutoring centers and other academic resources such as text-to-speech software can successfully complete college. Once these students graduate and gain the degree they need to enter their chosen career, they will have these resources to use at work as well.

Throughout this book, LeDerick shared his journey through the many challenges that he faced as he was preparing for his career. Many students with hidden disabilities face similar challenges as they prepare for their transition from high school to college and careers. Some teachers doubted whether LeDerick, who spent the majority of the time in separate special education classrooms, could successfully complete college. However, other teachers and his parents encouraged him to attend a quality college program that had supports for students with learning disabilities. LeDerick was empowered to enroll in college, and being successful in college gave him the confidence to believe in himself. In turn, he has empowered millions of other students to dare to dream for their ideal career goal. LeDerick is passionate about addressing the misperception that learning disabilities are synonymous with being unmotivated or unable.

Margo was not identified as a high school student with ADHD, and no one ever doubted that she would be successful in college. Yet her daughter, Anna, was labeled in high school as a special education student. Schools gave her a label, and along with that label came low expectations. Her Mom had to fight to keep her in college track courses. Now Anna has finished her Master of Science degree and is teaching other students how to believe in themselves and use technology to accommodate their vision impairments. Margo and Anna are committed to sharing how having ADHD provides many advantages. For example, they both develop creative solutions to complex problems facing schools and students today. Because of their passion and skills, many students with disabilities have the opportunity to prepare to enter their dream career.

CONCLUSION

Employment outcomes for students with hidden disabilities leave much room for improvement. More than 32% of young adults with learning disabilities and 34% with ADHD were not employed 8 years following their exit from high school. Those who obtained employment were more likely to be working in food service and sales jobs than in education, engineering, or science careers (Newman et al., 2011). Clearly, the majority of students with hidden disabilities are not achieving quality employment outcomes that could be considered their dream career.

Yet, more than one third of entrepreneurs report having disabilities. These entrepreneurs scored higher on risk-taking measures and developed enhanced communication and delegation skills, in part, as a compensatory strategy that resulted from having a disability (Logan, 2009). Successfully employed adults with disabilities use a variety of supports that range from technology to natural supports. Teachers must help students recognize and use natural supports that are available to all students but may not be recognized as a viable support for students with hidden disabilities.

Educators, parents, and employers must maintain high expectations for students to continually increase their academic and employment goals. Young adults with hidden disabilities can be empowered to dare to dream for their very own dream career by keeping expectations high for students who experience learning challenges and providing positive role models of successfully employed adults with disabilities who have achieved a variety of quality employment outcomes. Improving employment outcomes must begin with a belief that students with hidden disabilities have the right to dream for careers that match their interests, abilities, and passions. Once students believe that they can obtain their dream career, then they will have the motivation needed to gain the skills to enter those careers.

The Last Transition

Disability Pride and Quality Relationships

with Bill Bauer

7

"The better I understand myself,
the better people can understand me."
—Scott, 25, person with dyslexia, ADHD, and TBI

IDEA 2004 states that transition planning has the long-term goal of preparing students with disabilities for postsecondary education, employment, and independence. These are certainly important milestones for every person, regardless of how they are labeled. Researchers reported, however, that quality of life is directly related to the quality of social relationships that people have with family members, coworkers, significant others, and friends (Clifton, Anderson, & Schreiner, 2006; Diener, 2000). After all, having a house or apartment of one's own is just the frame placed around the picture of independent living. The myriad relationships and interactions experienced under one roof is what gives that picture color and turns the house into a home. Likewise, meaningful employment provides the fulfillment of receiving compensation for using one's talents and skills, but that income is ultimately used to support the growth and development of family and friends. Although today's educators have many responsibilities to teach required academic skills that are assessed and reported in student and even school report cards, the most critical skill for navigating life may be the ability to understand oneself and develop quality relationships. A person's self-concept, social skills, and the ability to develop authentic relationships are on the other side of the report card—the side that is often neglected in today's educational system of academic accountability. This chapter provides teachers with the rationale and tools to help students with hidden disabilities gain the knowledge, skills, and abilities to develop disability pride and authentic and meaningful relationships with others.

THE JOURNEY TO DISABILITY PRIDE

Students have their own set of values and beliefs that have been instilled by their families, communities, and experiences. Each student will be at different points on his or her journey to disability pride because of this diverse set of conditions. For example, if students' parents are overprotective and unwilling to instill a sense of independence, then teachers may have students who are not self-determined and lack self-advocacy skills. Or, if parents and students are in denial that a disability exists, then students may think that they are not very smart and use that as a rationale for academic difficulty. These types of behavior can hinder students' quest to self-determination and improved self-concept.

Teachers can help students navigate their path to disability pride by teaching them what their disability is, how it affects their learning, and how to use accommodations, technology, and other supports to compensate for the impairments that their disabilities create. If students fall off or get stuck on their path to disability pride, then teachers can help the students get back on the pride path before they become too involved in maladaptive behaviors. With a strong sense of encouragement, teachers and parents can provide the support needed to help students gain and maintain disability pride.

Self-Concept: Assisting Students to Discover Who They Are

Teachers, parents, and others who work with students with hidden disabilities must understand that every student has his or her own unique set of strengths, interests, skills, and needs. Students walk into class with their own self-concept of who they are. Students' self-concept is a combination of what others have told them, what they have discovered about themselves as they experience success and failure, and what the culture has told them through social, print, and digital media (Clifton et al., 2006). Businesses use media to sell products by encouraging people to compare themselves with models, actors, and athletes who are prettier, smarter, or more athletic (Clifton et al., 2006). These comparisons often leave teenagers feeling inadequate, isolated, and even depressed. These feelings of inadequacy can be reinforced by social networking sites such as Facebook, Twitter, and Instagram where teens are bombarded with messages (some inadvertent) that range from cyberbullying to selfies that scream, "Look what fun I am having! What is wrong with you?"

Researchers reported a link between social networking and depression or poor self-esteem (Schurgin-O'Keeffe & Clark-Pearson, 2011; Van Pelt, 2015). Other researchers reported that social networking sites can be an innovative avenue for identifying students at risk for depression and combating stigma surrounding mental health conditions (Moreno, Jelenchick, & Becker, 2011). Teaching students to develop healthy, asset-based self-concepts to not only see their strengths and talents clearly but also acknowledge and compensate for their weaknesses is essential to developing healthy self-concepts. Students are ready to develop healthy relationships once they know and accept who they are without apologizing for their challenges and need for supports.

Students with hidden disabilities have challenges that are inherently related to their disability. There are some disabilities that, depending on how they are expressed, will make the building and cultivation of relationships more difficult. For example, students with autism have a developmental disability that significantly affects verbal and nonverbal communication and social interaction. Students with speech-language impairments have a communication disorder that makes it difficult to clearly express themselves. Students with learning disabilities have difficulty understanding or using spoken or written language, which makes it difficult to listen, think, speak, read, write, or spell. Students may find building and maintaining relationships difficult, given these challenges, and teachers may need to provide specially designed instruction to teach students about their disabilities as well as the ability to clearly communicate about their abilities and disabilities. Even if a student with a hidden disability shows an aversion to some kinds of interpersonal connections, educators and families can expect appropriate social-communication skills while respecting a range of cognitive diversity within their classes. Gaining an awareness of the various stages of disability pride will help teachers, parents, and students increase their ability to successfully navigate relationships and their communities.

Where Are Students on the Path to Disability Pride?

Helping students assess where they are on their path to disability pride requires an understanding of the students' disability and each stage of disability pride. This includes an awareness of their strengths and challenges and how these characteristics affect their self-concept. Teachers promote the development of healthy self-concepts by helping students gain an awareness of common disability characteristics (see Chapter 1), the stages of disability pride (see Table 7.1 and Chapter 2), and how positive role models and mentoring can deepen students' awareness (see Chapter 3). Using the path to disability pride figure to help students connect experiences they have had with stages of disability pride will increase their awareness of their disability and how their choices affect their disability pride. The foundational skills that will help students find success within education and employment settings, as well as build strong relationships within their families and community, are embodied within the stages of the path to disability pride.

Teachers and parents can help students navigate through the stages of disability pride by teaching the vocabulary and providing many examples and nonexamples of people with hidden disabilities at the various stages of disability pride. Use the variety of vignettes provided throughout the chapters to generate discussions on the various stages of disability pride. Tips for Teaching 7.1 contains a summary of teaching strategies to increase students' understanding of disability pride vocabulary and stages.

Table 7.1. Stages of disability pride

Stages	Path of disability acceptance	Path of disability rejection
Challenges at school, at home, or with friends	Grief, confusion, frustration	Grief, confusion, frustration
Referral for evaluation or counseling	Searches for answers and solutions	Does not cooperate with evaluation process
Identification of hidden disability: learning disabilities, attention-deficit/hyperactivity disorder, autism spectrum disorder, speech-language, emotional disturbance	Initial sadness or relief of diagnosis to explain challenges that transcends into appreciation of additional resources and services	Denial or refusal of resources, services, medication, or modifications Frustration continues
Awareness of disability characteristics Supports and accommodations identified Positive role models with similar diagnosis identified	Acceptance: Positive role models promote optimism and hope Use of medication and/or accommodations result in achievement gains	Denial and refusal of assistance Rejection of supports Search for rebel peer group to find acceptance and a sense of belonging
Gain self-advocacy skills Increased comfort in discussing disability among peers with and without disabilities	Disability pride grows System values students for individual assets Interests, passions, and preferences unfold	Rejection of establishment's decisions Self-medication to deal with anger and frustration Leads to addiction if not controlled
Disability pride: Shares disability experiences openly and advocates for accommodations Participates in a disability community	Pays forward as mentor for others with hidden disabilities to promote disability pride	Maladaptive behavior • Underachievement • Drug use/abuse • Underemployment • Challenging relationships

Tips for Teaching

Assisting Students on Their Path to Disability Pride

- *Vocabulary.* Teach the vocabulary highlighted in Table 7.1.: 1) exploration: challenges, searching, and awareness; 2) acceptance: disclosure, supports, self-advocacy, and disability community; 3) nonacceptance: disability shame, rejection, rejecting supports, maladaptive behavior, and risk of underachievement.
- *Use peer models.* Invite peers to share their path to disability pride.
- *Discuss disability pride.* Depending on students' comfort level and stage of disability pride, discuss the following questions in one-to-one meetings or a small group of students with disabilities.
  - Can you tell me how you became aware of your disability?
  - What stages on the path to disability pride have you experienced?

(continued)

(continued)

- What stage on the path to disability pride are you at now?
- Can you tell me of a time when you felt shame?
- Can you share a time when you felt proud?
- *Complete your personal disability pride figure.* Provide students with a blank disability pride figure (see Figure 2.1) and ask them to label the stages from their own journey. Use the questions provided to prompt discussions.

ASSISTING STUDENTS ON THEIR PATH TO DISABILITY PRIDE

Research studies demonstrate that including students with disabilities in general education classrooms has benefits for students with and without disabilities (Cole, 2006; Frattura & Capper, 2006). Teachers who implement a number of the strategies suggested in Table 7.2 will promote the development of disability pride among students with disabilities. If these strategies are implemented in inclusive settings, then disability awareness will increase for students with and without hidden disabilities. Strategies are suggested for each stage of disability pride. These can be implemented in one-to-one conversations with individual students, through small-group discussions, or integrated within class discussions. Remember to leave it up to the student to disclose. Once adults or peer models disclose, students often will feel more comfortable opening up about their disability.

Table 7.2.   Strategies to assist students to develop disability pride acceptance

Incorporate guest speakers with hidden disabilities into their classes to speak about both their career and the effect their disability has had on their career choices and adult life. This educates both students with and without hidden disabilities and provides another avenue for students with disabilities to see successful adults with disabilities.

Develop a peer mentor program that matches students or adults with similar disabilities who are further along on their disability pride path with students that are beginning their journey.

Coordinate parent workshops that explain disability pride and provide testimonials from adults and students who share their disability pride journey. Invite parents to share their own journey of raising a child with disabilities.

Be an example of an inclusive teacher who accepts and values students with disabilities and maintains high expectations. Students with disabilities will begin to accept themselves when teachers (and others) accept them as people with strengths and talents. Find commonalties among the students with disabilities and their peers.

Disclosure

Allow students to talk about their strengths, interests, and successes in class. Allow them to also talk about any difficulties they may have at the moment.

Have students complete an All About Me worksheet or PowerPoint presentation that shares students' strengths, talents, hobbies, interests, goals, needs, and challenges.

Students are more alike than different. Share and celebrate both similarities and diversity among students.

(continued)

Table 7.2.   *(continued)*

Using supports and accommodations
Review the supports, services, and accommodations with students. Take a look at their individualized education programs (IEPs), and make sure that appropriate services and supports are in place. Update student supports at least annually.

If students are planning on making the transition to college, then explain the difference between supports allowed in college versus K–12 schools. For example, college students receive accommodations, but the curriculum and assessments are not modified to ensure they are appropriate. All students receive the same course material and must take the same tests. Encourage college-bound students to use the supports that will be available in college and wean them off of any modifications provided (e.g., modified tests, paraprofessionals who sit with students in class).

Encourage students to participate and engage in inclusive classes in which the general education curriculum is offered.

Self-Advocate
Encourage students to lead their own IEP meetings. Provide support and structure for their IEP participation through curricula such as the *Self-Directed IEP* (Martin, Marshall, Maxson, & Jerman, 1996) or *Whose Future Is It Anyway?* (Wehmeyer & Palmer, 2011).

Teach students how to self-advocate using scripts, role plays, and video examples (see Chapter 4).

When students want to participate in an extracurricular or curricular event, encourage them to find out more about the events and what it takes to join the event or group.

Create an environment in which students feel comfortable discussing their feelings, wants, and needs

Start a self-advocacy club for students with hidden disabilities to discuss and practice their self-advocacy skills.

Connect to the disability community
Encourage students to join various social media outlets related to their disability, including blogs, Facebook, and Twitter. Wider social networks encourage awareness and education.

Encourage students to research others who have had their disability (see Chapter 1).

Encourage wider social networks with students with and without disabilities who are supporters or ambassadors of inclusive efforts.

Become familiar with disability culture, history, and the types of disabilities represented in the classroom. The more a teacher knows about the disability, its strengths, and its limitations, the better he or she can encourage students to become the best they can be and promote an avenue to success.

Disability pride
Encourage students to research and/or present on their disability in class or in the community.

Encourage social activism and social change in ways that benefit the disability culture.

Find out when and where the state's Youth Leadership Forum is held. Help students apply for this conference. Encourage the students to reflect and/or present to a class or community about the experiences they had at the conference.

Teaching Social-Emotional Learning Skills

> "There is no more detrimental disability than one of lacking social relationships. The heartbeat of understanding and empathy allows us to share our wants, needs, expectations, and thoughts with our family, friends, and others."
> —Bill Bauer, professor with a hearing impairment

Students can gain and maintain disability pride by reducing the number of embarrassing situations by developing strong social-communication skills. Teach students to engage in conversations by actively listening and using appropriate nonverbal skills such as maintaining eye contact, respecting personal space, and using appropriate voice volume. Learning and practicing these skills with teachers, coaches, support staff, and peers while in school may prevent embarrassing situations later in life. Students with hidden disabilities and many of their typically developing peers can benefit from interventions that teach social-emotional skills to successfully interact with the people around them.

Social-emotional learning is defined as

> the process through which children and adults acquire and effectively apply the knowledge, attitudes, and skills necessary to understand and manage emotions, set and achieve positive goals, feel and show empathy for others, establish and maintain positive relationships and make responsible decisions. (Weissberg & Cascarino, 2013, p. 10)

CASEL identified five interrelated competencies, including self-awareness, self-management, social awareness, relationship skills, and responsible decision making. Students' ability to self-regulate their emotions and negotiate social interactions with teachers, classmates, support staff, and family members can have a huge impact on their performance in the classroom. Furthermore, developing social-emotional competence can have an exponential effect on the success youth encounter throughout their lives (Michaels & Hagen, 2014). Because of the importance of social-emotional competency, many schools are making a concerted effort to give their students the training needed to make positive choices to build quality relationships with others.

Teachers should observe how all their students interact in order to help them develop quality relationships. Some students, depending on their disability, may find it difficult to reach the social expectations of their teachers and peers. Actively listening, maintaining eye contact, and respecting other people's personal space are examples of social interaction skills that students with hidden disabilities may find difficult. These social skills can be taught and strengthened with support.

Bill Mentors and Advocates for Students with Disabilities

I can empathize with my students with disabilities because I have a disability myself. I knew what I needed to become successful. I aligned myself with successful people with disabilities and rarely took "no" for an answer. I also knew of the many attitudinal, physical, and social barriers that existed. I spent most of my teaching and administrative career eradicating those barriers and providing avenues for success for all people with disabilities for whom I was responsible. It is engrained in my persona to advocate for all people with disabilities. It should be a priority for educators to find mentors for children with disabilities—someone they can look up to and someone who believes in them.

Maladaptive behavior is a stage within the path of disability shame. Students who have reached this stage may engage in social activities that lead to school failure or drug or alcohol abuse. For example, students brag that they did not study for an examination, did not complete homework assignments, skip classes, or come to school drunk or high. Life skills training is a social-emotional learning intervention that can help youth in grades 6–12 avoid the pitfalls of maladaptive behavior. Life skills training teaches the social-emotional skills to build self-esteem, equip youth

> **Text Box 7.1**
>
> Examples of several of the most widely used social-emotional learning interventions, as well as their economic impact, can be found in *The Economic Value of Social and Emotional Learning*, which was released by the Center for Benefit-Cost Studies of Education at Columbia University's Teachers College (see http://cbcse.org/wordpress/wp-content/uploads/2015/02/SEL-Revised.pdf).

with the skills needed to resist peer pressure, and generally improve social-emotional competence to reduce anxiety and improve health outcomes (Belfield et al., 2015). Many mentoring programs provide opportunities for students to develop and practice social-emotional skills. See Chapter 3 for descriptions of mentoring programs to assist students in developing these skills.

Tips for Teaching

Activity to Promote Safe Conversation

Use the following activity to teach social-emotional skills to students. Role-play both positive and negative examples of nonverbal skills such as maintaining eye contact, respecting personal space, and using appropriate voice volume. Demonstrate how what you say and how you say it are critical elements of conversation.

- Place a green, yellow, and red poster board on the wall. Brainstorm appropriate versus inappropriate conversation topics with the class. Divide potential conversation starters into three categories:
    1. Appropriate topics on a green "go" poster: Where are you from? What are your favorite foods? What sports do you like?
    2. Caution topics on a yellow "caution" poster: past relationships, politics, tragic current events, family issues
    3. Inappropriate topics on a red "stop" poster: medical history, the amount of money someone makes, sexual conversation
- Role-play conversations from the previous lists, and have students model appropriate conversations using verbal and nonverbal skills. For example, demonstrate how to match the tone of voice to the message expressed. Demonstrate how the reaction will differ when different tones are used. For example, if someone uses a bored voice to give someone a compliment, then the receiver may not believe what was said, or he or she may even be insulted. Demonstrate how the inflection needs to match the message. Then, have students practice using appropriate verbal and nonverbal skills.

DISABILITY PRIDE'S IMPACT ON RELATIONSHIPS

I will be the first person to admit that my relationship history up until the point in which
I really started to get to know myself and started to get to know my disability could
probably be described as an unmitigated disaster. That is okay. Historically speaking, it
was. I was in relationships with people who did not understand me, which it is hard to
understand someone when they do not even understand themselves. Let's be honest,
that is just not a conducive situation for anyone. Everyone has their own stuff that they are
dealing with on any given day—work, school, jobs, emotions, stuff that has happened in
their past. Everyone comes to the playing field with stuff; it is just how it goes. You cannot
deal with someone else's stuff, if you are not dealing with your own stuff. (See Figure 7.1
for Andee's Path to Disability Pride concerning relationships.)
—Andee Peabody, doctoral student in Bioinfomatics

Seeing students' quality relationships with other people is one of the benefits
of helping students progress through the stages on the path of disability pride.
The quality of a person's relationships can also be a good gauge of his or her
overall self-esteem.

Communicating one's wants and needs is one of the most important skills
that must be exercised within a healthy relationship. Schultz (2014) stated that
many adults try to hide their learning disabilities from potential friends or ro-
mantic partners, including spouses, but significant others usually eventually

❶ Andee calls her past relationships unmitigated disasters
❷ No one understood the nature of her disability
❸ Andee states that she is understanding how her brain works
❹ Andee communicates to her boyfriend how she is getting to know herself; she shares her self-awareness
❺ Andee shares with others what it is like to have ADHD and verbalizes the supports needed to successfully communicate
❻ Andee learns to advocate for what works for her in both personal and professional settings

Figure 7.1. Andee's Path to Disability Pride.

Tips for Teaching

Assisting Students with Self-Disclosure in Relationships

Review the following suggestions with students who are learning to disclose in their relationships.

- *Disclose early.* It can be challenging to know when to disclose, whether in professional or personal relationships. Delaying disclosure can often cause a person with a hidden disability to feel anxious and fearful that his or her hidden disability will make itself apparent in a way that causes disability shame. Disclosing early can take away nervousness and allow a person with a hidden disability to just be him- or herself.

- *Talk about the positive.* Many people will only think about deficits when they meet someone with a disability. It can be useful for a person with a hidden disability to talk about his or her accomplishments and the supports and strategies he or she uses to be successful when disclosing to someone socially. Talking about challenges is also important, but the conversation should focus on a person's assets.

- *Practice makes perfect.* Talking to people can be difficult, particularly when dating. All self-disclosure is an art, so disclosing will become easier the more practice a person has talking with new people about him- or herself and working to build meaningful connections.

- *Build a network of support.* Family members, mentors, and friends may be willing to provide support. A person with a hidden disability must do his or her part to contribute to healthy relationships. Keep a balance between giving and taking. The individual should look for people who have accepted his or her disability the same way that the person accepted his or her disability as he or she moved toward disability pride.

- *Use supports in a relationship.* Ask and negotiate for help with challenges related to a disability. Students should contribute by using their strengths to complete tasks that they can do. If they struggle with paying the bills and their partner agrees to pay the bills, then they could volunteer to do the cooking or laundry.

find out. It is better for someone to share his or her disability with significant others in order to build trust earlier in the relationship, rather than later. Self-disclosure is one of the most critical stages of disability pride. Many students with hidden disabilities must practice with numerous teachers and peers to acquire the skills and confidence to disclose in academic, employment, and social settings. Tips that can be shared with students to help them disclose within the context of their relationships are found in Tips for Teaching.

Out to Dinner: LeDerick's Wife Supports Him in Gaining a Distraction-Free Table

I have reached an age in which I do not have to worry about a teacher suddenly asking me to read out loud, and I have learned to avoid professional situations that would be made difficult due to my learning disability. My learning disability makes itself known when my wife and I go out to dinner. Restaurants are full of distractions. Sports bars and large chain restaurants tend to have walls covered with oddball objects and large televisions that all scream for my attention, and even quiet restaurants have tables full of people talking or large windows looking out at a constantly changing streetscape. The part of my brain that is drawn to movement and sound is often in overload when I walk into a restaurant. I allow my senses to chase after every side conversation, flickering screen, and bouncing child when I am alone or out with my brother, but when I am on a date with my wife, I need to treat our conversation as if I was taking a math quiz. I often need a few accommodations in order to perform at my best, just like a math quiz.

Because I disclosed to my wife while we were dating, she is aware of my challenges and helps to support my needs. So, when we find ourselves in a restaurant and we make our way to our table, the first thing she will say to me is, "Are you happy with your seat?" This question is a code that we have developed and it can be translated to, "Are you going to be distracted by that television?" "Would you like to move to a more quiet area?" "Would you like to take my seat so you are not facing the window?" My wife's inquiry does two very important things—it reminds me to pay attention to our conversation, and it gives me permission to take control of my environment before it starts to take control of me.

Gaining Professional Support Through Mental Health Resources

Students' unmet mental health needs interfere with learning and developing healthy relationships. Approximately 20% of children and youth demonstrate a need for mental health services, although only one third of these children receive services (Barrett, Eber, & Weist, 2013). Many adults with hidden disabilities are living with a host of feelings that are directly or indirectly related to disability shame. Treatment from a mental health professional is one of the most effective supports a person can utilize to help him or her reconcile feelings of shame, nervousness, or anxiety. Whether it is therapy with a counselor or psychologist, the use of medication prescribed by a psychiatrist, or another form of support, students may need assistance to help them manage their feelings to gain and maintain disability pride.

Teachers should work with their school counselors or social workers when they are concerned about students' mental health. School counselors are trained on how to identify, assist, and refer students for mental health counseling, when needed. Consider talking to the school counselor if an elementary student appears excessively withdrawn and depressed, does not respond to special attention and attempts to draw him or her out, or exhibits extreme signs of anxiety, such as excessive clinging, irritability, or eating or sleeping problems for more than 1 month (American School Counselor Association, 2014). Talk to the high school counselor or special education supervisor if an older student exhibits these or similar behaviors:

- Is disoriented (e.g., if he or she is unable to give his or her own name, town, and the date)

- Is severely depressed and withdrawn

- Excessively uses drugs or alcohol

- Is unable to care for him- or herself (e.g., does not eat, drink, bathe, or change clothes)

- Reports feeling hopeless and out-of-control or fears hurting self or others.

Teachers often spend more time with their students than any other professional, and sometimes more time than parents have to spend with their children. An aware and supportive teacher can assist students on their path to disability pride by learning about the various types of hidden disabilities and the number of successful adults who have similar disabilities. Helping students gain an asset-based approach to learning that builds on their strengths while compensating for their challenges is an essential step to preparing students for their transition to college and careers.

CONCLUSION

The journey to disability pride may take years for some students, whereas others may gain a positive and asset-based understanding of their disability within a matter of months. The coauthors know by experience, however, that maintaining disability pride can be challenging when individuals continue to test and stretch their limits with professional and personal goals. Sometimes those feelings of self-doubt and fear return when people are overcommitted, tired, or challenged. Gaining an understanding of one's own path of disability pride helps minimize disability shame. Building honest and authentic relationships within disability communities, professional networks, and families is instrumental in providing the support needed to make the transition back on the path of disability pride. It is only with disability pride that individuals are able to dare to dream and meet their potential.

References

Achieve. (n.d.). *What is college- and career-ready?* Washington, DC: Author.

American School Counselor Association. (2014). *Mindsets & behaviors for student success: K-12 college and career readiness standards for every student.* Alexandria, VA: Author.

Association on Higher Education and Disability. (2012). Supporting accommodation requests: Guidance on documentation practices, April, 2012. Hunterville, NC: author.

Alston, R.J., Bell, T.J., & Hampton, J.L. (2002). Learning disability and career entry into the sciences: a critical analysis of attitudinal factors. *Journal of Career Development, 28(4),* 263–275.

Anderson-Inman, L., & Horney, M.A. (2007). Supported eText: Assistive technology through text transformations, *Reading Research Quarterly,* 42:153–160.

Applebee, A.N., Langer, J.A., Nystrand, M., & Gamoran, A. (2003). Discussion-based approaches to developing understanding: Classroom instruction and student performance in middle and high school English. *American Educational Research Journal, 40(3),* 685–730.

Arnold, L.E. (2004). *A family's guide to attention-deficit/hyperactivity disorder.* Newtown, PA: Handbooks in Health Care.

Associated Press. (2005). *U.S. college drop-out rate sparks concern.* Retrieved from http://www.nbcnews.com/id/10053859/ns/us_news-education/t/us-college-drop-out-rate-sparks-concern/#.VpkjsfkrKUk

Association for Career and Technical Education. (2010). What is "career ready?" Alexandria, VA: Author.

Autor, D. (2014). Skills, education and the rise of earnings inequality among the other 99 percent. *Science 23,* 843–851.

Axelrod, E., Campbell, G., & Holt, T. (2005). *The best practices guide in mentoring youth with disabilities.* Boston, MA: Partners for Youth with Disabilities.

Baer, R.M., Flexer, R.W., Beck, S., Amstutz, N., Hoffman, L., Brothers, J., Stelzer, D., & Zechman, C. (2003). A collaborative follow-up study on transition service utilization and post-school outcomes. *Career Development for Exceptional Individuals, 26,* 7–25.

Baio, J. (2014). *Prevalence of autism spectrum disorder among children aged 8 years—autism and developmental disabilities monitoring network, 11 sites, United States, 2010.* Atlanta: GA: Center for Disease Control and Prevention, 63, 1–21. SS02. Retrieved from http://www.cdc.gov/mmwr/preview/mmwrhtml/ss6302a1.htm on Dec 17, 2015.

Balcazar, Y., Bradford, B., & Fawcett, S. (1988). Common concerns of disabled Americans: Issues and options, In M. Nagler (Ed.). *Perspectives on disability* (pp. 3–12). Palo Alto, CA: Health Markets Research.

Barnard-Brak, L., & Sulak, T.N. (2010). Online versus face-to-face accommodations among college students with disabilities. *American Journal of Distance Education, 24,* 81–91.

Barrett, S., Eber, L., & Weist, M. (Eds). (2013). *Advancing education effectiveness: Interconnecting school mental health and school-wide positive behavior support.* Retrieved from http://www.pbis.org/common/pbisresources/publications/Final-Monograph.pdf

Battistich, V., Schaps, E., & Wilson, N. (2004). Effects of an elementary school intervention on students' "connectedness" to school and social adjustment during middle school. *The Journal of Primary Prevention, 24(3),* 243–262.

Belfield, C., Bowden, B., Klapp, A., Levin, H., Shand, R., & Zander, S. (2015). *The economic value of social and emotional learning.* New York, NY: Columbia University.

Benz, M., Lindstrom, L., & Yovnoff, P. (2000). Improving graduation and employment outcomes of students with disabilities: Predictive factors and student perspectives. *Exceptional Children, 66(4),* 509–529.

Berry, D., & O'Conner, E. (2009). Behavioral risk, teacher-child relationships, and social skill development across middle childhood: A child-by environment analysis of change. *Journal of Applied Developmental Psychology, 31(1),* 1–14.

Blackorby, J., Hancock, G.R., & Siegel, S. (1993). *Human capital and structural explanations of post-school success for youth with disabilities: A latent variable exploration of the National Longitudinal Transition Study.* Menlo Park, CA: SRI International.

Bolt, S.E., & Thurlow, M.L. (2004). Five of the most frequently allowed testing accommodations in state policy: Synthesis of research. *Remedial and Special Education, 25*(3), 141–152.

Bridgeland, J.M., Dilulio J.J., & Morison K.B. (2006). *The silent epidemic: Perspectives of high school dropouts.* Retrieved from http://www.saanys.org/uploads/content/TheSilent Epidemic-ExecSum.pdf

Brown, S. E. (2003). Movie stars and sensuous scars: Essays on the journey from disability shame to disability pride. New York, NY: People with Disabilities Press , pp. 80–81.

Brown, S.E. (2011). *Disability culture: Beginnings. A fact sheet.* Retrieved from http://www .instituteondisabilityculture.org

Bruce, M., & Bridgeland, J. (2014). *The mentoring effect: Young people's perspectives on the outcomes and availability of mentoring.* Washington, DC: Civic Enterprises with Hart Research Associates for MENTOR: The National Mentoring Partnership.

Brune, J.A., & Wilson, D.J. (2013). *Disability and passing: Blurring the lines of identity.* Philadelphia, PA: Temple University Press.

Bulgren, J.A., Marquis, J.G., Deshler, D.D., Lenz, B.K., & Schumaker, J.B. (2013). The use and effectiveness of a question exploration routine in secondary level English language arts classrooms. *Learning Disabilities Research and Practice, 28*(4), 156–169.

Burgstahler, S. (2003). The role of technology in preparing youth with disabilities for postsecondary education and employment. *Journal of Special Education Technology, 18,* 7–19.

Burgstahler, S., & Chang, C. (2007). Promising interventions for promoting STEM fields to students who have disabilities. *Review of Disability Studies: An International Journal, 5*(2), 29–47.

Burgstahler, S., & Cronheim, D. (2001). Supporting peer-peer and mentor-protégé relationships on the Internet. *Journal of Research on Technology in Education, 34*(1), 59–74.

Burgstahler, S., Moore, E., & Crawford, L. (2011). Report of the AccessSTEM/ Access Computing/DO-IT longitudinal transition study (ALTS). Retrieved from http:// washington.edu/doit/Stem/tracking3.html

Butterworth, J., Hagner, D., Kiernan, W., & Schalock, R. (1996). Natural supports in the workplace: Defining an agenda for research and practice. *Journal of The Association for Persons with Severe Handicaps, 21*(3), 103–113.

Cameron, J. (1982). *For all that has been: Time to live and time to die.* New York, NY: Macmillan.

Cameto, R., Levine, P., & Wagner, M. (2004). *Transition planning for students with disabilities: A special topic report from the National Longitudinal Transition Study–2.* Menlo Park, CA: SRI International.

Cantley, P., Little, K., & Martin, J. (2010). *Me! Lessons for teaching self awareness and self advocacy version 2.0.* Norman, OK: Zarrow Center for Learning Enrichment.

Carter, E.W., Austin, D., & Trainor, A.A. (2011). Factors associated with the early work experiences of adolescents with severe disabilities. *Intellectual and Developmental Disabilities, 49,* 233–247.

Carter, E.W., Trainor, A., Ownes, L., Sweden, B., & Sun, Y. (2010). Self-determination prospects of youth with high incidence disabilities: Divergent perspectives and related factors. *Journal of Emotional and Behavioral Disorders, 18,* 67-81. Doi: 10.1177/1063426609332605

Cho, E, Roberts, G.J., Capin, P., Roberts G., Miciak, J., & Vaughn, S. (2015). Cognitive attributes, attention and self-efficacy of adequate and inadequate responders in a fourth grade reading intervention. *Learning Disabilities Research & Practice, 30*(4), 159–170.

Clifton, D.O., Anderson, E., & Schrieinger, L.A. (2006). *Strengths quest: Discover and develop your strengths in academics, career and beyond.* New York, NY: Gallup Press.

Cole, C. (2006). *Closing the achievement gap series: Part III. What is the impact of NCLB on the inclusion of students with disabilities?* Bloomington, IN: Center for Evaluation and Education Policy.

Collaborative for Academic, Social, and Emotional Learning. (2015). *The 2015 CASEL guide: Effective social and emotional learning programs: Middle and high school edition.* Chicago, IL: Author.

Coppola, G. (2007, December 12). *Why dyslexics make great entrepreneurs.* Retrieved from http://www.bloomberg.com/bw/stories/2007-12-12/why-dyslexics-make-great-entrepreneursbusinessweek-business-news-stock-market-and-financial-advice

Cosier, M., Causton-Theoharis, J., & Theoharis, G. (2013). Does access matter? Time in general education and achievement for students with disabilities. *Remedial and Special Education, 34*(6), 323–332.

Crawford, P. (2012). *Experts ponder the meaning of increases in inclusion for special education students.* Retrieved from www.publicconsultinggroup.com

Diedrich, D. (2014). I'm a scientist with learning disabilities and that's okay! http://www.huffingtonpost.com/collin-diedrich/im-a-scientist-with-learn_b_5517718.html.

Diener, E. (2000). Subjective well-being: The science of happiness and a proposal for a national index. *American Psychologist, 55*(1), 34–43.

Doren, B. (2014). *Parental expectations for students with disabilities.* Retrieved from www.wcer.wisc.edu

Dubois, D.L., & Karcher, M.J. (Eds). (2013). *Handbook on youth mentoring.* Thousand Oaks, CA: Sage Publications.

Dukes III, L.L., Koorland, M.A., & Scott, S.S. (2009). Making blended instruction better: Integrating universal design for instruction principles in course design and delivery. *Action in Teacher Education, 31*(1), 38–48.

Durlofsky, P. (2014). *Can too much social media cause depression?* Retrieved from www.mainlinetoday.com

Dusenbury, L. (2014). What are the key features of high-quality standards for SEL? Chicago, IL: Collaborative for Academic, Social, and Emotional Learning.

Eby, L.T., Hoffman, B., Sauer, J. B., Baldwin, S., Kinkade, K.M., Maher, C. P., Curtis, S., Allen, T.D., Baranik, L.E., & Morrison, M.A. (2012). An interdisciplinary meta-analysis of the potential antecedents, correlates and consequences of protégé perceptions of mentoring. *Psychological Bulletin, 139*(2), 441–476.

Education for All Handicapped Children Act of 1975, PL 94-142, 20 U.S.C. §§ 1400 *et seq.*

Effective practices matrix (2015). Charlotte, NC: University of North Carolina at Charlotte, National Technical Assistance Center on Transition. Retrieved on December 29, 2015 from *http://www.transitionta.org/sites/default/files/effectivepractices/EP_Matrix_print_12_4_2015.pdf*

Ellis, D. (2002). *Becoming a master student* (10th ed.). New York, NY: Houghton Mifflin.

Evidence based practices for transition youth. (n.d.). Columbus, OH: Ohio Employment First. Retrieved on December 29, 2015 from http://www.ohioemploymentfirst.org/up_doc/Evidence_Based_Practices_for_Transition_Youth.pdf

Evidence-based predictors for post school success. (n.d.). Columbus, OH: Ohio Employment First. Retrieved on December 29, 2015 from http://www.ohioemploymentfirst.org/up_doc/Evidence_Based_Predictors_for_Post_school_Success3_25_15.pdf

Eye to Eye Strategic Business Plan. (2014). New York, NY: Eye to Eye National office.

Faggella-Luby, M., Lombardi, A., Lalor, A., & Dukes, L.L. (2015). Methodological trends in disability and higher education research: A historical analysis of the *Journal of Postsecondary Education and Disability. Journal of Postsecondary Education and Disability, 27*(4), 357–368.

Field, S., & Hoffman, A. (1994). Development of a model for self-determination. *Career Development for Exceptional Individuals, 17,* 159–169.

Field, S., Martin, J.E., Miller, R., Ward, M.J., & Wehmeyer, M.L. (1998). *A practical guide to teaching self-determination.* Reston, VA: Council for Exceptional Children.

Fitzgibbon, C., & O'Connor, B. (2002). *Adult dyslexia: A guide for the workplace.* New York, NY: Wiley.

Flink, D. (2014). *Thinking differently: An inspiring guide for parents of children with learning disabilities.* New York, NY: HarperCollins.

Frattura, E., & Capper, C. (2006). Segregated programs versus integrated comprehensive service delivery for all learners. Assessing the differences. *Remedial and Special Education, 27*(6), 355–364.

Getzel, E.E., & Webb, K.W. (2012). Transition to postsecondary education. In M.L. Wehmeyer & K.W. Webb (Eds.), *Handbook of adolescent transition education for youth with disabilities* (pp. 295–311). New York, NY: Routledge Taylor and Francis Group.

Ghosh, R., & Reio, T.G. (2013). Career benefits associated with mentoring for mentors: A meta-analysis. *Journal of Vocational Behavior, 83,* 106–116.

Goldberg R. J., Higgins E. L., Raskind M. H., & Herman K. L. (2003). Predictors of success in individuals with learning disabilities: A qualitative analysis of a 20-year longitudinal study. *Learning Disabilities Research & Practice, 18,* 222–236. doi:10.1111/1540-5826.00077

Grandin, T. (2006). *Thinking in pictures: My life with autism.* New York, NY: Vintage Books.

Grandin, T. (2010, February). *Temple Grandin: The world needs all kinds of minds* [Video file]. Retrieved from http://www.ted.com/talks/temple_grandin_the_world_needs_all_kinds_of_minds

Gregory, A., & Ripski, M. (2008). Adolescent trust in teachers: Implications for behavior in the high school classroom. *School Psychology Review, 37*(3), 337–335.

Grindstaff, J. (2012). *Developing positive character strengths.* Retrieved from www.autismdigest.com

Grigal, M., & Hart, D. (2010). Think college! Postsecondary education options for students with intellectual disabilities. Baltimore, MD: Paul H. Brookes Publishing Co.

Habib, D. (2013, July). *Who cares about Kelsey? A documentary.* Retrieved from whocaresaboutkelsey.com

Halpern, A.S., Herr, C.M., Wolf, N.K., Lawson, J.D., Doren, B., & Johnson, M.D. (1995). *NEXT S.T.E.P.: Student transition and educational planning. Teacher manual.* Eugene, OR: University of Oregon.

Halpern, A.S., Yovanoff, P., Doren, B., & Benz, M.R. (1995). Predicting participation in postsecondary education for school leavers with disabilities. *Exceptional Children, 62,* 151–164.

Heal, L.W., & Rusch, F.R. (1995). Predicting employment for students who leave special education high school programs. *Exceptional Children, 61,* 472–487.

Henderson, B. (2011). *The blind advantage: How going blind made me a stronger principal and how including children with disabilities made our school better for everyone.* Cambridge, MA: Harvard University Press.

Herrera, C., Vang, Z., & Gale, L.Y. (2002). *Group mentoring: A study of mentoring groups in three programs.* San Francisco, CA: Public/Private Ventures.

Horne, L. (2011). *Dare to dream.* Retrieved from http://www.lederick.com

Individuals with Disabilities Education Act (IDEA) of 1990, PL 101-76, 20 U.S.C. §§ 1400 *et seq.*

Individuals with Disabilities Education Improvement Act (IDEA) of 2004, PL 108-446, 20 U.S.C. §§ 1400 *et seq.*

Izzo, M.V., Earley, J.A., McArrell, B., & Yurick, A.L. (2014). *The Ohio State University Nisonger Center e-mentoring program replication guide* (2nd ed.). Retrieved from http://go.osu.edu/ementoring.

Izzo, M.V., & Lamb, P. (2003). Developing self-determination through career development activities: Implications for vocational rehabilitation counselors. *Journal of Vocational Rehabilitation, 19*(2), 71–78.

Izzo, M.V., Earley, J., McArrell, B, & Yurick, A.L. (2012). *E-mentoring program: Improving achievement and transition outcomes.* Columbus, OH: Ohio State University Nisonger Center.

Izzo, M.V., Murray, A.J., Day, K., Yurick, A.L., & Ransom, S. (2014). *E-mentoring program* (2nd ed.). Retrieved from http://go.osu.edu/ementoring

Izzo, M.V., Murray, A., Priest, S., & McArrell, B. (2011). Using student learning communities to recruit STEM students with disabilities. *Journal of Postsecondary Education and Disability, 24*(4), 301–316.

Izzo, M.V., Rissing, S.W., Andersen, C., Nasar, J.L., & Lissner, L.S. (2011). Universal design for learning in the college classroom. In W.F.E. Preiser & K.H. Smith (Eds.), *Universal design handbook* (2nd ed., pp. 31–39). New York, NY: McGraw-Hill.

Izzo, M.V., Yurick, A., Nagaraja, H.N., & Novak, J.A. (2010). Effects of a 21st-century curriculum on students' information technology and transition skills. *Career Development for Exceptional Individuals, 33*(2), 95–105.

James, D.J., & Glaze, L.E. (2006). *Mental health problems of prison and jail inmates.* Washington, DC: U.S Department of Justice, Office of Justice Programs.

Ju, S., Zhang, D., & Pacha, J. (2012). Employability skills valued by employers as important for entry-level employees with and without disabilities. Retrieved from http://www.whocaresaboutkelsey.com/the-issues/statistics

Kalambouka, A., Farrell, P., & Dyson, A. (2007). The impact of placing pupils with special educational needs in mainstream schools on the achievement of their peers. *Educational Research, 49*(4) 365–382.

Kamil, M.L., Borman, G.D., Dole, J., Kral, C.C., Salinger, T., & Torgesen, J. (2008). *Improving adolescent literacy: Effective classroom and intervention practices: A practice guide* (NCEE #2008-4027). Washington, DC: National Center for Education Evaluation and Regional Assistance, Institute of Education Sciences, U.S. Department of Education.

Karpur, C.H., Caproni, & Sterner, (2005). An overview of the TIP model. Retrieved from http://tipstars.org/OverviewofTIPModel.aspx

Kaufmann, B., & Stuart, C. (2007). *Road to self-sufficiency: A guide to entrepreneurship for youth with disabilities.* Washington, DC: National Collaborative on Workforce and Disability for Youth, Institute for Educational Leadership.

Kennedy, P.J., & Fried, S., (2015). *A common struggle: A personal journey through the past and future of mental illness and addiction.* New York, NY: Blue Rider Press.

Kluth, P. (2010). *You're going to love this kid!* Baltimore, MD: Paul H. Brookes Publishing Co.

Kochhar-Bryant, C., Bassett, D., & Webb, K. (2009). *Transition to postsecondary education for students with disabilities.* Thousand Oaks, CA: Corwin Press.

Koerth-Baker, M. (2013, October 15). *The not-so-hidden cause behind the ADHD epidemic.* Retrieved from http://www.nytimes.com/2013/10/20/magazine/the-not-so-hidden-cause-behind-the-adhd-epidemic.html?_r=0.

Kohler, P. (1996). *Taxonomy for transition programming.* Champaign, IL: University of Illinois.

Koplewicz, H.S. (2014). Foreward. In D. Flink (Ed.), *Thinking differently: An inspiring guide for parents of children with learning disabilities* (pp. vii–x). New York, NY: HarperCollins.

Larson, K.C. (2015). *Rosemary: The hidden Kennedy daughter.* New York, NY: Houghton Mifflin Harcourt.

Larsson, H., Chang, Z., D'Onofrio M., & Lichtenstein P. (2014). The heritability of clinically diagnosed attention deficit hyperactivity disorder across the lifespan. *Psychological Medicine, 44*(10), 2223–2229. Doi: 10.1017/S00332917113002493.

Leddy, M.H. (2010). Technology to advance high school and undergraduate students with disabilities in science, technology, engineering, and mathematics. *Journal of Special Education and Technology, 25*(3), 3–8.

Lee, A. (2002). A comparison of postsecondary science, technology, engineering, and mathematics (STEP) enrollments for students with and without disabilities. *Career Development for Exceptional Individuals, 34,* 272–282.

Lee, I.H., Rojewski, J.W., Gregg, N., & Jeong, S. (2015). Postsecondary education persistence of adolescents with specific learning disabilities or emotional/behavioral disorders. *Journal of Special Education, 49,* 77–88.

Lee, J., Grigg, W., and Donahue, P. (2007). *The Nation's Report Card: Reading 2007* (NCES 2007-496). National Center for Education Statistics, Institute of Education Sciences, U.S. Department of Education, Washington, D.C.

Leong, C.K. (1992). Enhancing reading comprehension with text-to-speech (DECtalk) computer system. *Reading and Writing: An Interdisciplinary Journal, 4,* 205–217.

Leonhardt, D. (2014, May 27). *Is college worth it? Clearly, new data shows.* Retrieved from http://www.nytimes.com/2014/05/27/upshot/is-college-worth-it-clearly-new-data-say.html.

Levinson, E.M., & Palmer, E.J. (2005). Preparing students with disabilities for school-to-work transition and postschool Life. *Principal Leadership, 5*(8), 11–15.

Logan, J. (2009). *Dyslexic entrepreneurs: The incidence: Their coping strategies and their business skills.* New York, NY: Wiley.

Lundberg, I., & Olofsson, A. (1993). Can computer speech support reading comprehension? *Computers in Human Behavior, 9,* 282–293.

Madaus, J.W., Banerjee, M., & Hamblet, E.C. (2010). Learning disability documentation decision making at the postsecondary level. *Career Development for Exceptional Individuals, 33,* 68–79.

Madaus, J.W., Lalor, A.R., Gelbar, N., & Kowitt, J.S. (2014). The Journal of Postsecondary Education and Disability: From past to present. *Journal of Postsecondary Education and Disability, 27*(4), 347–368.

Martin, J.E., Marshall, L.H., Maxson, L.M., & Jerman, P.L. (1996) *The self-directed IEP* (2nd ed.). Longmont, CO: Sopris West Educational Services.

Martin, J.E., van Dycke, J.L., Christensen, W.R., Greene, B.A., Gardner, J.E., & Lovett, D.L. (2006). Increasing student participation in IEP meetings: Establishing the self-directed IEP as an evidenced-based practice. *Exceptional Children, 72,* 299–317.

May, A.L., & Stone, C. A. (2010). Stereotypes of individuals with learning disabilities: Views of college students with and without learning disabilities. *Journal of Learning Disabilities, 43,* 483–499.

Mazzotti, V.L., Rowe, D.A., Cameto, R., Test, D.W., & Morningstar, M.E. (2013). Identifying and promoting transition evidence-based practices and predictors of success: A position paper of the division of career development and transition. *Career Development and Transition for Exceptional Individuals, 36,* 140–151.

McConnell, A.E., Martin, J.E., Juan, C.Y., Hennessey, M.N., Terry, R.A., el-Kazimi, N.A.,… Willis, D.M. (2012). Identifying nonacademic behaviors associated with post-school employment and education. *Career Development and Transition for Exceptional Individuals, 36,* 174–187.

McIntosh, K., Horner, R.H., Chard, D.J., Boland, J., & Good III, R.H. (2006). The use of treading and behavior screening measures to predict nonresponse to school-wide positive behavior support: A longitudinal analysis. *School Psychology Review, 34,* 275–291.

McLaughlin, M.J. (2012). Access for all: Six principles for principals to consider in implementing CCSS for students with disabilities. *Principal.* Retrieved from http://www.naesp .org/sites/default/files/McLaughlin_2012.pdf

Meinzen, S., & Meinzen, S. (2013). *The organic entrepreneur economy: The entrepreneur and community infrastructures that fix and grow economies immediately.* Kansas City, MO: Evis Consulting.

Mellard, D.F., Fall, E.E., & Woods, K.L. (2013). Relation and interactions among reading fluency and competence for adult education learners. *Learning Disabilities Research and Practice, 28,* 70–80. doi:10.1111/ldrp.12008

Mentor: National Mentoring Partnership. (2005). *How to build a successful mentoring program using the elements of effective practice.* Retrieved from www.mentoring.org/ program_resources/elements_and_toolkits

Michaels, C., & Hagen, E. (2014). *Social and emotional learning: Implications for enhancing children's mental health.* Minneapolis, MN: University of Minnesota Extension.

Miranda, A., Tarraga, R., Fernandez, M.I., Colomer, C., & Pastor, G. (2015). Parenting stress in families of children with autism spectrum disorder and ADHD. *Exceptional Children 82*(1) 81–95.

Moreno, M.A., Jelenchick, L.A., & Becker, T. (2011). Feeling bad on Facebook: Depression disclosures by college students on a social networking site. *Depress Anxiety, 28*(6) 447–455.

Murawski, W.W., & Swanson, H.L. (2001). A meta-analysis of co-teaching research: Where are the data. *Remedial and Special Education, 22,* 258–267.

National Center for Education Statistics. (2009). *Number and percentage distribution of students enrolled in postsecondary education institutions, by level, disability status, and selected student and characteristics: 2003-2004–2007-2008.* Retrieved from http://nces.ed.gov/programs/ digest/d09/tables/dt09_231.asp

National Center for Learning Disabilities, (nd). *Executive Function 101.* Retrieved from https://www.understood.org/en/learning-attention-issues/child-learning-disabilities/ executive-functioning-issues/ebook-executive-function-101

National Collaborative for Workforce and Disability for Youth. (2009). *The 411 on disability disclosure: A workbook for families, educators, youth service professionals (YSPs) and other adult allies who care about youth with disabilities.* Washington, DC: Institute for Educational Leadership.

National Council on Disability. (2011). *Rising expectations: The developmental disabilities act revisited.* Washington, DC: National Council on Disability.

National Institute of Mental Health. (2013). *Attention deficit/hyperactivity disorder.* Bethesda, MD: National Institute of Mental Health, NIH Publication No. TR 13-3572.

Nelson, J.R., Benner, G.J., Neill, S., & Stage, S.A. (2006). Interrelationships among language skills, externalizing behavior, and academic fluency and their impact on the academic skills of students with EBD. *Journal of Emotional and Behavioral Disorders, 14,* 209–216.

Nelson, L.L. (2014). *Design and deliver: Planning and teaching using universal design for learning.* Baltimore, MD: Paul H. Brookes Publishing Co.

Newman, L.A., & Madaus, J.W. (2015). Reported accommodations and supports provided to secondary and postsecondary students with disabilities: National perspectives. *Career Development and Transition for Exceptional Individuals, 38,* 173–181.

Newman, L., Madaus, J., & Javitz, H. (2015). *Impact of postsecondary supports on college completion for students with learning disabilities and those who are deaf or hard of hearing. Propensity modeling analyses: A quasi-experimental design findings from the National Longitudinal Transition Study–2 (NLTS–2).* Poster presented at the Council for Exceptional Children Convention, San Diego, CA.

Newman, L., Wagner, M., Cameto, R., & Knokey, A.M. (2009, April). *The post-high school outcomes of youth with disabilities up to 4 years after high school: A report of findings from the National Longitudinal Transition Study–2 (NLST–2).* Retrieved from www.nlts2.org/reports/2009_04/nlts2_report_2009_04_complete.pdf

Newman, L., Wagner, M., Knokey, A.-M., Marder, C., Nagle, K., Shaver, D., Schwarting, M. (2011). *The post-high school outcomes of young adults with disabilities up to 8 years after high school: A report from the National Longitudinal Transition Study–2 (NLTS–2).* Menlo Park, CA: SRI International.

No Child Left Behind Act of 2001, PL 107-110, 115 Stat. 1425, 20 U.S.C. §§ 6301 *et seq.*

National Secondary Transition Technical Assistance Center. (nd). *Predictors of post-school success.* Retrieved from http://www.nsttac.org/content/predictors-post-school-success

Nurmi, J.E., Salmela-Aro, K., & Koivisto, P. (2002). Goal importance and related achievement beliefs and emotions during the transition from vocational school to work: Antecedents and consequences. *Journal of Vocational Behavior, 60,* 241–261.

Ohio Center for Autism and Low Incidence. (2015). *Autism Internet modules.* Columbus: OH. Author. Retrieved from http://www.autisminternetmodules.org/ on December 19, 2015.

Ohio Department of Education. (2004). *High-quality high schools: Preparing all students for success in postsecondary education, careers and citizenship.* Columbus, OH: author. Retrieved from ftp://ftp.ode.state.oh.us/Publication/High%20Quality%20High%20Schools.2004.pdf

Ohio Department of Jobs and Family Services. Ohio Means Jobs. (n.d.). Retrieved from https://jobseeker.ohiomeansjobs.monster.com/

Ohio's State Board of Education Task Force on Quality High Schools. (2004). *High quality high schools: Preparing all students for success in postsecondary education, careers and citizenship.* Columbus, OH: Ohio Department of Education.

OSEP Technical Assistance Center on Positive Behavioral Interventions and Supports (October 2015). *Positive Behavioral Interventions and Supports (PBIS) Implementation Blueprint: Part 1- Foundations and Supporting Information.* Eugene, OR: University of Oregon. Retrieved from www.pbis.org.

Parr, M. (2013). Text-to-speech technology as inclusive reading practice: Changing perspectives, overcoming barriers. *Learning Landscapes, 6,* 303–322.

Planty, M., Hussar, W., Snyder, T., Kena, G., Kewalramani, A., Kemp, J., & Dinkes, R. (2009). *The condition of education 2009* (NCES 2009-081). Washington, DC: National Center for Education Statistics, Institute of Education Sciences, U.S. Department of Education.

Powers, L.E., Geenen, S., Powers, J., Pommier-Satya, S., Turner, A., Dalton, L., & Swank, P. (2012). My life: Effects of a longitudinal, randomized study of self-determination enhancement on the transition outcomes of youth in foster care and special education. *Children and Youth Services Review, 34,* 2179–2187.

McKlin, T., Engelman, S., & Ranade, N. (2013). *Ohio's STEM Ability Alliance Summative Evaluation Report.* Atlanta: GA: The Findings Group, LLC.

Repetto J.B., & Andrews, W.D. (2012). Career development and vocational instruction. In M.L. Wehmeyer & K.W. Webb (Eds.), *Handbook of adolescent transition education for youth with disabilities* (pp. 156–170). New York, NY: Routledge.

Rimm-Kaufman, S. (2014). *Improving students' relationships with teachers to provide essential support for learning.* Retrieved from http://www.apa.org/education/k12/relationships.aspx

Rose, D.H., & Meyers, A. (2002). *Every student in the digital age: Universal design for learning.* Alexandria, VA: Association for Supervision and Curriculum Development.

Safren, S.A., Sprich, S., Mimiaga, M.J., Surman, C., Knouse, L., Groves, M., & Otto, M.W. (2010). Cognitive-behavioral therapy vs. relaxation with educational support for medication treated adults with ADHD and persistent symptoms: A randomized controlled trial. *Journal of the American Medical Association, 305*(8), 875–880.

Sailor, W. (2014). Advances in schoolwide inclusive school reform. *Remedial and Special Education, Online First.* doi:10.1177/0741932514555021

Sanford, C., Newman, L., Wagner, M., Cameto, R., Knokey, A.-M., & Shaver, D. (2011). *The post-high school outcomes of young adults with disabilities up to 6 years after high school: Key findings from the National Longitudinal Transition Study–2 (NLTS–2).* Menlo Park, CA: SRI International.

Saylor, T. (2013, November). *My journey to self-determination.* Retrieved from www.dcdt.org/DCDT-Program-2013-FINAL.pdf

Schultz, J.J. (2014). *Managing social-emotional issues of adults with learning disabilities.* Pittsburgh, PA: Learning Disabilities Association of America.

Schurgin-O'Keeffe, G., & Clarke-Pearson, K. (2011). Clinical report: The impact of social media on children, adolescents, and families. *American Academy of Pediatrics, 127*(4), 800–804.

Schwarz, A. (2013). *The selling of attention deficit disorder.* Retrieved from http://www.nytimes.com/2013/12/15/health/the-selling-of-attention-deficit-disorder.html

Sevo, R. (2011). Basics about disabilities and science and engineering education. Atlanta, GA. Under the direction of Robert L. Todd, Center for Assistive Technology and Environmental Access, Georgia Institute of Technology.

Shandra, C.L., & Hogan, D.P. (2008). School-to-work program participation and the post-high school employment of young adults with disabilities. *Journal of Vocational Rehabilitation, 29,* 117–130.

Shaw, S.F., Madaus, J.W., & Dukes III, L.L. (2010). *Preparing students with disabilities for college success: A practical guide to transition planning.* Baltimore, MD: Paul H. Brookes Publishing Co.

Sheff, D. (2013). *Clean: Overcoming addiction and ending America's greatest tragedy.* Boston, MA: Houghton Mifflin.

Shifrer, D. (2013). Stigma of a label: Educational expectations for high school students labeled with learning disabilities. *Journal of Health and Social Behavior, 54*(4), 462–480.

Shogren, K.A. (2013). *Self-determination and transition planning.* Baltimore, MD: Paul H. Brookes Publishing Co.

Shogren, K.A., Wehmeyer, M.L., Palmer, S.B., Rifenback, G.G., & Little, T.D. (2015). Relationship between self-determination and post-school outcomes for youth with disabilities, *Journal of Special Education, 48,* 256–267.

Silver-Pacuilla, H., Ruedel, K., & Mistrett, S. (2004). *A review of technology-based approaches for reading instruction: Tools for researchers and vendors.* Washington, DC: American Institute for Research.

Sipe, C.L. & Roder, L.E. (1999). *Mentoring in school-age children: A classification of programs.* Philadelphia, PA: Public/Private Ventures.

Sitlington, P.L., & Clark, G.M. (2006). *Transition education and services for students with disabilities* (4th ed.). Boston, MA: Pearson Education.

Smart, J. (2001). *Disability, society and the individual.* Austin, TX: PRO-ED.

Snow, K. (n.d.). *To ensure inclusion, freedom, and respect for people with disabilities, we must use people first language.* Retrieved from http://www.disabilityisnatural.com/

Solanto, M.V. (2011). *Cognitive-behavioral therapy for adult ADHD: Targeting executive function.* New York, NY: Guilford Press.

Solanto, M.V., Marks, D.J., Wasserstein, J., Mitchell, K., Abikoff, H., Alvir, J.M., & Kofman, M.D. (2010). Efficacy of meta-cognitive therapy for adult ADHD. *American Journal of Psychiatry, 167*(8), 958–968.

Sowers, J., Powers, L.E., & Shpigelman, C.N. (2012). *Science, technology, engineering, and math (STEM mentoring for youth and young adults with disabilities: A review of the research* [Monograph]. Portland, OR: Regional Research Institute on Human Services, Portland State University.

Stetser, M., & Stillwell, R. (2014). *Public high school four-year on-time graduation rates and event dropout rates: School years 2010–11 and 2011–12.* Washington, DC: National Center for Education Statistics.

Swaner, L. E., & Brownell, J.E. (2008). *Outcomes of high impact practices for underserved students: A review of the literature.* Washington, DC: Association of American Colleges and Universities.

Test, D.W., Fowler, C., & Kohler, P. (2012). *Evidence-based practices and predictors in secondary transition: What we know and what we still need to know.* Retrieved from http://www.nsttac .org/sites/default/files/assets/pdf/pdf/ebps/ExecsummaryPPs%20Jan2013.pdf

Test, D.W., Fowler, C.H., Wood, W.M., Brewer, D.M., & Eddy, S. (2005). A conceptual framework of self-advocacy for students with disabilities. *Remedial and Special Education, 24,* 43–54.

Test, D.W., Kemp-Inman, A., Diegelmann, K., Hitt, S.B. & Bethune, L. (2015). Are online sources for identifying evidence-based practices trustworthy? An evaluation. *Exceptional Children, 82,* 58–80.

Test, D.W., Mazzotti, V.L., Mustian, A.L., Fowler, C.H., Kortering, L.J., & Kohler, P.H. (2009). Evidence-based secondary transition predictors for improving post-school outcomes for students with disabilities. *Career Development for Exceptional Individuals, 32,* 160–181. doi:10.1177/0885728809346960

The Ohio State University Nisonger Center. (2014). *E-mentoring program* (2nd ed.). Retrieved from http://go.osu.edu/ementoring

Thompson, R.B., Corsello, M., McReynolds, S., & Conklin-Powers, B. (2013). A longitudinal study of family socioeconomic status (SES) variables as predictors of socio-emotional resilience among mentored youth. *Mentoring and Tutoring: Partnership in Learning, 21*(4), 378–391. doi:10.1080/13611267.2013.855864

U.S. Department of Commerce, U.S. Census Bureau. (2002). *The big payoff: Educational attainment and synthetic estimates of work-life earnings.* Washington, DC: Government Printing Office.

U.S. Department of Education. (2010). *Race to the top: Application for Phase 2 funding.* Washington, DC: Author.

U.S. Department of Education. (2011, May 27). *A blueprint for reform.* Retrieved from http:// www2.ed.gov/policy/elsec/leg/blueprint/blueprint.pdf

U.S. Department of Education, Office of Civil Rights. (2011). *Students with disabilities preparing for postsecondary education: Know your rights and responsibilities.* Retrieved from http:// www2.ed.gov/about/offices/list/ocr/transition.html

U.S. Department of Education, Office of Civil Rights. (2014, March 21). *Civil rights data collection: Data snapshot (college and career readiness).* Retrieved from www2.ed.gov/about/ offices/list/ocr

U.S. Department of Education, Office of Special Education and Rehabilitative Services, Office of Special Education. (2014). *36th annual report to congress on the implementation of the Individuals with Disabilities Education Act.* Washington, DC: Author.

U.S. Department of Education, Office of Special Education and Rehabilitative Services. (2006, August 14). *34 CFR parts 300 and 301 assistance to states for the education of children with disabilities and preschool grants for children with disabilities: Final rule.* Retrieved from http://www2.ed.gov/legislation/FedRegister/finrule/2006-3/081406a.pdf

U.S. Department of Labor, Office of Disability Employment Policy. (2005). *Opening doors to all candidates: Tips for ensuring access for applicants with disabilities.* Retrieved from http:// www.dol.gov/odep/pubs/fact/opening.htm

U.S. Government Accountability Office. (2003). *College completion: Additional efforts could help education with its completion goals.* Washington, DC: U.S. Government Printing Office.

Van Naarden Braun, K., Christensen, D., Doernberg, N., Schieve, L., Rice C., Wiggins, L, Schendel, D., Yeargin-Allsopp, M. (2015). Trends in the prevalence of autism spectrum disorder, cerebral palsy, hearing loss, intellectual disability, and vision impairment, metropolitan Atlanta, 1991–2010. *PLoS ONE 10*(4): e0124120. doi: 10.1371/journal. pone.01224120

Van Pelt, J. (2015). *Is Facebook depression for real.* Retrieved from http://www.socialworkto day.com/archive/exc_080811.shtml

Van Reusen, A.K., Bos, C.S., Schumaker, J.B. & Deshler, D.D. (1994). *The self-advocacy strategy for education and transition planning.* Lawrence, KS: Edge Enterprises.

Villa. R., Thousand, J., & Nevin, A. (2013). *A Guide to Co-Teaching: New Lessons and Strategies to Facilitate Student Learning* (3rd ed). Thousand Oaks, CA: Corwin Press.

Wagner, M., Marder, C., Blackorby, J., Cameto, R., Newman, L., Levine, P., & Davies-Mercier, E. (2003, November). *The achievements of youth with disabilities during second-*

ary school. Retrieved from http://www.nlts2.org/reports/2003_11/nlts2_report_2003_11_complete.pdf

Wagner, M., Newman, L., Cameto, R., Garza, N., & Levine, P. (2005). *After high school: A first look at the postschool experiences of youth with disabilities. Retrieved from* www.nlts2.org/reports/2005_04/nlts2_report_2005_04_complete.pdf

Wagner, M., Newman, L., Cameto, R., & Levine, P. (2005). *Changes over time in the early post-school outcomes of youth with disabilities.* Retrieved from www.nlts2.org/reports/2005_06/nlts2_report_2005_06_complete.pdf

Wagner, M., Newman, L., Cameto, R., Levine, P., & Marder, C. (2007). *Perceptions and expectations of youth with disabilities.* Retrieved from www.nlts2.org/reports/2007_08/nlts2_report_2007-08_execsum.pdf

Walker, A., Kortering, L., Fowler, C., Rowe, D., & Bethune, L. (2013). *Age appropriate transition assessment toolkit,* (3rd ed.). Charlotte, NC: National Secondary Transition Technical Assistance Center. Retrieved on Dec. 29, 2015 from http://www.transitionta.org/sites/default/files/transitionplanning/TransitionAssessmentToolkit.pdf

Ward, M.J. (1996). Coming of age in the age of self-determination: A historical perspective on self-determination. In D. Sands & M.L. Wehmeyer (Eds.), *Self-determination across the life span: Theory and practice.* Baltimore, MD: Paul H. Brookes Publishing Co.

Wehby, J.H., Falk, K.B., Barton-Arwood, S., Lane, K.L., & Colley, C. (2003). The impact of comprehensive reading instruction on the academic and social behavior of students with emotional and behavioral disorders. *Journal of Emotional and Behavioral Disorders, 11,* 225–238.

Wehmeyer, M.L. & Kelchner, K. (1995). *The Arc's Self-Determination Scale.* Arlington, TX: The Arc National Headquarters.

Wehmeyer, M.L., Little, T.D., Lopez, S.J., & Shogren, K.A. (2011). *The adolescent self-determination scale-short form.* Lawrence, KS: Kansas University Center for Developmental Disabilities.

Wehmeyer M.L., & Webb, K.K. (Eds.). (2013). *Handbook of adolescent transition for youth with disabilities.* New York, NY: Routledge.

Wehmeyer, M.L., & Palmer, S.B. (2003). Adult outcomes for students with cognitive disabilities three-years after high school: The impact of self-determination. *Education and Training in Developmental Disabilities, 38,* 131–144.

Wehmeyer, M.L., & Palmer, S.B. (2011). *Whose future is it anyway? A comprehensive, research-based, self-determination curriculum.* Verona, WI: Attainment Company.

Wehmeyer, M.L., Palmer, S.B., Lee, Y., Williams-Diehm, K., & Shogren, K. (2011). A randomized-trial evaluation of the effect of whose future is it anyway? On self-determination. *Career Development for Exceptional Individuals, 34,* 45–56.

Wehmeyer, M.L., Palmer, S.B., Shogren, K.A., Williams-Diehm, K., & Soukup, J. (2013). Establishing a causal relationship between interventions to promote self-determination and enhanced student self-determination. *The Journal of Special Education, 46,* 195–210. doi:10.1177/0022466910392377

Wehmeyer, M.L., & Schwartz, M. (1997). Self-determination and positive adult outcomes: A follow-up study of youth with mental retardation or learning disabilities. *Exceptional Children, 63,* 245–255.

Weissberg, R. P., & Cascarino, J. (2013). Academic learning + social emotional learning = national priority. *Kappan, 95,* 8–13.

Williams, D. *Somebody, Somewhere.* New York, NY: Three Rivers Press, 1994, p. 186.

Williams, L. (2013). *Could illiteracy and the lack of effective reading strategies be the hidden cause of crime?* Retrieved from www.districtadministration.com

Williamson, G.L. (2004). *Student readiness for postsecondary options.* Durham, NC: MetaMetrics.

Wood, L.L., Sylvester, L., & Martin, J.E. (2010). Student-directed transition planning: Increasing student knowledge and self-efficacy in the transition planning process. *Career Development and Exceptional Individuals, 33,* 106–114.

Yu, J., Huang, T., & Newman, L. (2008, March). *Facts from NLTS–2: Substance use among young adults with disabilities.* Menlo Park, CA: SRI International.

Zhao, C.M., & Kuh, G.D. (2004). Adding value: Learning communities and student engagement. *Research in Higher Education, 45,* 115–138.

Index

Note: *b* indicates boxes, *f* indicates figures, *t* indicates tables.

Academic adjustments in college, 119, 120, 120*b*, 121–122
Acceptance stage
  accommodations/supports and, 54
  attention-deficit/hyperactivity disorder (ADHD) and, 142
  assisting students with, 155*t*–156*t*
  awareness and, 154*b*–155*b*, 154*t*, 155*t*
  case studies, 46–47, 73
  overview, 50–52, 53*f*
Accommodations
  acceptance and, 54
  case studies, 146
  college and, 102–103, 116, 117, 119–122, 120*b*, 126*b*, 128
  overview, 156*t*
  stigma and, 80–81
  transition planning and, 102–108, 104*b*, 106*b*, 107*f*
  see also Supports
ADA, *see* Americans with Disabilities Act of 1990 (PL 101-336)
Adam the designer, 145–146, 147*f*
ADHD, *see* Attention-deficit/hyperactivity disorder
Adolescent Self-Determination Scale, 33*t*, 35*t*
Advocacy, 36–37, 86, 135–136, 161–162
  see also Self-advocacy
Age Appropriate Transition Assessment Toolkit, 94–95
AHEAD, *see* Association on Higher Education and Disability
AIR, *see* American Institutes for Research Self-Determination Scale
Alcohol abuse, *see* Substance abuse
Americans with Disabilities Act (ADA) of 1990 (PL 101-336), 118, 118*t*, 119
The American Institutes for Research (AIR) Self-Determination Scale, 33*t*
Andee, 82–84, 85*f*, 115, 126, 159
Anna
  challenges, 40
  diagnosis, 43–44
  disability support services, 129–130
  educational performance, 6, 7
  emergency room, 48–49
  medication, 106
  rejecting supports, 46–47

  self-disclosure, 52, 53*f*
  special education, 45–46, 100–101
  supports for all students, 103
Anxiety
  college and, 121
  mental health resources and, 161–162
  transition planning and, 20*b*
Art mentoring program, 74, 75–77
ASDs, *see* Autism spectrum disorders
Assessments
  for college, 118*t*, 122
  cost of evaluations, 6
  of learning style, 104
  location on path to pride and, 157, 154*b*–155*b*, 158*t*
  of personality, 137*b*
  of self-determination, 33*t*–34*t*
  for transition planning, 92*b*, 94–96
Asset-based approach
  awareness and, 41–42, 42*t*
  to college majors/careers, 126–127
  conversation on disability and, 101, 102*b*
  to social relationships, 160*b*
Association on Higher Education and Disability (AHEAD), 119*b*, 129
Athletics, 97, 129–130
Attention-deficit/hyperactivity disorder (ADHD)
  autism with, 16
  behavior problems and, 20*b*, 21
  college and, 115
  definition, 28
  disability category of, 4
  employment outcomes and, 138
  executive function skills and, 141–143, 143*f*
  expectations and, 44
  famous people with, 27*b*
  learning disabilities with, 14, 131–132, 145, 146
  mentoring and, 69, 74, 75–77
  overview, 12–14
  tips for teaching, 14*b*–15*b*
  web sites/resources, 28, 29*b*
Attention-deficit/hyperactivity disorder (ADHD) case studies
  careers, 137, 140–142, 146, 151–152
  college, 115, 126, 127, 128–130
  criminal behavior, 19, 25

Attention-deficit/hyperactivity disorder
    (ADHD) case studies—continued
  diagnosis, 6, 13, 43–44
  disability shame, 45–49
  educational performance, 6, 7
  management, 30
  mentoring, 65, 70–74, 70b, 79, 82–84, 85f
  Path to Disability Pride, 36–37, 40, 43–44,
      45–49, 52, 53–54, 55
  social relationships, 160
  transition planning, 100–101, 102, 103,
      106
Auditing college classes, 132–133
Autism spectrum disorders (ASDs)
  definition, 3t, 4
  famous people with, 16, 17, 27b
  social relationships and, 157
  tips for teaching, 17b–18b, 20b
Avoidance, 21
Awareness stage
  careers and, 127
  college and, 115, 120
  disability awareness, 102b, 159
  disability shame and, 162
  examples, 72
  overview, 41–44, 42t
  Path to Pride Disability and, 108–109,
      109b, 156–157, 154b–155b, 158t, 5

Bauer, Bill, 70–74, 70b, 101, 161
Behavior problems
  autism and, 17
  life skills training and, 161–162, 160b
  in maladaptive behavior stage, 38f,
      47–49, 154b–155b, 155t
  overview, 18–19
  reasons for, 19, 21–22, 22b, 23b
  tips for teaching, 20b, 22b
Best Evidence Encyclopedia, 11t
Best Practices Guide on Mentoring Youth
    with Disabilities, 87
Bipolar personality, 25–26, 27b
Boredom, 21
Breaks from class, 20b

Career(s)
  assessment for, 95–96
  asset-based approach to, 126–127
  employment outcomes, 138, 140–141,
      153
  empowering students for, 152–153
  entrepreneurship, 144–146
  executive function skills and, 141–143,
      143f
  exploring options, 97, 109b, 136–137,
      135b–136b, 139f
  identity development and, 135–136

  mentoring and, 68–69, 80b
  natural supports and, 150–152
  readiness for, 136–137
  technology supports, 147–150
  transition planning and, 91b, 95–96, 97
Career(s) case studies
  attention-deficit/hyperactivity disorder
      (ADHD), 137, 140–142, 146, 151–152
  learning disabilities, 97, 135–136, 145,
      149–150, 152–153
Career Days, 136b
Career One Step, 91b
Career schools, 119
CAST, 11t
CCSS, see Common Core State Standards
Celebrities, see Famous people with
    learning differences
Center on Response to Intervention, 11t
Challenges stage
  in adulthood, 90
  awareness of, 154b–155b, 154t, 155t
  deficit-based approach and, 101
  disability shame and, 124–125
  examples, 72, 77, 124, 125f
  identity development and, 42
  maintaining pride and, 58–59
  overview, 38f, 39–40
  persistence/supports and, 132
Choice/Maker Self-Determination
      Assessment, 34t
Chris, 143
Climate of schools, 11t–12t, 25, 80–81
Coaching executive function skills, 143
Cognitive-Behavioral Therapy for Adult ADHD
      (Solanto), 142
Collaboration, 117–119, 118t, 119b
College
  academic adjustments, 119, 120, 120b,
      121–122
  accommodations/supports and, 102–103,
      116, 117, 119–122, 120b, 126b, 128
  climate of, 80–81
  getting started on campus, 121–125, 124f
  importance of, 115, 117
  mentoring and, 68, 80b
  modifications and, 105, 117, 121
  readiness for, 136–137
  strategies for success, 125–133, 126b, 128b
  transition planning and, 12t, 91b, 92b, 109b
  web sites/resources, 119b
College case studies
  attention-deficit/hyperactivity disorder
      (ADHD), 115, 126, 127, 128–130
  EnVisionIT curriculum, 96
  learning disabilities, 51–52, 54–55, 64–65,
      112–113, 122–123, 131–133
College Navigator, 91b
Common Core State Standards (CCSS),
      17b–18b

Communication
    disability normalized, 99, 100
    disability pride and, 26
    self-advocacy skills and, 110*b*–111*b*
    teaching skills for, 17*b*–18*b*, 160–161,
        160*b*
Comprehension (reading), 10*b*
Confidence, 21
Connection to disability community stage
    awareness and, 154*b*–155*b*, 154*t*, 155*t*
    examples, 73
    overview, 56–58, 57*f*, 156*t*
    Path to Disability Pride and, 111–113
Coping strategies, 23*b*
Costs of evaluations, 6
Co-teaching, 50
Criminal behavior
    disability shame and, 48
    emotional disturbance and, 18–19, 49
    positive behavior interventions and
        supports (PBIS) and, 25
    reading and, 11
Curricula, 33*t*–34*t*, 78*b*, 95–96

Daniel, 128–129
"Dare to Dream" (Horne), 59, 60*b*–61*b*,
    135–136
Deafblindness, 3*t*, 4*t*
Deafness, 3*t*, 4*t*
Debating class, 99
Decision making
    in college, 117
    in self-disclosure, 56, 123–124, 159, 160*b*
Deficit-based approach, 42, 42*t*, 101
Delegation of work tasks, 141, 145, 151
Denial, 44, 144*b*–145*b*
Depression
    bipolar personality, 25–26, 27*b*
    case studies, 9–10, 46, 48, 107, 107*f*
    mental health resources and, 161–162
    social media and, 156
Developmental Disabilities Assistance
        and Bill of Rights Act of 1975
        (PL 94-103), 31
Developmental Disabilities Councils, 31
Diedrich, Collin, 152–153
Different ability, 29
    see also Learning differences
Disability
    adulthood challenges and, 90
    definition, 25, 26
    normalizing, 99–101, 102*b*
    prevalence of, 2, 3*t*–4*t*, 4
    special education and, 45
Disability awareness, 102*b*, 159
    see also Awareness stage
Disability community, *see* Connection to
    disability community stage

Disability pride
    case studies, 36–37, 45–49, 74, 124, 125*f*
    maintaining, 58–59, 59*b*, 162
    mentoring and, 63, 68–69, 74, 162
    movement for, 31–32, 33*t*–35*t*, 36–37
    overview, 50–58, 53*f*, 57*f*, 156*t*
    path to, 37, 38*f*, 39
        see also Path to Disability Pride
    reframing disability, 25–26, 27*b*, 28, 29–30
    shame and, 38*f*, 44–49
    social relationships and, 158–160, 159*f*,
        160*b*
    strategies for, 159–162, 5–156*t*, 160*b*
    transition planning and, 97–113
        see also Transition planning and
            disability pride
    transition to, 39–44
Disability pride movement, 31–32, 33*t*–35*t*l,
    36–37
Disability safe list, 132*b*
Disability shame stage
    assisting students in, 154*b*–155*b*, 155*t*
    awareness and, 42, 42*t*, 162
    case studies, 45–49, 72–73
    challenges and, 124–125
    identity development and, 37, 38*f*, 39
    mental health resources and, 161–162
    see also Stigma
Disability support services (DSS)
    documentation to, 121–122, 129
    laws on, 119, 120
    meeting regularly with, 129, 130
Disclosure, *see* Self-disclosure stage
Documentation for college, 121–122, 129
DO-IT Center, 11*t*, 87
Dropouts
    criminal behavior and, 19
    reading and, 11
    reasons for, 23–25, 24*b*
    substance abuse and, 49
    web sites/resources, 11*t*
Drug abuse, *see* Substance abuse
DSS, *see* Disability support services
Dyslexia
    accommodations and, 122
    case studies, 70–74, 70*b*, 147–149, 149*f*
    famous people with, 27*b*
    mentoring and, 74, 75–77
Dysphagia, 70–74, 70*b*

Education for all Handicapped Children
        Act of 1975 (PL 94-142), 32
Einstein, Albert, 8, 27*b*
Electronic mentoring, 66, 67, 69, 77–79, 78*b*,
    80*b*
Embarrassment, 48, 53–54, 160–161
Emotional disturbance
    definition, 3*t*

Emotional disturbance—continued
    overview, 18–19, 20b
    substance abuse and, 49
Emotional self-regulation, 157
Employment joy factor, 140–141
Employment outcomes, 138, 140–141, 153
    see also Career(s); Outcomes
Empowerment
    for careers, 152–153
    disability normalized, 100
    disability pride and, 26, 28
Entrepreneurship, 144–146
Environmental model, 41
EnVisionIT curriculum, 95–96
The E-Mentoring Program, 77–79, 78b, 80b, 87
Evaluations, 6
    see also Assessments
Evidence-based practices, 11t–12t
    see also Tips for teaching
Executive function skills, 14b–15b, 141–143,
    143f
Exit exam requirement, 108
Expectations of teachers/parents
    acceptance and, 5
    learning disabilities/attention-deficit/
        hyperactivity disorder (ADHD) and,
        44
    outcomes and, 7, 112–113
Eye to Eye, 69, 74, 75–77, 85–86, 87

Families
    acceptance and, 5
    dropping out and, 24b
    expectations of, 7, 44, 112–113, 5
    at individualized education program
        (IEP) meetings, 50
    labeling and, 7
    mentoring benefits for, 66f
    support by, 148, 160b
    tips for teaching, 147b
Famous people with learning differences, 27b
FAPE, see Free appropriate public
    education
Flink, David, 75–77, 78f, 85–86, 128b
Foreign language requirement, 127
Foundations of Successful Youth
    Mentoring, 87
The 411 on Disability Disclosure, 34t
Free appropriate public education (FAPE),
    32
Functional model, 41

Goals
    for careers, 137, 138b, 152–153
    postsecondary education as, 115
    transition planning and, 90, 92b, 94–96,
        97, 98b, 109b, 113

Grandin, Temple, 16, 17, 27b
Gratification, 21
Group mentoring, 66, 67, 69

Hearing impairments
    case studies, 101, 161
    college and, 103
    definition, 3t
Hidden disabilities
    careers, 135–153
    college life, 115–133
    identification of, 1, 5–7
    mentoring, 63–87
    overview, 1–30
    Path to Disability Pride, 31–61
    prevalence of, 4–5, 13, 16
    social relationships, 155–162
    transition planning, 89–113
    see also specific aspects of hidden disabilities
High school diploma status, 108
High school versus college, 118t
Horne, LeDerick,
    acceptance, 51–52
    anger, 46
    career interests, 97
    challenges, 39–40, 107
    college, 54–55, 122–123, 132–133
    conduct/music teacher, 21
    "Dare to Dream," 59, 60b–61b, 135–136
    daring to dream, 135–136
    disability community, 57, 57f, 58
    disability shame, 45–46, 48, 107, 107f
    educational experiences, 8–10, 39–40
    embarrassment/fear, 48
    evaluation/diagnosis, 8–10, 40–41, 43
    failing successfully, 132–133
    high school regular diploma, 109
    individualized education program (IEP)
        meeting, 56
    inclusive honors class, 99
    learning disability management, 30
    mentors, 64–65
    natural supports, 151
    parental involvement, 112–113
    path to success, 94
    restaurant table distractions, 160–161
    self-advocacy, 36
    self-awareness, 108
    special education, 45
    study skills class, 131
    transition challenges, 107

IDEA, see Individuals with Disabilities
    Education Act of 1990
    (PL 101-476); Individuals with
    Disabilities Education Improvement
    Act of 2004 (PL 108-446)

Identity development
  acceptance stage and, 51
  careers and, 135–136
  case studies, 48
  challenges stage and, 42
  disability shame and, 37, 38f, 39
  see also Path to Disability Pride
IEP, see Individualized education
      program
I'm Determined.org, 34t
Imparato, Andy, 25–26, 27b
Impulsivity, 21
Inclusion
  benefits of, 5, 5b
  disability awareness and, 155
  disability normalized, 99
  in study skills class, 131
Individualized education program (IEP),
      109b, 113
Individualized education program (IEP)
      meetings, 50, 56, 96–97
Individuals with Disabilities Education Act
      (IDEA) of 1990 (PL 101-476), 32
Individuals with Disabilities Education
      Improvement Act (IDEA) of 2004
      (PL 108-446)
  attention-deficit/hyperactivity disorder
      (ADHD), 13–14
  college versus high school, 118t, 119
  disability categories, 2, 3t–4t, 4
  transition planning, 90, 152
Informational interviews, 138b, 139f
Intellectual disabilities, 3t, 16
Interests, 16, 97, 135b–136b
Interrupting, 20b
Interviewing employees/employers, 138b,
      139f
Invisible disabilities, see Hidden disabilities
iPads, 104b, 131–132
iPhone, 150
IRIS Center, 91b
Izzo, Margo Vreeburg
  attention-deficit/hyperactivity disorder
      (ADHD) management, 30
  advocacy/self-advocacy, 36–37
  career, 137, 140–141
  employment joy factor, 140–141
  executive function skills, 141–142, 143f
  identification of attention-deficit/
      hyperactivity disorder (ADHD), 13
  individualized college courses, 127
  medication support, 55
  mentoring, 65, 79
  natural supports, 151–152
  self-disclosure, 53–54, 151–152

JAN, see Job Accommodation Network
Job-related factors in dropping out, 24b

The Job Accommodation Network (JAN),
      91b

Kelsey, 19, 25
Kindle, 150

Labeling
  acceptance stage and, 51, 77b
  case studies, 8–10
  owning the label, 77b
  stigma and, 6–7
Learned helplessness, 49
Learning differences, 27b, 28–29, 70–74, 70b
Learning disabilities
  accommodations and, 122
  attention-deficit/hyperactivity disorder
      (ADHD) with, 14, 131–132, 145, 146
  careers and, 144
  college and, 103, 115
  definition, 3t, 4
  employment outcomes and, 138
  expectations and, 44
  famous people with, 27b
  mentoring and, 64, 69, 74, 75–77
  overview, 8–11, 10b, 11t–12t
  social relationships and, 157
Learning disabilities case studies
  careers, 97, 135–136, 145, 149–150,
      152–153
  college, 51–52, 54–55, 64–65, 112–113,
      122–123, 131–133
  conduct, 21
  disability community, 57, 57f
  disability shame, 45–46, 48, 107, 107f
  labeling, 8–10
  learning disability management, 30
  mentoring, 64–65, 70–74, 70b
  Path to Disability Pride, 36, 39–41, 43,
      45–46, 48, 51–52, 54–55, 56, 57, 57f, 58
  social relationships, 160–161
  transition planning, 94, 97, 99, 107, 107f,
      108, 109, 112–113
Learning styles, 104, 137b
Life skills training, 161–162, 160b

Maladaptive behavior stage
  awareness of, awareness and, 154b–155b,
      154t,
  life skills training and, 161–162, 160b
  overview, 38f, 47–49
  see also Behavior problems
Materials organization, 15b
Me! Lessons for Teaching Self-Awareness/
      Self-Advocacy, 34t
Medical model, 41
Medications, 43–44, 55, 105–106

Meltdowns, 20b
Memory loss, 70–74, 70b
Mental health resources, 161–162
Mental retardation, *see* Intellectual
    disabilities
Mentoring
    acceptance and, 5
    autism and, 17b–18b
    benefits of, 65–68, 66f, 84–85, 86
    disability pride and, 63, 68–69, 74, 162
    The E-Mentoring Program, 77–79, 78b, 80b,
        87
    Eye to Eye, 74, 75–77, 85–86, 87
    Ohio STEM Ability Alliance Program,
        80–82
    outcomes from research, 68–69
    overview, 63–64
    Path to Disability Pride and, 70–74, 70b,
        74b
    role models and, 64–65
    support and, 160b
    by teachers/staff, 50, 66f
    types of, 65–68, 66f
Mentoring case studies
    attention-deficit/hyperactivity disorder
        (ADHD), 65, 70–74, 70b, 79, 82–84,
        85f
    learning disabilities, 64–65, 70–74, 70b
    social relationships, 161–162
Modifications
    college and, 105, 117, 121
    transition planning and, 156t
Moore, Graham, 97–98
Motivation, 10b
Multiple disabilities, 3t

National Center for Learning Disabilities,
    11t
National Center on UDL, 11t
National Collaborative on Workforce and
    Disability/Youth, 91b
National Dropout Prevention Center, 11t
National Mentoring Partnership, 87
National Technical Assistance Center on
    Transition (NTACT), 12t, 91b
Natural supports, 150–152
Nelson, Scott
    business started, 145, 146
    mentoring, 70–74, 70b, 74b, 75f
    transition planning, 104
Nonacceptance stage
    awareness and, 154b–155b, 154t,
        155t
    overview, 38f, 44–45
Nonverbal communication skills, 160b
NTACT, *see* National Technical Assistance
    Center on Transition

OCALI Transition to Adulthood
    Guidelines, 91b
OCALL.org, 104b
Ohio Employment First Transition
    Planning, 91b
Ohio STEM Ability Alliance Program
    (OSAA), 80–82, 124, 125f
The Ohio State University E-Mentoring
    Program, 35t, 77–79, 78b, 80b, 87
One-to-one mentoring, 66–67
Organization, 14b–15b, 71, 141–142
Orthopedic impairment, 4t
OSAA, *see* Ohio STEM Ability Alliance
    Program
Other health impairments, 4t, 5
Outcomes
    emotional disturbance and, 18–19
    employment, 138, 140–141, 153
    executive function skills and, 141–143,
        143f
    expectations of parents and, 7, 112–113
    high school diploma status and, 108–109
    inclusive classrooms and, 99
    of mentoring, 68–69, 79–80, 80b
    positive behavior interventions/supports
        (PBIS) and, 25
    postschool success, 126–127
    reading and, 11
    self-determination and, 96
    student learning communities (SLCs)
        and, 128
    substance abuse and, 49
    transition planning and, 90, 93–94, 113

PADD, *see* Protection and Advocacy for
    Developmental Disabilities
Parents, *see* Families
Passions, 16, 135b–136b
Path to Disability Pride
    accommodations/supports provided,
        102–108, 104b, 106b, 107f
    disability community building, 111–113
    disability normalized, 99–101, 102b
    disability shame, 38f, 44–49
    disability/strengths/limitations
        awareness, 108–109, 109b
    maintaining pride, 58–59, 59b
    mentoring and, 70–74, 70b, 74b, 75f
    reframing disability, 25–26, 27b, 28, 29–30
    self-determination/disclosure/self-
        advocacy, 109–111, 110b–111b
    social relationships and, 156–157,
        154b–155b, 155t
    strategies to assist students, 159–162,
        155t–156t, 160b
    tips for teaching, 144b–145b, 154b–155b
    transition to, 39–44

Path to Disability Pride case studies
  attention-deficit/hyperactivity disorder
      (ADHD), 36–37, 40, 43–44, 45–49, 52,
      53–54, 55
  framework examples, 53f, 57f, 72–74, 75f,
      78f, 82–84, 85f, 107f, 125f, 143f, 149f
  learning disabilities, 36, 39–41, 43, 45–46,
      48, 51–52, 54–55, 56, 57, 57f, 58
PBIS, see Positive behavior interventions
      and supports
Peabody, Andee, 82–84, 85f, 115, 126, 159
Peer tutoring, 103
People First Language Resources, 92b
Persistence, 106b, 132
Person-Centered Planning, 92b
Personality assessment, 137b
Pineda, Victor Santiago, 28
PL 93-112, see Rehabilitation Act of 1973
PL 94-103, see Developmental Disabilities
      Assistance and Bill of Rights Act of
      1975
PL 94-142, see Education for all
      Handicapped Children Act of 1975
PL 101-336, see Americans with Disabilities
      Act (ADA) of 1990
PL 101-476, see Individuals with Disabilities
      Education Act (IDEA) of 1990
PL 108-446, see Individuals with Disabilities
      Education Improvement Act (IDEA)
      of 2004
Planning, 142
  see also Transition planning
Positive behavior interventions and
      supports (PBIS), 12t, 25
Postsecondary education, see College
Proactive involvement, 106b
Procrastination, 142
Promising Practices Network, 12t
Protection and Advocacy for
      Developmental Disabilities (PADD),
      31

Readiness for college/career, 136–137
Reading
  case studies, 39–40, 71
  disabilities and, 10–11, 10b
  mentoring and, 79
  tips for teaching, 10b, 15b
Refusal, 20b
Rehabilitation, vocational, 120–121, 122
Rehabilitation Act of 1973 (PL 93-112), 118,
      118t, 119
Reinforcement of self, 142
Rejecting supports stage
  awareness and, 154b–155b, 154t,
  overview, 38f, 46–47
Resources, see Web sites and resources

Risk of underachievement stage
  awareness of, 154b–155b, 154t, 155t
  careers and, 136
  overview, 38f, 49
Role models
  acceptance and, 5
  autism and, 18b
  awareness and, 41–42
  of conversing safely, 160b
  mentors as, 64–65
Role playing, 20b, 110–111

Sarah, 124, 125f
Scaffolding by mentors, 84
Scarlet letter case study, 45
School factors in dropping out, 24b
School-to-prison pipeline, 18–19
Scott
  business started, 145, 146
  mentoring, 70–74, 70b, 74b, 75f
  transition planning, 104
Script for self-advocacy, 126b
SDAi, see Self-Determination (SD)
      Assessment internet
Searching stage
  awareness and, 154b–155b, 154t
  overview, 38f, 40–41
Section 504 of the Rehabilitation Act of 1973
      (PL 93-112), 118, 118t, 119
Self-Advocacy Clubs, 112
Self-advocacy stage
  awareness and, 108, 154b–155b, 154t
  benefits of, 84–85
  case studies, 36–37, 74, 82–84, 85f
  college and, 82–84, 85f, 102–103, 118t
  at individualized education program
      (IEP) meetings, 56
  overview, 32, 55–56, 156t
  plan development, 125–126, 126b
  transition planning and, 109–111,
      110b–111b
  web sites/resources, 34t, 35t, 112
The Self-Advocacy Strategy, 35t
Self-awareness, see Awareness stage
  Self-concept, 153, 154b–155b, 154t
  see also Awareness stage; Identity
      development
Self-determination
  benefits of, 84–85
  individualized education program (IEP)
      meeting and, 96
  overview, 32, 33t–35t
  Path to Disability Pride and, 156
  transition planning and, 109–111,
      110b–111
Self-Determination (SD) Assessment
      internet (SDAi), 33t

Self-directed individualized education program (IEP), 35*t*, 96

Self-disclosure stage
  assisting students in, 159, 5
  awareness and, 154*b*–155*b*, 154
  benefits of, 128
  case studies, 52, 53–54, 53*f*, 73, 151–152
  college and, 116, 121, 123–124
  decisions in, 56, 123–124, 159, 160*b*
  role playing and, 110–111
  social relationships and, 157, 159, 160*b*
  transition planning and, 109–111, 110*b*–111*b*
  web sites/resources, 34*t*

Self-management plans, 22*b*
Self-regulation, 160–161
Self-talk, 22*b*–23*b*
Settings for self-advocacy, 110*b*
Sign language, 127
SLCs, *see* Student learning communities
Smartphones, 103–104, 150
Social emotional learning, 156–157, 160*b*
Social media, 156*t*

Social relationships
  autism and, 16–17
  case studies, 161–162
  disability pride and, 158–160, 159*f*, 160*b*
  location on path to pride and, 157, 158*b*–159*b*, 158*t*
  quality of life and, 155
  self-concept and, 156–157, 158*b*–159*b*
  self-talk and, 23*b*
  strategies for disability pride and, 159–162, 155*t*–156*t*, 160*b*
  teaching skills for, 17*b*–18*b*, 20*b*, 156–158, 160*b*

Social skills
  autism and, 16–17
  self-talk and, 23*b*
  teaching, 17*b*–18*b*, 20*b*, 156–158, 158*b*
Social-emotional learning skills, 156–158, 158*b*
Soft Skills to Pay the Bills, 92*b*
Solanto, Mary, 142
Specific learning disabilities, *see* Learning disabilities
Speech-language impairments, 4*t*, 157
Spelling, 39–40, 71, 147–149, 149*f*
STEM disciplines
  case studies, 124, 125*f*, 152–153
  mentoring program for, 80–82
  student learning communities and, 128
S.T.E.P. (Student Transition and Education Planning), 34*t*
Stigma
  disability shame and, 44, 46
  labeling and, 6–7
  supports and, 41, 44, 48, 50, 54, 80–81
  see also Disability shame stage

Strength-based approach, *see* Asset-based approach
Student learning communities (SLCs), 81–82, 128
Study skills classes, 130–131
Substance abuse, 48, 49, 161–162
Suicidal thoughts, 46, 48, 161–162
Summary of performance, 122
Supports
  acceptance and, 54
  awareness of, awareness and, 154*b*–155*b*, 154*t*
  for careers, 147–150
  challenges stage and, 132
  college and, 102–103, 116, 117, 119–122, 120*b*, 128
  disability support services (DSS), 119, 120, 121–122, 129, 130
  by families, 148, 160*b*
  for learning styles, 104
  medications as, 55, 105–106
  mentoring and, 160*b*
  natural, 150–152
  overview, 156*t*
  positive behavior interventions and, 12*t*, 25
  rejecting supports stage, 38*f*, 46–47, 154*b*–155*b*, 154*t*
  stigma and, 41, 47, 50, 54, 80–81
  transition planning and, 102–108, 104*b*, 106*b*, 107*f*, 156*t*
  using supports stage, 54–55, 73–74, 156*t*
  see also Accommodations
System navigation skills, 108

Tasks
  delegation of, 144, 148, 150
  organization of, 14*b*–15*b*
  self-talk and, 23*b*
TBI, *see* Traumatic brain injury
Technology
  for careers, 147–150
  case studies, 82–84, 85*f*, 146, 147–150, 149*f*
  in college, 82–84, 85*f*, 120*b*, 131–132
  disability normalizing and, 100
  emotional disturbance and, 20*b*
  transition planning and, 103–104, 104*b*
TEDx, 12*t*
Testing accommodations, 104–105
  see also Assessments
Think College, 12*t*, 92*b*
Time organization, 14*b*, 141–142
Tips for teaching
  awareness, 102*b*
  behavior problems, 20*b*, 22*b*
  conversing safely, 160*b*
  culture of disability pride, 59*b*
  emotional disturbance, 20*b*

executive function skills, 14b–15b
goal setting/attainment, 109b
interests/passions, 135b–136b
Path to Disability Pride, 144b–145b,
    158b–159b
persistence/proactive involvement, 106b
reading, 10b, 15b
self-advocacy skills, 110b–111b, 126b
self-disclosure, 160b
social-communication skills, 17b–18b
Tonti, Stephen, 27b, 28, 29b
Transition Assessment and Goal Generator,
    92b
Transition planning
    anxiety and, 20b
    assessments for, 94–96
    behavior problems and, 22b
    careers and, 91b
    college and, 12t, 91b, 92b, 109b
    disability pride and, 97–113
    goals and, 90, 92b, 94–96, 97, 98b, 109b, 113
    IDEA on, 32, 90, 152
    individualized education program (IEP)
        meeting and, 96–97
    mentoring program for, 77–80, 80b
    overview, 89–90, 113
    predictors/practices for success, 93–94
    resources, 33t–35t, 92b
    supports allowed and, 156t
    tips for teaching, 20b, 22b, 102b, 106b,
        110b–111b
    transition services definition, 90, 91b–92b
Transition planning and disability pride
    accommodations/supports provided,
        102–108, 104b, 106b, 107f
    disability community building, 111–113
    disability normalized, 99–101, 102b
    disability/strengths/limitations
        awareness, 108–109, 109b
    overview, 97–99
    self-determination/disclosure/
        self-advocacy, 109–111, 110b–111b
Transition planning case studies
    attention-deficit/hyperactivity disorder
        (ADHD), 100–101, 102, 103, 106
    EnVisionIT, 96
    hearing loss, 101
    learning disabilities, 94, 97, 99, 107, 107f,
        108, 109, 112–113
Transition to Independence Process Model,
    92b
Traumatic brain injury (TBI), 4t, 5, 70–74,
    70b, 75f
Tutoring, 64–65, 103

UDL, see Universal design for learning
Underachievement risk, 38f, 49, 136,
    158b–159b, 158t
Universal design for learning (UDL), 11t,
    50, 105
Using supports stage, 54–55, 73–74, 156t
    see also Supports

VARK questionnaire, 104
Visual impairments, 4t, 79
Vocabulary, 10b, 154b
Vocational rehabilitation, 120–121, 122
Vocational schools, 119
Voice recorders, 131–132
Voice-to-text features, 103–104

Weakness-based approach, see
    Deficit-based approach
Web sites and resources
    Association on Higher Education and
        Disability (AHEAD), 119b
    attention-deficit/hyperactivity disorder
        (ADHD), 28
    autism spectrum disorders (ASDs), 17
    "Dare to Dream," 61b
    E-Mentoring Curriculum, 78b
    emotional learning, 160b
    evidence-based practices, 11t–12t
    inclusion, 5b
    iPad apps, 104b
    learning style assessment, 104
    mentoring, 87
    Nelson, Scott, 70b
    rights/responsibilities of college students,
        119b
    school climate, 11t–12t, 25
    self-determination, 33t–35t
    transition planning, 33t–35t, 91b–92b,
        94–95
    vocational rehabilitation offices, 122
What Works Clearinghouse, 12t
Who Cares About Kelsey?, 12t, 19
Whose Future Is it Anyway?, 35t
Word processing software, 150

Youth Leadership Forums (YLFs), 111–112,
    156t
Youthhood, 92b

Zarrow Center, 92b